Water Resources Administration in the United States

in the United States

Policy, Practice, and Emerging Issues

This book was sponsored by the
American Water Resources Association

in cooperation with the
AWRA National Capital Section

Co-Sponsored by

American Public Works Association

U.S. Bureau of Reclamation

U.S. Fish and Wildlife Service

Interstate Council on Water Policy

Salt River Project

U.S. Soil and Water Conservation Service

Tennessee Valley Authority

U.S. Environmental Protection Agency

Water Resources Administration in the United States

Policy, Practice, and Emerging Issues

Selected Papers from the
American Water Resources Association
National Forum on Water Management Policy
June 28 - July 1, 1992
Washington, D.C.

Martin Reuss, Editor

American Water Resources Association / Michigan State University Press

East Lansing
1993

All Michigan State University Press books are produced on paper which meets the requirements of American National Standard of Information Sciences—Permanence of paper for printed materials ANSI Z23.48-1984

Michigan State University Press
East Lansing, Michigan 48823-5202

Printed in the United States of America

01 00 99 98 97 96 95 94 93 1 2 3 4 5 6 7 8 9 10

Library of Congress Cataloging-in-Publication Data

Water resources adminstration in the United States: policy, practice and
    emerging issues / edited by Martin Reuss.
        p.   cm.
    Includes bibliographical references and index.
    ISBN 0-87013-333-0 (alk. paper)
    1. Water resources development—Government policy—United
States. 2. Water quality management—Government policy—United
States. I. Reuss, Martin. II. American Water Resources Association.
HD1694.A5W323   1993
333.91'00973—dc20
                                                          93-7668
                                                             CIP

Dedicated to the memory of Abel Wolman

Contents

Floodplain Management

Risks and Uncertainties

America's Water Infrastructure Needs

Where Do We Go from Here?

List of Figures

List of Tables

Acknowledgments

This book is the final product of the National Forum on Water Management Policy, a conference sponsored by the American Water Resources Association (AWRA). Federal co-sponsors included the Environmental Protection Agency, Bureau of Reclamation, Soil Conservation Service, Tennessee Valley Authority, and the Fish and Wildlife Service. The Army Corps of Engineers also substantially contributed to the Forum's success. Nonfederal co-sponsors included the American Public Works Association, the Interstate Council on Water Policy, and the Salt River Project. Martin Reuss, the editor of this volume, served as the Forum's general chair. Gerald D. Seinwill was technical chair. Janet Bowers and Carl H. Gaum helped raise funds and resolve administrative issues.

The editor expresses his gratitude to David W. Moody, president of the AWRA in 1992, for his constant encouragement and helpful advice during the preparation of this volume. Julie L. Loehr, the editor in chief of Michigan State University Press, capably and cheerfully oversaw final editing and publication.

Introduction

Martin Reuss

The articles in this book are revisions of papers presented at the National Forum on Water Management Policy, held in Washington, D.C., from 28 June to 1 July 1992 and organized by the American Water Resources Association (AWRA). Not all papers could be included, but those that are cover some of the most important water resources questions facing U.S. politicians and planners in the last decade of the twentieth century, and they explicitly highlight the importance of interdisciplinary, intergovernmental cooperation.[1] Although the Forum registration was open to everyone, all paper presenters and commentators were invited speakers. They include some of the leading practioners, policymakers, and academics in the field. To insure an interdisciplinary approach, Forum organizers invited geographers, political scientists, and historians to give papers, as well as the engineers, hydrologists, and economists more commonly found in water policy meetings. Also, efforts were made to insure that local, state, and federal agencies were represented. Multidisciplinary, interagency, and intergovernmental, the Forum provided an unusual opportunity to bring deeper perspective and new ideas to the critical area of water policy. The AWRA and Forum co-sponsors hope that this book will expand the dialogue by engaging a broad audience of concerned citizens throughout the country.

Of course, conferences on water policy are nothing new. Indeed, perhaps their most striking feature is their predictable recurrence. Since before the Civil War, every few years some professional, private, or public organization sponsors a water policy conference. The flurry of recommendations following each conference, often ending in bureaucratic oblivion rather than in substantive change, reflects futility as much as ambition. The United States seems historically incapable of establishing a water policy and certainly has not found the key to reconciling rational natural resource administration with its pluralist, federalist system of government.

However, the National Forum on Water Management Policy resulted from recent concerns whose complexity sets it off from some of its lineal ancestors. The issues are difficult to define, no less resolve. Public demands on water—a finite resource—and on public services grow, yet most Americans resist tax increases to pay for new services and remain suspicious of government itself. Public sensitivity to issues of environmental degradation and water quality increase, but so do worries over an adequate, reliable water supply. The infrastructure requires repair and replacement, especially in urban areas, but the costs overwhelm government budgets. When one strips away all the complex socioeconomic issues, the fundamental water resources question is the same as in other natural resource areas: how to protect the environment while allowing for economic growth. The issue is summed up in the term "sustainable development," and, as Arthur E. Williams of the Army Corps of Engineers and LaJuana S. Wilcher of the Environmental Protection Agency indicate, the challenge is daunting.[2]

The emphasis of the Forum was on water management policy. This was for good reason. While policies concerning planning and construction are important, the "big dam era" is behind us. The future promises far less construction of major water projects and more emphasis on environmental enhancement, recreation, water quality, and urban water use. Both the management and design of water projects must maximize efficiency. If new facilities are necessary, their design and construction must respond to dozens of environmental laws and to growing demands on limited government budgets. Clearly, before we can make more efficient use of water, we must make management itself more efficient.

This is being done in a number of ways. Cooperative interagency agreements assign agencies specific roles and eliminate misunderstandings in water management. Watershed management—an idea that goes back to the Progressive Era at the beginning of the century, but never fully implemented—is now receiving new attention. The approach focuses on planning and managing projects to optimize water use throughout the entire river basin. In the Progressive Era, the concept mainly addressed questions dealing with the allocation of available water for specific purposes, such as navigation, hydropower, irrigation, and domestic water use. More recently, the concept envelops both water quality and quantity issues.

The challenges facing Americans today in water resources beg for innovative solutions and new institutional approaches. As one example, safeguarding America's water and preserving its wetlands involve regulations that raise basic constitutional questions yet to be fully answered either in the judicial or legislative branches. These issues include the delimitation of state versus federal jurisdiction and the rights of private owners of wetlands to compensation when government prohibits development of their property. In another area, public officials are investigating market forces, such as tax breaks for water

2

conservation or additional assessments for using water above a certain amount, in efforts to regulate demand and conserve water. Meanwhile, new ways are being found to resolve disputes. Rather than appealing to the courts, aggrieved parties appear more willing to negotiate. This is particularly true of Indian claims, where the federal courts seem increasingly hostile to the plaintiff's position.[3] In many cases, government agencies can assume the role of "honest broker" in these negotiations. Also, there are more efforts to develop public-private organizations to insure continuous citizen involvement in water resources issues. The authors in the section on "Trends in Water Resources Management" analyze some of these new developments from their own particular perspective.

Certainly, no consideration of water management can ignore the role of government. Frustrated private citizens, occasionally with the support of bureaucrats and politicians, periodically question the ability of governmental institutions to resolve intertwined water resource issues. They raise issues about the appropriate level of government to make decisions relating to local water use, or about the adequacy of the public review process in developing operational plans. President Ronald Reagan's "New Federalism" turned to state governments and private businesses to shoulder more of the financial and management burden for water resources construction, operation, and maintenance. Most states welcomed increased involvement in planning and managing federal water projects, but were predictably unenthusiastic about contributing more money. The Reagan philosophy was reflected in the Water Resources Development Act of 1986, which established new cost-sharing formulae, increased user fees, and authorized hundreds of new projects.[4] Bory Steinberg presents some of the implications of this legislation in his paper. A key issue for the 1990s is how well the states can meet the new management and financial burdens placed on them. A related issue is the appropriate role of states in protecting water resources against environmental degradation. The problem becomes more complicated when more than one state is affected or when states lack the capability or will to enforce regulations.

The appropriate distribution of powers between the state and federal governments has been a point of contention ever since the United States gained its independence, as Robert Kelley suggests in his presentation. In all likelihood, disputes will continue. The issue is wrapped up in conflicting notions of federalism. Do we have dual federalism in this country, in which, according to one political scientist, there are "two separate federal and state streams flowing in distinct but closely parallel channels"?[5] Or does cooperative federalism more accurately define the nation's governing structure? This structure calls for the federal government and states to share activities, including planning, financing, and implementation. More recently—its beginnings can be traced to the 1930s and it became recognized in the 1950s—the term "intergovernmental relations" (IGR) has come to describe many federal-nonfederal programs. The major difference between federalism and intergovernmental relations is that the latter stresses *administration*, rather than policymaking, and is characterized by cooperative programs and often by large federal grants.[6] Relevant examples include federal funds for state water research centers or for wastewater treatment plants. The emphasis is on solving specific social and natural resource problems, and the programs call for the effective utilization of professional expertise at all levels of government.[7] While this approach has the capability of stimulating and sustaining change quickly and effectively, there are drawbacks, most of which can be seen in the field of water resources.

One problem is that professional administrators at all levels of government occasionally may find it difficult to reconcile their loyalty to a program with their loyalty to political superiors, for political objectives may conflict with apolitical administrative agendas. Also, while administrators closest to the problem may feel most competent to make decisions, federal officials just as strongly believe that they should oversee activities involving the federal budget, which, as Bruce Long points out, must be stretched further and further to accomodate the increasing demands being made on it. A third problem is that the system of intergovernmental relations does not eliminate, and may exacerbate, the competition among agencies at various levels of government. State agencies (such as departments of public works and natural resources) will fight for control of programs, and federal agencies will also battle for administrative control. Fourth, IGR may actually lead to a deterioration of relations. This can result from fundamental disagreements over level of funding or choice of program beneficiaries. More often, it results from one level of government believing that it has unfairly and unwisely been left out of the administrative "loop," i.e., state agencies believed that they should have had greater control over some of President Lyndon B. Johnson's block grant programs that sent federal funds directly to local governments. This direct federal-local link is a feature of what is sometimes called "creative federalism."[8] Finally, and perhaps most important, the system often confuses the public and results in lack of accountability. It is often difficult to know which government (local, state, or federal), no less which agency, is in charge. In sum, the resolution of water resources issues must be placed in the context of ongoing discussions about the future of American federalism.

When all is said, however, good water management, incorporating the notion of "sustainable development," necessitates more than changes in administration. It requires new environmental values. Historically, this country has lauded individual initiative and development. It has praised those who "pushed back the frontier" and "conquered nature." Projects were—and are—justified principally in terms of economic development. This is the ideology of the pioneer. It ignores the finiteness of both financial and natural resources. The approach is, in fact, an anachronism for a nation whose present and future well-being requires stewardship, not conquest, of the environment. Future projects must minimize environmental degradation. Flora, fauna, and aesthetic and recreational enjoyment need to be considered as carefully as gross national product, regional development, and individual income. In their articles, James M. Wright and Don L. Porter of the Tennessee Valley Authority and L. Scott Tucker, Executive Director of the Urban Drainage and Flood Control District, which includes the city of Denver, present practical management approaches to balance economic, environmental, aesthetic, and recreational concerns.

A number of factors, then, compel a reexamination of water policy in this country. These include changing values, shifting financial burdens, decaying infrastructure, degraded environment, and greater reliance on local and state governments. Western water users initiated the present round of conferences, just as they did in the early twentieth century, when, along with hydropower developers, they agitated for multipurpose river development. In her article, Holly Stoerker outlines the development of these conferences, emphasizing the important, indeed crucial, role states must play in developing and regulating water resources.

Neither from the economic nor the environmental point of view can the nation afford irresponsible and inefficient water use. Structural and policy changes are necessary, most participants in the National Forum on Water Management Policy seemed to agree, although technology offers some remedies. The Forum focused on *policy*, and the recommendations produced by the Forum's eight issue groups (see Appendix A) were intentionally limited to policy. Recommendations could be for either legislative or administrative changes and for any level of government.[9]

In developing this Forum, organizers faced the problem of selecting from a large number of issues those that seemed particularly pressing and controversial. The topics selected represent a consensus, but certainly each individual would have developed a slightly different list if he or she had sole control of the program. Likewise, while engineers, policymakers, and social scientists were well-represented at the Forum, natural scientists were not, as noted by several speakers, and this may have lent some bias to the proceedings. We can only hope that future conferences may fill some of the gaps left by the National Forum. Readers are reminded that the views of the authors are their own and not necessarily those of their agency, organization, or business, or of the American Water Resources Association, or any of the co-sponsors of the National Forum on Water Management Policy.

Over a hundred years ago, Woodrow Wilson, in his classic essay, "The Study of Administration,"[10] formulated what remains the fundamental challenge facing government officials at all levels:

> The question for us is, how shall our series of governments within governments be so administered that it shall always be to the interest of the public officer to serve, not his superior alone but the community also,

with the best efforts of his talents and the soberest service of his conscience? How shall such service be made to his commonest interest by contributing abundantly to his sustenance, to his dearest interest by furthering his ambition, and to his highest interest by advancing his honor and establishing his character? And how shall this be done alike for the local part and for the national whole?"

Wilson then added, "If we solve this problem we shall again pilot the world."

Wilson no doubt thought that social scientists would "solve this problem." Subsequent events proved otherwise; public administration has not gotten easier with time. To be sure it is rarely simple in a democratic, heterogeneous society, especially in the area of water management, where decisions may effect areas far removed from the watershed. Yet, manage we must, even while knowing how frustrating it can be. Proper management, like proper planning, allows for the emergence of new objectives, the empowerment of new groups, and the political involvement of the traditionally less articulate. It is necessary if projects are to serve equitably *all* the people in a region. In short, water management decisions, like others in public administration, must be based on some notion of justice.

The Forum and this book are dedicated to the memory of Abel Wolman. In a career spanning more than 70 years, Wolman, who died in 1989 at the age of 96, was one of this country's premier water resources planners. Perhaps best known for his work in sanitary engineering, and in particular for his pioneer research in using chlorination to purify water, Wolman also served as chief engineer of the Maryland Department of Health, professor of the department of sanitary engineering at Johns Hopkins, and chairman of the Water Resources Committee of the Natural Resources Committee during the New Deal of President Franklin D. Roosevelt. He constantly sought more data, decrying both the absence of analysis of completed projects and the inadequate planning of projects yet to be built.

Wolman firmly believed that rational administration would—and government should—improve society through the wise application of engineering and science. He thought that national policy should serve the country as a whole and that projects of purely local benefit should be financed by local interests. A cautious advocate of new federal-state relationships to oversee resource development, Wolman understood the advantages of local *management* (not necessarily, planning) over centralized administration.[12]

There is evidence in Abel Wolman's public career of a dynamic tension not uncommon to the career of water resources planners to this day. On one hand, there is the philosophical Wolman counseling caution, due regard for the public weal, and citizen participation. He undoubtedly agreed with a 1937

National Resources Committee publication on drainage basin planning that noted, "Through the democratic process, with participation in planning for the future of the areas in which they live, our citizens have found opportunity to make known their needs and to see how their requirements may get together in a general plan."[13] On the other side, there is Wolman, the rational engineer, wishing, in the words of one his reports, "to provide a sound and nationwide outline for securing the greatest beneficial use of the water resources of each major drainage basin in the United States,"[14] a matter that becomes messy when it extends beyond purely engineering matters of water control into public socioeconomic issues that spill over hydrological boundaries. However, Wolman understood better than some of his contempories the obligations of the engineer as an agent of social change. Indeed, for Wolman the distinction between social and technical engineering loses meaning. The responsible engineer will know something of human relations and will seek to apply his technical knowledge to social improvement. For Wolman, the engineer's ongoing social responsibility toward the public is at least as important as technical responsibility for project design and construction. Certainly, the same may be said of the administrators and policymakers who pass the laws and develop the regulations that often determine the fate of specific projects and of water resources development in general.

Notes

1. Some of the papers not included are summarized in the essays by Bory Steinberg and Holly Stoerker.
2. For more on sustainable development, see World Commission on Environment and Development, *Our Common Future* (New York, 1986).
3. On this, see Lloyd Burton, *American Indian Water Rights and the Limits of Law* (Lawrence, KS, 1991), 35-62.
4. See Martin Reuss, *Reshaping National Water Politics: The Emergence of the Water Resources Development Act of 1986* (Fort Belvoir, VA, 1991).
5. Jane Perry Clark, *The Rise of a New Federalism* (New York, 1938), as quoted in Daniel J. Elazar, "Federal-State Collaboration in the Nineteenth-Century United States," in *Cooperation and Conflict: Readings in American Federalism,* eds. Daniel J. Elazar, R. Bruce Carroll, R. Lester Levine, Douglas St. Angelo (Itasca, IL, 1969), 83.
6. Deil S. Wright, "A Century of the Intergovernmental Administrative State: Wilson's Federalism, New Deal Intergovernmental Relations, and Contemporary Intergovernmental Management," in *A Centennial History of the American State*, ed. Ralph Clark Chandler (New York, 1987), 234-42.
7. For a provocative history of federalism to the mid-1960s, see Harry N. Scheiber, *The Condition of American Federalism: An Historian's View,* U.S. Senate, Subcommittee on Intergovernmental Relations, Committee on Government Operations, Committee Print, 89th Cong., 2d sess. (Washington, D.C., 1966).

8. On this, see Wright, "A Century of the Intergovernmental Administrative State," 219-60; David M. Welborn and Jesse Burkhead, *Intergovernmental Relations in the American Administrative State: The Johnson Presidency* (Austin, TX, 1989), 165-98.
9. For another set of recommendations dealing with the same overall issues, see Leonard B. Dworsky, David J. Allee, and Ronald M. North, "Water Resources Planning and Management in the United States Federal System: Long Term Assessment and intergovernmental Issues," *Natural Resources Journal* 31, no. 3 (Summer 1991): 475-547; for recommendations on western water management specifically, see Marc Reisner and Sarah Bates, *Overtapped Oasis: Reform or Revolution for Western Water* (Washington, D.C., 1990), 111-43.
10. Woodrow Wilson, "The Study of Administration," *Political Science Quarterly* 11, no. 2 (June 1887): 197-222.
11. Ibid., 221.
12. For more on Wolman's life and philosophy, see Gilbert F. White, ed., *Water, Health and Society: Selected Papers by Abel Wolman* (Bloomington, IN, 1969).
13. National Resources Committee, *Drainage Basin Problems and Programs: 1937 Revision* (Washington, D.C., 1938), v; With the substitution of the word "fit" for "get," the same statement appears in a pamphlet intended for more widespread distribution. See, National Resources Committee, *Water Planning* (Washington, D.C., 1938), 1.
14. Abel Wolman, "Highlights of the National Water Resources Study," 2. Charles Merriam papers, box 209, folder 1, The Joseph Regenstein Library, The University of Chicago.

Multidisciplinary Perspectives on Water Resources Policy

The Context and The Process: How They Have Changed over Time

Robert Kelley

The participants in this panel have been asked to answer the question, "What does your discipline bring to water resources management?" Perhaps a brief story will offer an answer. In the early 1960s I was asked, "how had the flood control system in the Sacramento Valley, in the vicinity of Marysville and Yuba City where the Feather and Yuba rivers converge, evolved over time into its existing arrangements?" There had been a catastrophic nighttime levee break by Yuba City in 1955, many people had drowned in their homes, and hundreds of thousands of acres of land sat under water for months thereafter. Plaintiffs claiming tens of millions of dollars in damages insisted that the levee break occurred because the system was badly designed and that the state was liable.

To answer the question posed to me, I searched through public and private archives and library collections and hundreds of contemporary newspaper articles, through supervisors' minutes and court transcripts and committee hearings and official reports and maps made long ago. When I told the state's deputy attorney general that my testimony was ready, he said, well, we want to make sure you have got it right. So far as they could find out, this would be the first time a historian would testify not simply to state the origin of a single document, as had on occasion happened, but to tell a story, many hours long, about events he had not personally observed distilled from hundreds of documents. Why the levees were in their particular alignment was for local people buried in the mists of time. They had simply become natural facts, in place seemingly forever. In Yuba City, however, there was a venerable water engineer who had been at work there for sixty years. In a valley where, in its original, pre-levees condition, massive flooding was an almost annual event, creating in the centerline of the Sacramento Valley an inland sea one hundred miles long and many miles wide, it was natural to assume that from his long involvement in floods, and in subsequent efforts to plan and build new works, this man would be a fount of information.[1]

Accordingly, in a pretrial conference the young historian gave a dry run of his testimony before this Moses of water management in the valley, who it was presumed would certainly find much to say in criticism or at least by way of modifying or fleshing out the story. There was in any event a good deal of skepticism in the air about this whole undertaking. What indeed could the discipline of history bring to this particular problem in water resources management?

What is now called *public* history was then the newest of newcomers on the scene. Hardly anyone knew how powerful historical analysis could be in explaining not only great wars but any kind of complex public situation, even down to the uses made of particular pieces of property over time. Unknown to the courts and policymakers was the existence of an almost untapped national resource in the research skills taught in America's graduate programs in history. If mobilized in this new direction—that is, helping clients understand an issue before them—these skills were capable of producing in-depth historical explanations which would be disciplined, closely-reasoned, closely-packed. They could provide answers to crucial public questions which would be based on solid evidence drawn from every kind of source, not just those legal or economic or technical in nature.[2]

My presentation before the venerable Yuba City engineer took several hours. In it I recounted step-by-step the long, complex human narrative of the struggle local people had waged with their big rivers flood after flood: what they had done by way of levee building, why, and how, and when; their many debates in many settings, their decisions, their defeats, their successes, decade after decade, from far back in the 1850s when Americans first settled the Valley.

In a sense, the presentation aimed at creating a verbal version of time-lapse photography, in which over a few hours a century of change could in the mind's eye be seen to take place. My audience in that conference room listened in on local debates occurring just a block away but more than a hundred years before, then watched as short, low, narrow levees first appeared here and there on an unadorned natural landscape, in scraps and pieces. Thereafter, these first small structures grew and lengthened and shifted in location as the river announced in successive high waters how it would perform. Then, having been tailored to fit the rivers' actual flow patterns in that particular location, they thickened eventually into embankments more than a hundred feet wide and rose to heights of twenty-five feet, then extended up and down the river bank and joined together to form a connected system. In a long learning process people had come—by trial and error—to see where the barriers must be and how aligned, if the monster flows were to pass them by.

As Sacramento Valley juries in case after case were later to conclude, the process and the system when seen historically, as a human creation constructed painstakingly over time, did in fact make sense, the decisions were understandable. The flood control system, juries concluded, was reasonably designed. Yet during my pretrial presentation, the venerable engineer who for sixty years had been in the center of these events, and who had inherited a professional memory of earlier days from older engineers, did not at all behave as the attorneys had thought he would. He kept clapping his hand to his brow, and saying, "Is *that* what happened! Is *that* what happened!"

So it always is. There is a touching faith that we can simply find the oldest resident, in a community or a corporation or a government agency, and ask him or her. People think they know about the past; while in actual fact, they are constantly making use of it—or so they believe. They are forever saying, "as history tells us. . . ." In their minds they link up current events with earlier ones, that is, they make analogies with past events and act accordingly, analogies unquestioned, untested, and usually inappropriate and inaccurate. In reality, of course, their unassisted "memories" of local history, regional or organizational, their unaided assumptions about to the history of the social security system or the atomic energy complex, let alone water resource issues, subsist on a thin gruel of legend and myth and assumed "facts" accepted without question. People are surprised to learn how it *really* happened, when someone digs into the sources.[3]

Public History's Role

All public or private works or programs or policies are in reality far more complex in their origins and nuances and nature, and in their evolution into their current condition, than present-day occupants of positions of authority or supervision realize. To explain these always complicated and elusive matters, the discipline of history brings to the task *memory—reliable, accurate, documented, comprehensive* memory. History is grounded in actual documents, thus it stands up to the intense scrutiny of the courts—and more and more, that is where just about every issue involving water winds up. This is why public historians now do so much litigation support all over the United States.

Public historians bring memory that will form the foundation for wise and effective policy decisions, rather than policies founded on false assumptions about the past which are certain to fail, often because they reinvent some version of an earlier wheel that collapsed. Life is a process, not a condition, and that means it is a *historical* process, not a logical one. Being historical, life proceeds not formulaically, according to theory, but in a disorderly, multifactor, to many people confusing fashion.

In sum, historical testimony is now so powerful in the courts because it tells the story of actual people doing actual things in actual circumstances, which the law and our juries can understand and credit. There are entire public history consulting firms now in existence which have come rushing up over the past fifteen years to meet that need, among the many other purposes public history serves. Also, there are now hundreds of historians in the federal government—and most notably, from our point of view, in the Bureau of Reclamation and the U.S. Army Corps of Engineers, where digging out the "lessons learned" from history is the fundamental goal.

The field of action continues to expand. In a typical development, a number of years ago the courts began asking an unusual question in cases involving a particular law: what is the *legislative history* of that statute? Looking beyond just the words of the enactment as it stands on the page, which may be variously interpreted, what did the legislature apparently intend to achieve by passing that bill? And so an entire area of professional practice has sprung up for public historians—in this case at the initiative of the judges themselves, not of the attorneys or litigants.[4]

So, too, following the 1969 passage of the National Environmental Policy Act, and similar statutes in various states, historians have become part of the environmental impact review process. Also, there is land use history, called for peremptorily by the new laws on toxic wastes. This has recently summoned into existence yet another thriving area of professional involvement for public historians.[5] Private corporations have been finding how extraordinarily valuable the work of consulting historical firms—skilled in researching the history of individual companies—can be, illuminating, for example, their firm's corporate culture, or why it launched itself in particular directions and perhaps how it can shift those directions.

The Crucial Relevance Of Political Culture and the Human Factor

Historians offer perhaps most of all, when they are doing their job right, an insistent teaching that we must get a comprehensive command of the *context* if we are to understand human affairs. Of all the dynamics in the making and implementing of public policy, context is perhaps the most powerful, the most crucial, of all influences.[6] Accordingly, my purpose in this gathering now is to offer a historical perspective on the peculiar nature of, and the inner dynamics and enduring tensions to be seen within, the context for water resource managment in this country, why it is the way it is, and how it has changed over time.

I do so because my experience over many years in studying and working with people in water management has taught me that they have one large blind spot, a blind spot out of which trouble for which they have not made preparation seems to erupt at them as a great surprise, to cause them endless frustrations and difficulties. That blind spot concerns the *political culture* in which we are all embedded, and the *human factors* which operate in that setting.

American political culture is, and always has been, an almost unique phenomenon in the world.[7] It is mysterious and irritating, and the impulse among the technically and scientifically trained is to ignore it, to look the other way, to curse it and hope they can get around it in some way. No community of people is more central to water management than civil engineers, but engineering students, nationwide, are required to learn almost nothing of the political system, nor of the human factor in public affairs, as they might learn of these things from the humanities and the social sciences.

13

At the University of California, Santa Barbara, we have recently created a professional school to train environmental scientists and managers; and, as the planning of the school was essentially in the hands of scientists and technical people, the proportion of the curriculum which studies how public policies are actually made and implemented in the real world is very, very small. The assumption is that if a good technical solution is worked out, somehow it will be enacted—if only that baffling and essentially illegitimate barrier, *politics*, the motivating spirit of which is thought to be ignorance and perverse resistance, does not get in the way. One hears the experts asking, are they not aware that we are the people who really understand this problem? Why do they not simply let us get on with our job?

The trouble is that, as the historic record abundantly demonstrates, water management is becoming more, not less, political; the public and their elected representatives, through a growing complex of private and public agencies locally, regionally, statewide, and nationally, are getting more and more involved. The water management elite has less and less freedom of action in a society putting into practice, ever more with each passing decade, the powerful principles of the Declaration of Independence, the Constitution, and the Bill of Rights.

What do I mean by this remark? The reality is that the way we carry on our public policymaking in this country is exactly how, in these great documents, from our beginnings we intended it to be. Our system, purposefully, is very difficult to move in particular directions. Furthermore, its creators believed that that quality—how we do things—was one of our proudest boasts before the world. The father of the U.S. Constitution, James Madison, looked at the monarchies of Europe and pointed out that centralized, unchecked power is dangerous to human liberty. It must be limited or tyranny results. It must be split up into many warring elements, horizontally and vertically.[8]

Power, for the most part, must be left in the hands of each state and local community, said Madison's close ally, Thomas Jefferson. Inveterate democrat, eternal philosopher of all who believe in the wisdom of the people at large, Jefferson was convinced that elites in power are inclined always to exaggerate their own wisdom as against the people; that, because corrupted by their wealth and preeminence, they are at every moment seeking their own profit and aggrandizement.[9]

Thus, in the United States, power has always been managed in a special way: in our particular version of that form of government called *federalism*, it is consciously, rigorously diffused and localized as it is in no other developed nation. Why? Ultimately in order to free the individual to make his or her own way in life. That was a radical idea in the 1700s, when everywhere else in the world it was believed that the people were foolish and governments must have unchecked authority to *rule* them and tell them what to do—and it remains a daring idea today. Indeed, historians have recently recognized, almost to their surprise, how truly and enduringly radical, in these terms, were the American Revolution and the Constitution of 1787 and the Bill of Rights. That radicalism continues in many ways to set apart American life from anything seen abroad.[10]

14

Even the Canadians, let alone the British, are far different from us in this matter, for as a monarchy, even one governed by a democratically elected parliament, they give much more power and unchecked freedom of action to their central authorities—to, as it is often stated, the central elites. No other developed country but the United States, for that matter, breaks up and diffuses its banking institutions as we do, creating literally thousands of them so that they will compete with each other, let alone fragments social policy, land management, and education as we do.

No other country is so populistic and egalitarian and democratic as is the United States—for better or for worse, however one views these things. The Canadians have recently adopted a constitution and a charter of rights and freedoms, but they are quite candid about the fact that they make no attempt to put within protective, constitutionally unbreachable walls the rights of individuals the way we do in our Bill of Rights. They do this only for the rights of groups, not of individual persons, whose rights Parliament is free to invade any time it thinks it wise to do so. In fact, we also protect the individual's right to private property as does no other nation, again including the Canadians and the British.[11]

The Central Paradox

Some ninety years ago, in the Progressive Era—the years roughly from 1900 on into the 1920s—we put into our system the central paradox that faces all water policy makers even today. On the one hand, at the state level we vastly expanded the people's potential control over government by establishing the initiative and referendum, that is, we empowered the people at large to make law directly. At the same time, out of our new universities, especially out of our engineering schools, there came the concept that scientifically trained expertise, impersonal and above all nonpolitical, should be put to use solving society's problems. Furthermore, it should be put to use in an institutional arrangement which walled off the experts, as much as possible, from popular supervision or control, for there was a great distrust of the people's wisdom in this variety of progressivism. Thus, powerful, presidentially-appointed commissions and executive-branch agencies were created who directed reclamation and flood control projects, regulated railroad, telegraph, and telephone rates, or interest rates and the money supply, as well as logging and access to hydropower sites. In all of this, the idea of central *planning* was the core faith, planning led and put into effect by experts.[12]

Americans in the Progressive Era were widely enamored of these ideas. Furthermore, in a way quite foreign to their temper now, they were still remarkably ready to trust and defer to authority. The notion of a scientifically-planned context for rationally opening and making use of the nation's natural resources was thought admirable, save to the businessmen being regulated. Engineers were still the most widely admired products of our new universities, nationwide they were often thought to be figures of daring and ingenuity—think of their exploits in the incredible expansion of the railroads and the excavation and building of the

15

Panama Canal, for example—and the idea of national planning led by such people could be confidently regarded as the wave of the future.[13] So it went, through the First World War, the New Deal, and the early years after the Second World War.

Water development has been peculiarly marked by effective power being close-held in a few hands, by its reliance on procedures essentially undemocratic in nature, and generally inaccessible to the people at large. In my state of California, the city of Los Angeles, left essentially free by the federal and state governments to do what it wished to the water resources of peoples living far away, and guided by gifted if sometimes quite unscrupulous engineers who were given now-incredible powers to do whatever they wished, subject to ratifying bond-elections, built an enormous water-gathering system almost by fiat, despite local resistance.[14]

In the mid-1920s, when under a true Progressive Republican, Secretary of Commerce and later President Herbert Hoover, the federal government began actively midwifing the tapping of the Colorado River by seven western states, a kind of apogee in elite control was locally reached.[15] Southern California secured from Sacramento the creation of a Metropolitan Water District to distribute its share of that river's water while its governing board was almost completely walled off from direct popular control, so as to free up the experts to do what in their judgment they believed right and proper.[16] Meanwhile, no part of the federal government's work grew more dramatically, in response to the fertilizing impact of the faith in planning and expert leadership, than its vast programs of water resource development. The incredible explosion of dam and reservoir projects all over the continent stands as one of humanity's most formidable physical creations on the face of the earth.[17]

The paradox, however, was still there, creating tension. How, in a ferociously democratic society, could experts be given the free hand that successful planning required? In fact, they were not. Even in these bounteous times for water developers, the process was powerfully shaped and channeled by American political culture to head off in directions the planners, the experts, often did not want to go. This is the lesson from the past taught by a brilliantly researched and narrated history authored by a senior historian in the U.S. Army Corps of Engineers, Dr. Martin Reuss. In it Reuss tells us of the deep historical traditions and attitudes which shape federal water management in this country, and the institutional structure we created for it, reaching far back into the 1800s. Then, with that foundation, we follow, almost day by day, the extremely complicated, extraordinarily human, and intensely political story of the passage to enactment of that historic piece of legislation, the Water Resources Development Act of 1986. Again and again, as we learn from him, that central confrontation between democracy, as embodied in the Congress of the United States, and expertise looking toward rational efficiency, as embodied in the federal water agencies, has produced victories for Congress and defeats for the agencies. In Congress, the planning impulse coming from the executive branch has always been brought up short by the realities of our now two-centuries-old system for making public policy.[18]

Americans have clearly decided that water is much too vital, too important to everyone and to every community, to leave its management to the experts. For more than 150 years the people's representatives in Congress, like those in the legislative bodies in each state, have been *determined* to hold onto their policy-making prerogatives over water. Congress exercises that iron grip to this very day, and it will forevermore. From local water districts and city councils to state legislatures and the national Congress, making ultimate decisions concerning water is therefore almost uniquely a *legislative* matter.

Executive departments are always important, of course. They are major centers of expertise and leadership. When it comes to water, however, the people's elected representatives want both to shape water policy and to be its final authority, and so do the people themselves, when they have the chance, through the initiative process. From as far back as the 1820s and 1830s, this has been the crux of the story: Congress, driven by its complex and confusing multiplicity of dynamics, ideas, and interests, is the arena where the decision is principally made as to whether or not something is to be done, and precisely how.[19] Nowhere do we learn this lesson more strikingly than in the absorbing narrative Richard Allan Baker, the historian of the United States Senate, has given us of the work of that towering figure in water management policy in the 1950s and 1960s, Senator Clinton Anderson of New Mexico, who most decisively transferred the making of natural resources policy from the White House to Congress.[20]

Furthermore, as the distinguished University of Oklahoma water historian Donald J. Pisani is reminding us in a recent iconoclastic book, the states and their local governments have always held fast to a very large degree of authority over water management. In other words, the traditional historical narrative is wrong. Water historians have told a near-conspiratorial tale of growing federal domination in the matter of water, a story in which the states appear practically to fade into the background, but that is a delusive picture. A great deal of constitutional and legal authority over water has historically been actively retained in the states' hands; it still is, and will always be.[21]

There are long stretches of our history, in fact, when Washington's impact upon the states, in this regard, has been quite limited. Even the Reclamation Act of 1902, which for the first time empowered the federal government to build dams and plan and construct irrigation works, left control over water supplies in the state's hands. Though brought to this point bitterly complaining, the federal government has had to line up with everyone else and get its water rights for federal projects from the states.[22] In short, American federalism is alive and very well in water matters. James Madison's vision of the proper allocation of power in a free society governs us as much today as ever it did in the past.

If anything, the diffusion of power in this country has increased. State legislatures used to meet every two years for brief periods, and had almost no staff. Now many are practically full-time bodies with active, large staffs. Some states are even maintaining, in effect, foreign policies of their own, as they place permanent

17

trade offices in countries abroad. The historic innovation of the 1986 Water Resources Development Act was to establish cost-sharing with the states, which has had the surprising result, for such federal agencies as the Corps of Engineers, that they must henceforth share management over federal water projects with the states as well.[23]

To repeat: federalism is strengthening and growing in day-to-day impact in this country. In fact, scholars who in recent years have been mounting fresh studies of federalism and its powerful influence on events have been discovering that a flow toward federalism is a world-wide trend. From India around the world in both directions, certainly in the collapsing former Soviet Union and its empire, the striking reality of our time in nation after nation has been the devolution of authority from central to provincial and local governments.[24]

It is not surprising, then, that water is one of those subjects which as a policy question has become ever more intensely localized. Every water issue we may explore in American history began, of course, in a local community somewhere, and it is usually still there as a living problem. This huge realm in public policy continues to be managed in an arrangement that in some complicated fashion makes use of every level of government from local community through the state to Washington, D.C. Often, surprisingly, the situation features a direct link from the local community to Washington, as in Bureau of Reclamation projects, bypassing the states.

Thus the number of players involved in decisions has grown tremendously. As remarked earlier the freedom of elites in government and private enterprise to get what they want has been sharply reduced, put in the glare of pitiless publicity, wrenched out of their hands to share with ever more organized private and public agencies. Similarly, from the 1960s a vast nationwide upsurge of a newly sensitive environmental consciousness has shifted as in an earthquake all older foundations.

At the same time, a huge in-place institutional network creates mounting institutional drag. Steeply rising costs in construction and in all operations since the early 1970s and the rise of extremely expensive new competitors for public funds, as in health care and social security—let alone defense policy—have together sharply narrowed the range of elective appropriations. The fact that the farming population is down to less than 2 percent of the American people, while urban populations and their water needs and their political power in water policy decisions have grown tremendously, is a reality which has utterly transformed the nationwide political equation in all water matters. Business as usual in this arena is a thing of the past.

Then, as the rising tidal force which lifts all boats, in the latter decades of the twentieth century the American public has as never before become deeply involved in policy making and implementing. They have finally come fully alive to their potential powers in making public policy, and they *exercise* them. Wherever these powers, embodied most dramatically in the initiative and referendum process, are available—powers which the British and Canadian establishments

18

regard with horror—the public simply imposes new policies directly and in detail on all manner of public questions.

California's executive and legislature and its community of water experts found this out dramatically not long ago when after years of painstaking planning, governmental negotiations, and legislative enactment—even Governor Jerry Brown had approved the project—the people of the state on environmental grounds threw out bodily an enacted program for carrying Sacramento river water around the Sacramento-San Joaquin delta in a peripheral canal, its purpose being to deliver higher quality water to large farming interests and the urban peoples of Southern California.[25] Even the mighty Metropolitan Water District of Southern California is increasingly needing to take account of public desires and to let down the bars guarding its insulated system of elite control. Recently, for the first time we have been seeing contested elections to water boards, and longtime powerful figures sent packing as environmentally-oriented folks replace them.[26]

Summary

Water policymakers and managers, therefore, must take the political culture seriously, and train themselves—as well as student engineers—to understand and work with it, not as something illegitimate, but as something growing out of the very core of who we are. The political culture and human nature are much more decisive in the public equation than the benefit-cost analyses students in the technical fields are trained, almost alone, to conduct. Human affairs have a complexity far too great to be encompassed in such simple calculations; water planners, in an America increasingly flexing its democratic muscles and by daily exercise making them ever stronger, are being challenged to think in new ways.

The intense localism of our political culture, its fragmentation and diffusion of authority, and its commitment to individualism and private property and a strong and intrusive voice of the people, have without question changed water management drastically since the truly wide-open days of the nineteenth century and the first half of the twentieth. In this larger context, the deeper impulses are still so powerful and basic that they continue to produce a water management anarchy which makes it very difficult to get anything done. If we may be certain that any graph line will continue rising, it is that showing the power, in water management, of the political culture and of the human factor.

Notes

1. In Robert Kelley, *Battling the Inland Sea: American Political Culture, Public Policy, and the Sacramento Valley 1850-1986* (Berkeley, Los Angeles, & London, 1989), the story of the disciplining of the "inland sea," the reclaiming of the Sacramento Valley, and the building of its immense flood control system, is narrated at length. It draws heavily on the research conducted while writing consultant papers

for, and serving as an expert witness in, ten litigations over the years 1963-1985, cited therein.

2. The first graduate programs for training public historians were established at the University of California, Santa Barbara and at Carnegie-Mellon University (there, under the rubric "applied history") in 1976. There are now scores of them in the United States and elsewhere. The movement and profession of "public history" is now led by the National Council on Public History, which convenes annual national meetings attended by hundreds of public historians, and guided by the internationally-circulated professional and scholarly journal jointly sponsored by the NCPH and the University of California, Santa Barbara, *The Public Historian: A Journal of Public History,* now in its fourteenth volume. On public history's basic concept, see Robert Kelley, "Public History: Its Origins, Nature, and Prospects," *The Public Historian,* 1 (1978): 17-28. See also, Barbara J. Howe and Emory L. Kemp, eds., *Public History: An Introduction* (Malabar, FL, 1986); David F. Trask and Robert W. Pomeroy III, eds., *The Craft of Public History: An Annotated Select Bibliography* (Westport, CT, 1983); David B. Mock, ed., *History and Public Policy* (Malabar, FL, 1991).

3. These themes are richly developed in Richard E. Neustadt and Ernest R. May, *Thinking in Time: The Uses of History for Decision Makers* (New York and London, 1986).

4. See, Robert U. Goehlert and Fenton S. Martin, *Congress and Law-Making: Researching the Legislative Process,* 2d ed. (Santa Barbara, CA., 1989); Gwendolyn B. Folsom, *Legislative History: Research for the Interpretation of Laws* (Charlottesville, VA., 1972).

5. See, Shelley Bookspan, "History Requited: Historians and Toxic Waste," in Mock, ed., *History and Public Policy,* 75-96.

6. See, Garry D. Brewer and Peter deLeon, *The Foundations of Policy Analysis* (Homewood, IL., 1983): "Contextuality means understanding the relationship between the parts and whole of a problem ... we urge comprehensiveness by giving preference to the whole." (13) "The first factor is the *context of the problem.* . . .What are the environmental, normative, technological, and political constraints?. . .A primary consideration for the decision maker is the overall context. . . .The political culture of the system should be considered." (191-92). "A sensitive appreciation of specific, realistic contexts in which decisions are made and results are sought is a necessary prerequisite to understanding and action." (260)

7. The concept of "political culture," conceived to point to the reality that every governing system is "embedded" in the culture of a particular society, holds that governing institutions and political values are what they are in a given society because they "fit" the culture which gives them birth. The political scientist Gabriel Almond first proposed the concept in his "Comparative Political Systems," *The Journal of Politics* 18 (1956): 389-90. Historians have widely put it to use (see, "Introduction," in Robert Kelley, *The Cultural Pattern in American Politics: The First Century* [New York, 1979], 3-28).

8. See, Gordon W. Wood, *The Creation of the American Republic, 1776-1787* (Boston, 1969).

9. See, chapter 4, "The Inherited World View: Thomas Jefferson and the Ideology of Conflict," in Robert Kelley, *The Transatlantic Persuasion: The Liberal-Democratic Mind in the Age of Gladstone* (New York, 1969), 101-44; Merrill Peterson, *The Jefferson Image in the American Mind* (New York, 1960).

10. See, Gordon S. Wood, *The Radicalism of the American Revolution* (New York, 1992); Nathan O. Hatch, *The Democratization of American Christianity* (New Haven & London, 1989).
11. See, Seymour Martin Lipset, *Continental Divide: The Values and Institutions of the United States and Canada* (New York & London, 1990). For the Charter of Rights & Freedoms, compared with the U.S. Bill of Rights, consult 101-6.
12. The literature on the Progressive Era and its thinking is large. For the points here made, see: Stephen Skowronek, *Building a New American State: The Expansion of National Administrative Capacities 1877-1920* (Cambridge, Eng., 1982); Samuel Haber, *Efficiency and Uplift: Scientific Management in the Progressive Era* (New York, 1964); Otis L. Graham, Jr., *The Great Campaigns: Reforms and War in America 1900-1928* (Englewood Cliffs., NJ, 1971); Samuel P. Hays, *Conservation and the Gospel of Effiency: The Progressive Conservation Movement, 1890-1920* (Cambridge, MA, 1959); David J. Rothman, *Conscience and Convenience: The Asylum and its Alternatives in Progressive America* (Boston, 1980); Chapter 12, " A Policy Context Transformed: The Progressive Era and the Revival of Planning, 1902-1906," in Kelley, *Battling the Inland Sea,*. 247-72.
13. Raymond H. Merritt, *Engineering in American Society 1850-1875* (Lexington, KY, 1969).
14. William L. Kahrl, *Water and Power: The Conflict over Los Angeles' Water Supply in the Owens Valley* (Berkeley, Los Angeles, & London, 1982).
15. Norris Hundley, *The Colorado River Compact and the Politics of Water in the American West* (Berkeley, CA, 1975); Joan Hoff Wilson, *Herbert Hoover: Forgotten Progressive* (Boston, 1975).
16. Kazuto Oshio, a Fulbright doctoral student taking his work with me, is currently writing a history of the Metropolitan Water District, in which this dimension of its nature is explored.
17. The subject of two controversial recent works: Marc Reisner, *Cadillac Desert: The American West and its Disappearing Water* (New York, 1986), and Donald Worster, *Rivers of Empire: Water, Aridity, & the Growth of the American West* (New York, 1985).
18. Martin Reuss, *Reshaping National Water Politics: The Emergence of the Water Resources Development Act of 1986,* Institute of Water Resources, Water Resources Support Center, U.S. Army Corps of Engineers (IWR Policy Study 91-PS-1, Washington, D.C., 1991). See also, Daniel McCool, "Water Welfare and the New Politics of Water," *Halcyon/1992: A Journal of the Humanities* 14 (1992): 85-102.
19. Ibid., passim.
20. Richard Allan Baker, *Conservation Politics: The Senate Career of Clinton P. Anderson* (Albuquerque, NM, 1985).
21. Donald J. Pisani, "Water Law and Localism in the West," *Halcyon/1992,* 14 (1992): 33-56; and *To Reclaim a Divided West: The Dream and Reality of Irrigation, 1848-1902* (Albuquerque, NM, 1992).
22. Ibid.
23. See chapter 4, "Sharing the Burden," in Reuss, *Reshaping National Water Politics,* 145-99.
24. On this theme, see the published papers from the second and third Berkeley Seminar on Federalism: Harry N. Scheiber, ed., *Federalism: Studies in History, Law, and*

Policy (Berkeley, CA., 1988), and Harry N. Scheiber and Malcolm M. Feeley, eds., *Power Divided: Essays on the Theory and Practice of Federalism* (Berkeley, CA, 1989).

25. Discussed in Norris Hundley, *The Long Thirst: Californians and Water 1770s-1990s* (Berkeley, Los Angeles, and London, 1992).

26. Robert Gottlieb, "Thirst for Growth: Water Agencies in the West," *Halcyon/1992* 14 (1992): 73-84.

Economics and Water Resources

Allen V. Kneese

Introduction

My assignment is to describe and assess the contribution of economics to water management. This is a very large topic so, to meet space limitations, I will confine my discussion to water issues in the western United States and limit the topic further to mostly water quantity rather than quality matters. I should note, however, that the economics of water quality has been a large and influential area of research.

Water allocation institutions in the West were built up during a period of rapid water development and were designed to foster and aid that development. Prior appropriation law helped to provide a degree of security of supply so that private developers of irrigation had the incentive to commit capital and labor to the construction of diversion and distribution systems. Yet, the relationships between law, institutions, and development did not stop there.

Even after water sources were fully appropriated, agriculture continued to expand by developing supplies through the federal program to reclaim the arid West. The era of reclaiming arid lands began in the late nineteenth century, and the 1902 Reclamation Act established this objective as a national goal. The period following the Reclamation Act was one of heavily subsidized and increasingly centralized, large-scale irrigation projects. Long-term, interest-free financing based on "ability to pay" further institutionalized the notion that unappropriated and undeveloped water was itself free, with its only cost being the capital cost of constructing works and the subsequent operations and maintenance cost. The Bureau of Reclamation provided dams and diversion works on most major waterways in the West. Transbasin diversion projects were also commonplace. Special water districts were created to repay the federal government and to operate and maintain reclamation works. If projects experienced hardships, contract obligations were deferred. Regions that had political clout in Congress were usually treated most generously. Frequently, hydroelectric power production was part of these projects and was used as the "cash register" to subsidize irrigation water development.

The West is rapidly undergoing a major transformation with respect to water. Increasing water scarcity already has brought changes in western development and water-use patterns, and much greater changes are likely to occur in the future. In particular, the expansion of irrigated agriculture based on the availability of inexpensive water is ending.

Just a few decades ago supplies were sufficient to satisfy a rapid growth of water use throughout virtually all of the West. More recently, however, high costs and limited opportunities for developing new supplies have severely constrained the growth of offstream water use in many areas, especially where users are heavily dependent on diminishing supplies of groundwater. Total water withdrawals for all but hydroelectric generation rose 4.6 percent per annum from 1950 to 1960, compared to only 1.4 percent per annum from 1970 to 1980. Excluding the northern plains states of Kansas, Nebraska, and North and South Dakota, where water withdrawals nearly doubled over the last decade, water withdrawals rose only 0.9 percent per annum from 1970 to 1980.

Rights to most of the surface waters have been allocated, and with rising frequency, potential users are forced to compete for the same water. This competition has been intensified by the rising value that society is placing on instream water uses. In nearly half of the West's water resource subregions, the sum of instream use (defined as the flow at the discharge point of the subregion required to satisfy the higher of minimum needs to maintain fish and wildlife populations or navigational needs) and offstream consumption exceeds average yearly streamflow. Furthermore, since current levels of water consumption result in the groundwater mining of about 22.4 million acre-feet per year, future competition over supplies likely will intensify even in the absence of further growth in demand.

Approximately 90 percent of western water consumption is for the irrigation of about fifty million acres. As both the largest and a relatively low-value user, irrigation is the sector most directly affected by the changing water situation. Nonagricultural water consumption grew twice as fast as irrigation use from 1960 to 1980. Where water has become particularly scarce and expensive, water for irrigation has started to level off or even decline. In Arizona, for example, total irrigation water consumption declined by about 6 percent from 1970 to 1980, while consumption for other uses rose by 67 percent. Only in the northern plains did the growth of water consumption for irrigation exceed the growth for other uses during the last decade.[1]

My discussion will proceed in two parts. The first will focus on benefit-cost analysis, which was concerned with the economics of the allocation of public capital during the rapid development phase of water resources. While benefit-cost analysis is of historical interest and was first applied to the economic evaluation of water projects, it is now finding applications in many other areas of public decision making as well. The second part addresses the theory and practice of markets and pricing, a field that concentrates on the allocation of the water resource itself now that the era of massive water development is about over.

Benefit-Cost Analysis: The Historical Context

Introduction

Benefit-cost analysis, an applied welfare economics technique, has played a very large role historically in water resource economics and, more recently, in environmental economics. This mode of analysis initially was developed to evaluate water resources investments made by federal water agencies in the United States, principally the U.S. Bureau of Reclamation and the U.S. Army Corps of Engineers. The general objective of benefit-cost analysis in this application was to provide a useful picture of the costs and gains from making investments in water development. Here I briefly consider the history of this mode of analysis and show how its applications have evolved over time.

The intellectual father of the technique is often said to be Jules Dupuit, who in 1844 wrote a frequently cited study, "On the Measure of the Utility of Public Works."[2] In this remarkable article, Dupuit recognized the concept of consumer's surplus (a central concept in the modern application of benefit-cost analysis) and saw that consequently the benefits of public works are not necessarily equal to the direct revenues that the public works projects will generate.

Benefit-Cost Analysis and Water Resource Development

Early contributions to benefit-cost analysis generally came from the federal agencies responsible for water development. In fact, such agencies have long been aware of the need for economic evaluation of projects, and the benefit-cost procedure is now embodied in agency policy and in government legislation. As examples, in 1808 Albert Gallatin, President Jefferson's secretary of the treasury, issued a report on transportation programs for the new nation in which he stressed the need to compare the benefits and the costs of proposed waterway improvements. The Federal Reclamation Act of 1902, which created the Bureau of Reclamation (first called the Reclamation Service) and was aimed at opening the American West to irrigation, required analysis to establish the repayment capacity of projects.

In more recent times the Flood Control Act of 1936 has a special significance for the development of benefit-cost analysis. This statute declared the constitutional powers of the federal government to improve rivers in general and their watersheds for flood control purposes. It thus extended Corps of

Engineers operations to the many unnavigable streams along with navigable streams and their tributaries. The same flood control act provided that federal improvements for flood control could be undertaken "if the benefits to whomsoever they may accrue are in excess of the estimated costs. . . ." This provision effectively subjected all flood control projects of the Corps to a benefit-cost test, and made an excess of benefits over costs a requirement for authorization of a project. Whether the legislators who framed and enacted this statute knew it or not, with this provision they enshrined the "Kaldor-Hicks" potential compensation criterion in federal law. This criterion says that a project is economically justified if the beneficiaries could compensate the losers, whether they do so or not.

Although the statutory directive applied specifically only to flood control improvements by the Corps of Engineers and the Department of Agriculture, all water planning agencies soon adopted it for all water resources purposes. Each agency, however, adopted different and often inconsistent criteria for estimating benefits and costs.

A few years after the passage of the Flood Control Act of 1936, Congress provided a statutory basis for benefit-cost analysis by the Bureau of Reclamation. The Reclamation Project Act of 1939 authorized the secretary of the interior to take into account a variety of joint and alternative uses in the development of any reclamation project, including irrigation, power production, urban water supplies, flood control, navigation, and other miscellaneous purposes. It required that he consult with the Corps of Engineers on flood control and navigation features of projects and secure special congressional appropriations for such features.

Most significantly for our purposes, the 1939 act required the secretary of the interior to estimate the total benefits and costs of every multipurpose project, and required that the sum of benefits from a project at least cover the total project costs if congressional authorization for a project is to be secured. This law subjected Bureau projects, like those of the Corps of Engineers, to trial by benefit-cost analysis.

In 1946, the U.S. Federal Interagency River Basin Committee (a group composed of representatives of federal agencies with water resource responsibilities) appointed a subcommittee on benefits and costs to reconcile the practices of federal agencies in making benefit-cost analyses. This reflected the concern over the diverse practices of several agencies. In 1950, the subcommittee issued a landmark report entitled *Proposed Practices for Economic Analysis of River Basin Projects*. This volume was known affectionately to a generation of resource economists as the Green Book because of the color of its cover.[3] While never fully accepted either by the parent committee or the federal agencies, this report was remarkably sophisticated in its use of economic analysis and laid such an intellectual foundation for research and debate as to set it apart from other major reports in the realm of public expenditures.

This document also provided general guidance for the routine development of benefit-cost analysis of water projects that persists to the present day, a theme I will pick up again shortly.

Following this report came some outstanding publications from the research and academic communities. Several books appearing since the late 1950s have clarified the welfare economics concepts applicable to water resources development and use and have explored the fundamental rationale for government activity in the area. For example, Otto Eckstein's 1958 book, *Water Resources Development: The Economics of Project Evaluation,*[4] is outstanding for its careful review and critique of federal agency practice with respect to benefit-cost analysis. While naturally somewhat dated it remains a valuable reference.

In 1960, Jack Hirschleifer and collaborators prepared a clear exposition of principles together with applications to several important cases.[5] Other reports appeared during the early 1960s. In 1962, a group of economists, engineers, and hydrologists at Harvard University published an especially notable study which probed into applications of systems analysis and computer technology within the framework of benefit-cost analysis.[6] The intervening years have seen considerable additional work on the technique and its gradual expansion to areas outside the field of water resources.

Further Developments in the Federal Government

Meanwhile, back in Washington efforts to standardize benefit-cost practices in water projects continued. From the early 1950s to the early 1960s, the federal government issued two major documents of relevance. The first was Bureau of the Budget Circular A-47, developed in 1952 during the Truman administration and adopted by the Eisenhower administration the following year.[7] The second was Senate Document No. 97 which the Kennedy administration issued in 1962.[8] Neither differed substantially from the principles for national economic efficiency analysis set out in the Green Book, but they did reflect political differences between the two administrations. The Eisenhower administration wanted rules that would justify fewer projects, and the Kennedy administration wanted rules that would justify more projects. Thus the documents concerned themselves with such matters as appropriate discount rates and what types of benefits would be permissible for inclusion. This is one illustration of the fact that, as Mr. Dooley said of the Supreme Court, benefit-cost analysis "follows the election returns." More broadly, over the years economists have complained loudly that benefit-cost analysis is influenced by the self-interest of the agencies conducting it and their clientele groups. On the other hand, benefit-cost analysis has probably served to weed out the very worst water projects, and by presenting assumptions and data in an organized way it provides an opportunity for critics to question assumptions and data and to test the sensitivity of results to them. Such reanalysis has influenced decisions on public projects.

Also Senate Document 97 moved toward introducing multiobjective planning concepts into the evaluation process. It specified that three objectives should be included in water resource planning (1) national economic development, (2) resources conservation, and (3) the "well-being" of the people. The first (Green Book) objective came, in later discussions and documents, to be known as the NED objective. This thrust toward multiobjective planning was in practice a failure. The other objectives were given lip service; only NED was quantified in project evaluation.[9]

National interest in water resources planing peaked in the 1960s. This decade saw the great dam-building era in the Columbia, Missouri, and Colorado Basins, and enormous water works construction in California. In 1965 Congress passed the Water Resources Planning Act. Under the act, a Water Resources Council (WRC) was formed to report to the President and was charged with establishing principles, standards, and procedures for water resource and related land use planning. To guide this effort, the Council established four different objectives for water resource planning: (1) regional economic development, (2) the quality of the total environment, (3) the well-being of the people, and (4) NED. One assumes NED was put at the end to deemphasize it. However, of these stated objectives NED and environmental quality (EQ) were the only ones for which an actual planning procedure was outlined in the published document resulting from the Councils deliberations, *Principles and Standards for Planning Water and Related Land Resources* (P&S).[10] A.B. Jaffe described the new procedures in this way:

> To guide the water resource planing effort towards these dual objectives of National Economic Development (NED) and Environmental Quality (EQ), the P&S also establish for the first time a detailed planning process. Two of the required steps in the planning process, formulation of alternative plans and analysis of tradeoffs among these alternatives, deserve special attention. The required formulation of alternative plans must be conducted to ensure that at least one alternative designed to achieve the objectives of NED and one alternative designed to achieve the objectives of EQ be prepared. The impact of all plans on the NED objectives and the EQ objectives are to be evaluated by a "system of accounts." For each alternative project or program, the agency is to evaluate the beneficial and adverse effects on the NED objective and tabulate these in the NED "account" for that objective. The NED account is the B-C analysis presented in a disaggregated form so that the particular categories of costs and benefits can be seen. Similarly, the beneficial and adverse effects of each alternative on the EQ objective are tabulated in the EQ account. The EQ account should display effects on the environment, quantified as much as possible and described qualitatively where necessary.

Effects on Regional Development and Social Well-Being are also to
be displayed, but are not to be primary objectives.[11]

Actually, P&S procedures had little effect on agency practice which continued
to emphasize NED benefits in project evaluation. Efforts were made under the
Carter administration to tighten evaluation procedures and require more cost
sharing in federal projects by state and local entities. These points were somewhat moot however, since by then the great dam-building era was drawing to a
close and few major new federal projects were being proposed. In September
1981, President Reagan terminated the WRC.

At least he thought he had. Actually, the Council exists in law. However,
since the early days of the Reagan administration the Council has not met and
has no staff. Nevertheless it endorsed, by mail, the most recent guidance document from an interagency committee. The new document is entitled *Principles
and Guidelines*, as opposed to the previous *Principles and Standards*, but it is
still held to be binding on federal water resources agencies. For present purposes the main feature of this new document is its elevation of NED as the
sole object of the evaluation process while relegating the environment once
again to being an account.[12] It should be noted, however, that under the
National Environmental Policy Act of 1969 all major federal actions require
an "environmental impact statement." This is the primary way in which environmental considerations enter into the planning of new, and now rare, federal
water resource projects.

The most striking development in benefit-cost analysis in recent years has
been its increasing application to the environmental consequences of new
technologies and scientific and regulatory programs. For instance, the Atomic
Energy Commission used the technique to evaluate the fast breeder reactor
research and development program. The technique has also been applied to
other potential sources of hazard and environmental pollution. Its development
and application to environmental issues were accelerated by a Reagan administration directive requiring the benefit-cost analysis of "major" federal regulations. This directive remains in effect.

However, while benefit-cost analysis was limited largely to the relatively
straightforward problem of evaluating investment in water resources, economists actively debated the proper way of handling both empirical and conceptual difficulties with the technique. Some of the discussion centered on
technical issues such as ways to compute consumer surplus and estimate
demand functions for various outputs. For water projects these functions
included flood control, irrigation, navigations, municipal and industrial water
supply, and, later, recreation. Other issues more clearly related to questions of
value and equity, including whether the distribution of benefits and costs
among individuals needed to be addressed or whether it was adequate to consider only aggregates, as the 1936 Flood Control Act and the 1939 Federal

Reclamation Project Act directed. Another question focused on the appropriate discount rate to use on water projects.

Application of the technique to issues like the development of nuclear energy, the storage of atomic waste, man-induced climate change, and the regulation of toxic substances complicates both the empirical and value (ethical) issues found in water resource applications.[13]

Allocating Existing Supplies

As noted earlier, there are basically no more unallocated supplies of water in the arid West. This means attention is shifting away from development projects and associated economic evaluation problems to the efficient and equitable allocation and reallocation of existing supplies. Western water allocation institutions need to evolve toward greater reliance on economic incentives through the formation of markets and the improvement of pricing policies for publicly supplied wastes. Evidence shows that water use is sensitive to price, and demand-side management is increasingly important for balancing demand with supplies.

Water Marketing[14]

Economic theory says that competitive markets can efficiently allocate resources among competing uses over time, but the nature of the resource presents problems for establishing and relying on unfettered water markets. Thus, the manner and ease with which a region deals with increasing water scarcity depend largely on the institutions, that is, the policies, laws, organizations, and norms, governing the allocation and use of water.

State institutions, except where water is specifically in the purview of the federal government, establish the framework and determine an individual's rights to use and transfer water. Traditionally, however, state governments have not created conditions conducive to water marketing, but have often limited the role of economic incentives in the allocation of water use.

All state water law was initially based on the common law doctrine of riparian rights. This doctrine granted landowners the right to make "reasonable" use of water that bordered on or passed through their land as long as the use did not unduly inconvenience other riparian owners. By tying water rights to the land, the doctrine precludes markets. Water scarcity and the need to supply water to nonriparian lands caused the western states largely to abandon the doctrine of riparian rights in favor of the doctrine of prior appropriation— "first-in-time, first-in-right."

Although the appropriation doctrine was potentially an important step for creating clear, transferable property rights to water, the potential has yet to be fully realized because legal and administrative factors have obscured the nature and transferability of the rights. Among these factors are the beneficial-use provisions of the states' water laws. Rather than grant absolute ownership, the states granted rights to use water for "beneficial" purposes. Consequently, water rights that are not put to a beneficial use may be forfeited. Moreover, in some instances, sale of a right has been interpreted as evidence that the original user could no longer put the water to beneficial use. These provisions of western water law underlie the "use-it-or-lose it" attitude that characterizes many water users and discourages marketing and conservation.

Despite the institutional obstacles, which may be greatly exacerbated in the future by efforts to implement the Endangered Species Act, water rights do get transferred among users, and water marketing has become fairly common in many western states. Most western states permit water transfers if third parties are protected. Providing for these interests, however, can be time-consuming, costly and uncertain. Because the requisite legal and administrative hurdles add to the costs of a water transfer, the potential benefits generally have to be large to justify the effort and risk to the buyer and seller.

Recently, water marketing has increased, reflecting both the growing potential benefits of transfers and a more receptive posture toward water transfers. Laws to facilitate marketing of privately held water rights have been passed or are being considered. California now classifies water sales as a beneficial use. In 1988, Oregon's legislature passed a law that would permit any water right holder to implement conservation and apply to the Oregon Water Resources Commission for the right to sell the conserved water.[15] At the same time a bill to facilitate the transfer of water from irrigation to urban uses wended its way through the Texas legislature.[16]

Though increased marketing should be encouraged, free markets are not a panacea for efficient allocation of water over time. Two problems illustrate the limitations of markets and the challenges facing policymakers. First, third-party impacts associated with transfers need to be taken into account without unduly restricting marketing. Second, provision must be made for instream uses. Historically, instream uses were overlooked; appropriate water rights were established only by diverting water from its source. Streamflow depletion has directed attention to such values as hydroelectricity, recreation, and fish and wildlife habitat. Most western states have recently adopted measures to protect streamflows. These measures include reserving flows or granting rights for particular instream uses and directing agencies to review impacts before granting new rights. Still, the task of efficiently allocating water among instream and other uses is particularly complicated because instream uses such as fish and wildlife habitat are not marketed and thus, not easily valued. The values society attaches to these and other water uses change with population and income levels. The Endangered Species Act may be of particular significance in this connection.

Federally Supplied Water

As explained earlier, Congress established the Bureau of Reclamation early in this century to promote the development of irrigation in the arid and semiarid West. The Bureau provides full or supplemental irrigation for about 11 million acres, more than one-fifth of the total irrigated acreage. In 1975 it supplied 28.1 million acre-ft of water, 93 percent for irrigation.[17] Since the bureau accounts for nearly one-third of all surface and about one-fifth of total water deliveries in the 17 western states, improved efficiency in the use of this water could be important.

Although reclamation law originally intended for irrigators to pay for operation and maintenance plus construction, exclusive of interest charges, more than 90 percent of the capital costs of the Bureau's irrigation projects have been subsidized. With long-term contracts making no adjustment for inflation, payments on some projects no longer pay even for operation and maintenance.[18]

Irrigators fortunate enough to receive such inexpensive water have little or no incentive to conserve. Not only is water cheap, farmers who attempt to conserve risk losing their rights to the water. Federally subsidized water generally cannot be sold by a farmer or irrigation district at a profit. Under these conditions it is not surprising that the demand for Bureau of Reclamation water has been almost completely unresponsive to price changes.

The obstacles to moving toward marginal-cost pricing of federal water are large. For one thing, long-term supply contracts reduce the possibilities of flexible pricing. Another obstacle is that many reclamation projects are so inefficient from an economic point of view that many farmers could not survive a large price increase. Pricing policies that would shut down Bureau projects would probably not pass political muster.

Perhaps more likely than achieving higher prices for Bureau water is increased voluntary transfers of federal water both within and outside the conservation districts established to distribute the water. While such transfers are not common, Richard Wahl identified several transactions ranging from short-term rental or lease arrangements to permanent transfers.[19] There is even precedent for federal legislation to facilitate such transfers: during the 1976-1977 drought, Congress authorized temporary transfers of water from the Central Valley Project.

Although transfers do occur, their high transaction costs undoubtedly stymie many potentially beneficial ones. In Wahl's judgment, these costs stem mainly from lack of a clear Bureau policy about procedures for making transfers and its unwillingness to approve them. Wahl maintains that there is a considerable latitude for voluntary transfers within existing law if the Bureau were only willing to cooperate with interested trading parties and modify existing contracts that inhibit transfers. Such a policy shift would be consistent with the Bureau's *Assessment '87,* which concludes that "the Bureau's mission must change from one based on federally supported construction to one based on effective and environmentally sensitive resource management." Nevertheless, legislation extending the area and uses for federal water may be required to enable some of the most potentially beneficial exchanges.

Conclusions

The organizers of this session asked the authors to reply to two questions:
• What does your discipline bring to water resources management?
• How can we increase the application of your discipline to the management of water resources.

Given the context of my paper, I will address these questions with respect to water development and use in the West. Economics brings to the management of western water resources the constant reminder to planners, managers and legislators that water use presents a problem in the allocation of scarce resources. Early the emphasis was on scare capital. In this context benefit-cost analysis developed. Although economists often intensely criticized benefit-cost analysis as it was actually practiced, the approach probably did serve to eliminate some of the most inefficient potential projects. One vehicle for this is that it provides a framework and data that critics use to debate a project.

More recently the problem has become one of allocating existing, or even shrinking supplies of water. In this connection western water allocation institutions appear to be evolving in the desired direction. Several states either have passed or are considering legislation to encourage conservation and facilitate marketing of water rights. Further changes in state law and policy could help, and federal initiatives are needed to make federally supplied and controlled water responsive to both existing and changing supply and demand.

The hardest remaining problem in the economics of water allocation is how and to what extent to protect third parties affected by water transactions, including instream uses. A recent report from the National Research Council, *Water Transfers in the West: Efficiency, Equity, and the Environment,*[20] attempts to address this problem. The report suggests ways of providing third party participation in the transaction process.

Efforts to implement the requirements of the Endangered Species Act bring a new, large uncertainty into the water marketing picture. The federal act was passed in 1973, but it has made major waves in western water only within the last few years. Nearly all western water courses contain species that could be, and in some cases have been, declared threatened or endangered, and therefore require mandatory protection. Examples are several species of Columbia River salmon, snails in the Snake River, salmon in the Sacramento River, smelt in the San Francisco Delta, and Sqawfish in the Colorado River. In many cases proposed protective measures require provision of additional instream flows and/or major changes in the way reservoir systems are operated. Water rights, as noted earlier, are granted under state law, primarily under the prior appropriations system. These rights may be, in some cases, greatly threatened by efforts to implement the Endangered Species Act.

For example, *The Wall Street Journal* reports on efforts on the part of the Bureau of Reclamation to save the fast-disappearing winter run of Chinook salmon up the Sacramento River. These salmon are listed as threatened species under the Endangered Species Act.

> Moreover, the bureau is contemplating reducing deliveries to so-called "water rights holders"—farmers who owned water rights on the system's rivers before the Central Valley Project was constructed in the 1920s—by about half. That is a potentially explosive move, because water right holders, many of whom are among the biggest and most politically well-connected agricultural barons in the state have always maintained that water rights laws and guarantees made by the bureau assure that they can't receive less than 75 percent of their allotments in a given year, no matter how severe a drought is. The matter likely would end up in court.[21]

Uncertainty about impacts on right holders may persist for many years as litigation proceeds. This introduces a wild card into the water rights game. Since secure rights are essential to well functioning markets, efforts to implement the act may well put a damper on further development of the fledgling water markets.

Indeed efforts to protect endangered species and/or threatened ecosystems is likely to be *the* premier natural resources issue of the 1990s for economists and other pertinent disciplines.

Notes

1. Kenneth D. Frederick and Allen V. Kneese, "Reallocation by Markets and Prices" in *Climate Change and U.S. Water Resources,* ed. Paul E. Wagoner (New York, 1990).
2. Jules Dupuit, "On the Measurement of the Utility of Public Works," *International Economic Papers* 2 (nd). Translated from the French.
3. U.S. Federal Interagency River Basin Committee, Subcommittee on Benefits and Costs, *Proposed Practices for Economic Analysis of River Basin Projects*, (Washington, D.C., 1950).
4. Otto Eckstein, *Water Resource Development: The Economics of Project Evaluation* (Cambridge, MA, 1958).
5. Jack Hirshleifer, Jerome W. Milliam, and James C. De Haven, *Water Supply: Economics, Technology and Policy* (Chicago, 1960).
6. Arthur Maass, Maynard M. Hufschmidt, Robert Dorfman, Harold A. Thomas, Jr., Stephen A. Marglin, and Gordon Maskew Fair, *Design of Water-Resource Systems* (Cambridge, MA, 1962).

7. U.S. Bureau of the Budget, "Reports and Budget Estimates Relating to Federal Programs and Projects for Conservation, Development, or Use of Water and Related Land Resources," Circular A-47 (December 1952).

8. The President's Water Resources Council, *Policies, Standards, and Procedures in the Formulation, Evaluation, and Review of the Plans for Use and Development of Water and Related Land Resources* S. Doc. 97, 87th Cong., 2d sess. (1962).

9. For a more detailed discussion, see A. B. Jaffe, "Benefit-Cost Analysis and Multi-Objective Evaluation of Federal Water Projects," *Harvard Environmental Law Review*, 4, no. 58 (1980): 58-85.

10. 38 *Federal Register* 24.778 (1973).

11. Jaffe, "Benefit-Cost Analysis," 70.

12. Richard W. Wahl, "Water Marketing, Efficient Water Use, and the Bureau of Reclamation," paper presented at the Program on Comprehensive River Basin Management at the Annual Research Conference of the Association for Public Policy Analysis and Management, Austin, TX, 31 October 1986.

13. See Allen V. Kneese and Wiliam Schulze, "Ethics and Environmental Economics" in *Handbook of Natural Resources and Energy Economics,* eds. Allen V. Kneese and James L. Sweeney (Amsterdam, 1985).

14. The next two sections are based heavily on Frederick and Kneese, "Reallocation by Markets and Prices."

15. Joseph L. Sax, "The Constitution, Property Rights and the Future of Water Law" Western Water Policy Project, Disc. Ser. Paper 2, Natural Resources Law Center, University of Colorado School of Law (1990).

16. *Water Market Update* 1, no. 4 (1987).

17. U.S. Bureau of Reclamation, *Federal Reclamation Projects: Water and Land Resource Accomplishments, 1975, Summary Report* (Washington, D.C., 1976), 2.

18. Kenneth D. Frederick and J. C. Hanson, *Water for Western Agriculture* (Washington, D.C., 1982), 66-71.

19. Richard W. Wahl, *Promoting Increased Efficiency of Federal Water Use Through Voluntary Water Transfers,* National Center for Food and Agricultural Policy, Resources for the Future, Discussion Paper Series No. FAP87-02 (September 1987).

20. Committee on Western Water Management, *Water Transfers in the West: Efficiency Equity and the Environment* (Washington, D.C., 1992).

21. *The Wall Street Journal*, 14 February 1992.

Geographers and Water Resource Policy

Rutherford H. Platt

Introduction

Since the establishment of the first academic department of geography in the United States in 1903, American geographers have contributed fruitfully in many capacities to the evolution of the science and art of water resource management. On the physical side of the discipline, geographers as geomorphologists, hydrologists, and climatologists, have addressed problems relating to water balance, climate variability, fluvial hydrology under diverse climatic and geomorphic regimes, lake level fluctuation, coastal geomorphology, and groundwater hydrology. Since the 1972 Federal Water Pollution Control Act Amendments, physical water research has increasingly focused on issues of surface and groundwater quality, including the effects of non-point sources and toxic substances.

Geographers as social scientists (the primary focus of this paper) seek to apply the findings of physical geography and related sciences to the assessment, interpretation, and remediation of problems involving the human use of water as a resource. Geographers bring a unique disciplinary perspective to the analyis of water management which involves: (1) recognition of the importance of *spatiality* or areal distributions of physical and social phenomena, and their interdependence, (2) a sense of *scale* or hierarchy as reflected in the organization of both physical drainage systems (main stem, tributaries of descending orders) and the institutions of society (e.g., national, state, municipal, private) that share management authority over water resources (3) recognition of a broad range of *societal choices* in the pursuit of multiple and often competing functions or goals (e.g., hydropower, irrigation, habitat protection) employing multiple means (e.g. alternative adjustments to flood hazards),[1] and (4) a holistic or *interdisciplinary* perspective whereby geographers synthesize the insights of more specialized research related to water in such fields as the physical sciences, engineering, economics, ecology, and law.[2]

Early Contributions

The roots of geographical perspectives on water and land resources management antedate the formal emergence of academic geography in the United States. In 1864, George Perkins Marsh, an inquisitive Vermont lawyer, ambassador to Italy, and eclectic scholar, published his seminal treatise, *Man and Nature, Or, Physical Geography as Modified by Human Action.*[3]

This work reflected the influence of the contemporary German geographers Alexander von Humboldt and Carl Ritter, who widely documented the interaction of human and physical geography. Marsh blended exhaustive description of human-land and human-water relationships, drawn from antiquity, from contemporary Europe, and from the United States, with moralistic outrage at the pervasive degradation of "natural harmonies" at the hands of mankind. Geographer David Lowenthal has declared this work to be "the fountainhead of the conservation movement."[4]

Marsh devoted one fourth of the work to an examination of human use and abuse of water resources. Little escaped his attention: diking of the North Sea Coast; drainage of England's fenlands; the impact of deforestation on floodflow and sedimenation downstream; the impacts of land reclamation upon climate; groundwater contamination; loss of harbors due to siltation; and alternatives for coping with floods and coastal erosion.[5]

Marsh's legacy to future generations of natural resource scholars was attested in the dedication to him of the landmark mid-twentieth-century survey of global environmental issues, *Man's Role in Changing the Face of the Earth,* and in the establishment of the George Perkins Marsh Institute at Clark University in 1991.[6]

Another proto-geographer, who would vastly influence water resource policies in the American West, was, of course, John Wesley Powell. Beginning with his epic voyage down the Colorado River in 1869, Powell widely explored the western arid lands individually and as director of the "Geographical and Geological Survey of the Rocky Mountain Region," nominally under the Department of the Interior. Confronted by petty conflicts over the allocation of federal survey funding, Powell transcended the geologist's focus on micro-description of small areas to articulate a geographer's vision of "what the West must do to grow into a strong part of the American commonwealth" in the words of his biographer Wallace Stegner.[7]

Powell's 1878 *Report on the Lands of the Arid Region* challenged the national policy implicit in the Homestead Act and other federal lands legislation that applied an eastern template of settlement to the West.[8] Powell called for recognition of the vital role of land reclamation through irrigation that in turn demanded new cooperative and governmental institutions for beneficial development of scarce water resources. He thus helped to foster the progressive conservation doctrine of "wise use," as applied to national forests by Gifford

37

Pinchot and to water resources beginning with the Newlands Act of 1902, which established the Reclamation Service, later renamed the Bureau of Reclamation. Powell's legacy is anathema to advocates of wild and free-flowing rivers (likely including Marsh if he had lived a century later). However, Powell's call for scientific assessment of regional physical resources as a basis for public policies on settlement and economic growth anticipated twentieth century requirements for economic and environmental justification of proposed public actions, to which geographers would widely contribute.

According to Theodore Schad, "With the flowering of the conservation movement during the administration of President Theodore Roosevelt, the concept of comprehensive planning for multiple use of water resources was actively promoted."[7] Several national water commission reports during the period 1908-1912 reflected comprehensive planning, as did the first river basin plans prepared during the late 1920s by the Army Corps of Engineers under House Document 308.[10]

Harlan H. Barrows, one of the first generation of geographers trained at the intensely progressive University of Chicago, challenged his fledgling discipline in 1923 to "make clear the relationships existing between natural environments, and the distribution and activities of man" and to engage in "a comparative study of human adjustment to specific natural environments."[11] In 1933, President Franklin D. Roosevelt appointed Barrows to the new Mississippi Valley Committee. Thereafter, Barrows served on the water resources committees of a succession of New Deal national planning boards. His preface to the water portion of the 1934 National Resources Board Final Report was described by the chair of the Water Planning Committee, Abel Wolman, a half century later, as comprising "as good a philosophical statement on water resources management as could be written today".[12]

Another Barrows contribution to the water resources field was to invite a promising young graduate student to serve as staff to the Water Planning Committee in Washington. Based in the Executive Office Building next to the White House, Gilbert White plunged into the turbulent waters of policy debate swirling around economic justification of water projects, cost sharing among levels of government, upstream versus downstream approaches to flood control, single versus multiobjective planning, and executive branch versus congressional authority over water resource investments.[13] White later became the preeminent geographer in the field of water resources management.

The River Basin Tradition

The use of river basins and their subwatersheds as appropriate spatial units for data collection and policy formulation is a fundamental geographical notion that has run through water resources planning since the 1920s. Of course, river basins must not be viewed as self-contained islands unto themselves.

The harmonious reconcilation of water issues within river basins is hampered by various factors. One is the spatial nonconformity of political and physical systems whereby the jurisdiction of private and public water management institutions usually does not conform to the geography of watersheds. Another is the prevalence of out-of-basin water transfers, reflecting spatial discontinuity between regions of supply and demand, and the inequality of urban and rural political influence. Also, demands for basin resources such as recreation, agricultural products, timber, electrical power, fisheries, and natural habitat reflect the influence of socioeconomic and ecological systems extending far beyond the basin's boundaries. Comprehensive river basin management thus implies consideration not only of conditions within the basin in question, but a variety of geographic externalities as well.

Proposals for comprehensive river basin management, no matter how soundly developed, have seldom been effectuated through public action. Only once has the United States Congress established a multipurpose governmental institution with a jurisdiction coterminous with a major river basin, namely the Tennessee Valley Authority.[14] Opposition to "big government" and public power represented by TVA has prevented the creation of comparable basin-wide institutions elsewhere in the United States.[15]

The concept of the basin unit, however, has been widely utilized in national and regional water planning studies. A landmark among those studies and a benchmark in the evolution of American water policy was *Ten Rivers in America's Future,* prepared under the direction of geographer Edward A. Ackerman for the President's Water Resources Policy Commission in 1950 (Gilbert White was vice-chair of the commission).[16] Consistent with the priorities of the time, those ten case studies chiefly addressed hydropower, irrigation, navigation, flood control, and recreation, with comparatively little attention to water quality, aquatic habitat, groundwater, pricing, or aesthetics. Engineering approaches still dominated river management proposals, although nonstructural measures such as floodplain zoning were tentatively mentioned.

Frequently, as in the 1944 Pick-Sloan program for the Missouri River, lip service was paid to "basinwide planning." But the early post-World War II period was marked by a series of massive construction projects driven more by the political geography of congressional politics than by the physical and economic geography of river basins. According to Keith Muckleston:

> The term "basin planning" was widely used but less frequently employed as development tended to proceed on a project-by-project basis. This may be attributed to the non-reimbursability of most water-related outputs, the constituency orientation of Congress, the informal coalition between Western irrigation interests and southern flood control and navigation interests, and the absence of an effective coordinating mechanism.[17]

Numerous interstate compacts have been established to effectuate basinwide agreements regarding water, but most of these have involved the allocation of water in arid regions. Only in two river basins, the Delaware and the Susquehanna, have compacts been utilized to facilitate comprehensive basin management. Only one minor water-related compact has appeared since 1970.[18]

River basin planning received a new impetus from the 1965 Federal Water Resources Planning Act, as recommended by the 1961 *Report of the Senate Select Committee on National Water Resources.*[19] This law established the U.S. Water Resources Council and authorized the creation of federal-state river basin commissions, of which six were eventually formed (Ohio, Upper Mississippi, Missouri, Great Lakes, and two involving multiple basins: New England and Pacific Northwest). The Water Resources Council, a federal interagency collaborative body, prepared two National Water Assessments[20] that assembled a broad array of water resource data for individual river basins and regions, and for the nation. The Council achieved consensus on the use and estimation of the 100-year flood as a federal standard and promulgated *A Unified National Program for Floodplain Management.*[21] Its "Principles and Standards for the Evaluation of Water Resource Projects," adopted in 1973, earned the political hostility of advocates of projects suspended by President Carter's "hit list" in 1977.

The individual river basin commissions produced "comprehensive, coordinated, joint plans for water and related land resources" which however were merely advisory to federal, state, and local authorities.[22] All of the commissions were abolished along with the Water Resources Council by the Reagan administration in 1982. Numerous geographers, including the present writer, contributed as staff, advisory board members, or as consultants to the work of those organizations. With the demise of the river basin planning institutions established under the 1965 Act, the basin scale declined in prominence in American water planning in favor of more generic and place-specific topics of water research.

The river basin tradition, however, continued to influence comparative international studies of river basin development. In 1976, several American geographers joined with Soviet and other international colleagues in a floating symposium on the Volga River to consider what the world could learn from its experience with river basin development. Gilbert White[23] urged that geographers evaluate the successes and failures of past efforts to develop major rivers, emulating such examples as the study of the Lower Rio Grande by John Day.[24] Kieth Muckleston[25] and W.R. Derrick Sewell[26] espectively evaluated North American experience in the Columbia and Fraser River Basins. A decade later, White published the exemplar of river basin post-audits in his article on "The Environmental Effects of the High Dam at Aswan."[27]

Analysis of international river basins continues as a theme in American geography today. Philip P. Micklin of Western Michigan University recently examined the range of climatic, hydrologic, and economic issues posed by the dessication of the Aral Sea.[28] The 1992 Annual Meeting of the Association of American Geographers included a session organized by geographers at the University of Colorado (Jeffery W. Jacobs and James L. Wescoat, Jr.) and Auburn University (Richard W. Perritt) that examined response to potential climate change in four major river basins: the Mekong, Lower Indus, Zambezi, and the Plate.[29]

From Water Development to Water Management

The National Water Commission Report

A new direction in water resource planning was signalled by the monumental 1973 *Report of the National Water Commission*.[30] That study focused upon generic national policy issues, not river basins per se. Moreover it dealt primarily with economic, environmental, and legal issues, rather than technological solutions. As summarized by the Commission's Executive Director, Theodore M. Schad, "The basic philosophy expressed by the Commission is that the United States has enough water to meet essential demands, including aesthetic and environmental demands, but not enough to waste."[31] The report reflected the Commission's belief that "a change in emphasis from water development to preservation and enhancement of water quality and environmental preservation is underway and will continue in the future" and further that "all users of water who get an economic return for its use [should] pay the full cost of service and all polluters [should] pay the costs of abating their pollution."[32] Reflecting the shift in the Commission's emphasis from water development to comprehensive water management, its nine principal consultants included two geographers (Gilbert F. White and Edward A. Ackerman), two water planners (Maynard M. Hufschmidt and Irving K. Fox), two attorneys (Ralph W. Johnson and Edward Weinberg), a resource economist (Nathaniel Wollman), an international public health authority (Abel Wolman), and only one civil engineer (Harvey O. Banks).[33]

Flood Hazards

The transition from water development to water management reflected in the National Water Commission *Report* marked a reorientation of water research toward generic, albeit interrelated, water policy issues (e.g. flooding, water supply, water quality, irrigation) as distinct from comprehensive planning for specific river basins. One of the most prominent generic themes of water research by geographers since the 1960s has been "water as hazard" either in a state of excess (riverine and coastal flooding and erosion) or of deficiency (agricultural and urban drought). The University of Chicago Department of Geography published a series of monographs during the 1960s and

1970s by Gilbert White and his students and associates which examined diverse aspects of human perception of and adjustment to water as hazard. These included doctoral dissertations by Robert W. Kates,[34] Ian Burton,[35] John R. Sheaffer,[36] Thomas F. Saarinen,[37] Duane D. Baumann,[38] Shue Tuck Wong,[39] John C. Day,[40] James F. Johnson,[41] and James K. Mitchell,[42] among others. Several of these studies helped to pinpoint a fundamental weakness in structural approaches to riverine and coastal flood control—that dams, levees, seawalls, and similar devices convey a false sense of security and lead to intensification of land use in "protected" floodplains. While losses from average floods are reduced, floods that exceed the design level of the project or that break through weak points inflict catastrophic losses upon the development that the flood control structure attracted into the floodplain.[43]

The collective message of this research was delivered to Congress through the 1966 Report of the Bureau of the Budget Task Force on Federal Flood Control Policy,[44] that reflected the "range of choice" philosophy of the task force's chair, Gilbert White.[45] The report advocated a variety of measures to broaden the nation's response to the problem of floods. These included tentative support for a federal flood insurance program to be accompanied by floodplain management in participating communities.

Congress established the National Flood Insurance Program in 1968 and strengthened it in 1973, a year after Hurricane Agnes wreaked devastation in the Atlantic seaboard states. The program reflects a shift in national policy away from exclusive reliance upon structural flood control and toward a greater use of economic and legal incentives to use floodprone land more cautiously. Geographers continue to do research on flood hazards along our rivers, lakes, estuaries, and ocean coasts that refines nonstructural approaches at the federal, state, and local levels.[46] A number of studies and symposia have examined the causes and management implications of individual disasters such as Eve Gruntfest's work on the Big Thompson Canyon flood of 1976.[47] Other researchers have examined the relationship between flood hazards and property values in various communities.[48] My own flood-related research has addressed the institutional context of floodplain management, particularly at the regional and metropolitan scale.[49]

Water Quality

M. Gordon Wolman published two papers in *Science* in 1971 and 1987 that, respectively, mark the onset and perhaps the apex of the national commitment to water pollution abatement.[50] In the earlier paper, Wolman offered a geographical critique of the prevailing methods for collecting and appraising surface water quality data. Reviewing the sketchy data available for various rivers and estuaries for several water quality indices (dissolved oxygen, dissolved solids, sediment, temperature, radioactivity, pesticides, and trash and debris), he concluded that estimates of existing and potential pollution burdens on streams do not *ipso facto* indicate how such watercourses will in fact respond physically: "To a large extent, observations of the condition of river systems have been confined to measures of the quality of the flow itself and exclude descriptions of the bed, banks, and environs of the river."[51] Thus the actual environmental stress placed on riverine systems may be greater or less than expected, depending upon factors beyond merely the variation of pollution loadings.

Fifteen years and $100 billion later (spent on sewage treatment plants nationally), Smith, Alexander, and Wolman questioned the efficacy of the federal commitment to reduction of point source biochemical oxygen demand (BOD) as the primary approach to water quality improvement.[52] Based on data for 30 pollutants gathered at more than 300 monitoring sites between 1974 and 1981, the authors found a weak relationship between BOD reduction through wastewater treatment and reduction of dissolved oxygen deficit (DOD) in the monitored streams. They urged greater attention to non-point sources of suspended solids, nitrates, and salts and called for expansion and refinement of the nation's water quality monitoring system.

Geographers in governmental resource management agencies today are applying their spatial perspective and computer mapping skills to the achievement of water quality and related goals. James M. Omernik and his colleagues at the U.S. Environmental Protection Agency Research Laboratory at Corvallis, Oregon, are mapping ecoregions as alternatives to river basins as natural resources management units. Ecoregions are based on perceived patterns of land use, land surface forms, existing and potential natural vegetation, and soils. According to Omernik:

> The primary function of the ecoregion map is to provide a geographic framework for organizing ecosystem resources information. This framework should allow managers, planners, and scientists to: 1) compare similarities and differences of land/water relationships; 2) establish water quality standards that are in tune with regional patterns of tolerances and resiliences to human impacts; 3) locate monitoring, demonstration, or reference sites; 4) extrapolate from existing site-specific studies; and 5) predict the effects of changes in land use and pollution controls.[53]

More than merely a new cartographic tool, however, ecoregion maps help to establish and administer standards for regional aquatic biological quality which is poorly measured by conventional toxicological criteria.[54]

Christopher Lant and Jo Beth Mullens propose to broaden the measurement and evaluation of environmental quality of water bodies for purposes of recreation management.[55] They suggest that conventional water quality indices be supplemented by characteristics of "lake-river quality" that reflect physical, ecological, and aesthetic values.

Lant and Rebecca Roberts used a "willingness to pay" survey to evaluate public support for the retention of riparian greenbelts as natural buffer strips to enhance water quality, recreation, fisheries, and to reduce sedimentation and turbidity in middle western streams, lakes, and reservoirs.[56] Their research found that the "intrinsic values of a natural resource are large in economic terms, larger than the recreational values, and also large compared with [agricultural] use made of those natural resources."[57] They urge a shift in federal policy from subsidizing maximum crop production on such riparian lands to the encouragement of nonuse through incentives under the Conservation Reserve Program established in the Food Security Act of 1985.

Robert M. Hordon and his colleagues at Rutgers have further addressed the establishment of riparian buffer strips to protect public reservoirs through state or local regulations.[58] They advocate buffer strips to protect surface water supplies from non-point contamination from agriculture, urbanization, bank erosion, road salt, and leaking storage tanks. Under a contract with the New Jersey Department of Environmental Protection, the Rutgers group developed a model that related buffer width to overland flow velocity, as determined principally by slope and roughness.

W. Andrew Marcus, a fluvial geomorphologist, has specialized in the application of science to public policy in the regulation of contaminated aquatic sediments. In 1989, he called attention to the fact that conventional biological and chemical tests insufficiently define and measure sediment contamination.[59] He urged that hydrologic considerations also be addressed. No longer should geographers be content with bottom sampling of permanent water bodies. They should expand their treatment of the aquatic environment to include floodplains, wetlands, and other intermittent water features. Marcus recommended using two or more sampling techniques depending upon local hydrology. In a later article in the *Environmental Law Reporter*, he more fully developed the legal implications of alternate sampling methodologies for contaminated sediments.[60]

Based on a field study of the sediment budget of a tributary to Chesapeake Bay, Marcus and Kearney compared the contributions of fluvial runoff from uplands versus coastal erosion.[61] While the former contaminates critical spawning grounds and aquatic nurseries near river mouths, coastal erosion was found to be "the major contributor to the fine sediment load that generates turbidity problems, buries benthic habitats, and adsorbs and stores toxins."[62]

Drought and Water Conservation

The work at the University of Chicago on floods stimulated geographers' interest in other forms of natural hazards including drought. Two lines of geographic research have addressed water scarcity. One is concerned with urban water supply and the other with agricultural adjustments. Under the first heading, Resources For the Future in 1970 published *Drought and Water Supply*, the result of a joint study by geographers and resource economists at Clark University and Harvard.[63] This study examined the response of municipal and industrial water managers in Massachusetts to the Northeast Drought of 1962-1966. Surveys of 48 communities (four in depth) revealed their strong preference for supply augmentation strategies, including emergency sources, in contrast to demand management. Under the latter approach, outdoor water use was restricted on a temporary basis, but few officials expressed interest in raising the price of metered water or in reusing treated wastewater. Public water managers considered water scarcity unacceptable, regardless of its actual costs to society, and attempted to augment supplies at any cost to ensure an adequate, safe supply sufficient to meet increased demand without raising the consumer price.

The research and consulting activities of Duane Baumann at Southern Illinois University (who assisted in the 1970 Resources for the Future study) have facilitated demand forecasting and water conservation in the United States. Baumann, Benedykt Dziegielewski, and other colleagues have challenged the prevailing practice of linear extrapolation of per capita water demand to justify the need for future supply augmentation.[64] On behalf of the Institute for Water Resources of the Army Corps of Engineers, they developed disaggregated water-use models that show the varying socioeconomic characteristics of the residential population and that differentiate overall water demand by economic sector, season, climatic conditions, and other variables.[65] They have recently completed a manual for California Urban Water Agencies on *Evaluation of Urban Water Conservation Programs.*[66]

However, the gradual shift from supply augmentation to demand management evident in American urban water planning since 1970 has been driven not so much by the cost efficiency of the latter as by the political unfeasibility of the former. For instance, the Two Forks Dam proposed by the Denver Water Department was defeated not by cost effectiveness but because it would have destroyed one of the most popular trout fisheries in the West.[67] Jacque Emel at Clark University characterizes out-of-basin diversions such as Boston's Quabbin Reservoir (completed in the 1940s by the Metropolitan District Commission) as "commodification" of common resources and "domination of nature" for the benefit of "urban elites."[68] The history of the Boston Metropolitan water system since 1970, however, demonstrates a clearcut, though initially reluctant, conversion to demand management with further diversions being dropped from consideration.[69]

On the agricultural side of geographic research on drought, Thomas F. Saarinen[70] applied concepts of environmental perception drawn from behavioral psychology to explain how Great Plains wheat farmers individually cope with drought through such measures as stubble mulch, irrigation, and strip cropping. He found that perception of drought varies according to degree of aridity, amount of personal experience with drought, type of farm operation, and personality/age differences, with aridity being the primary variable. Newer practices such as stubble mulch varied spatially in usage according to the geographic principle of diffusion of innovation.

William Reibsame, Stanley Changnon, and T.R. Karl[71] evaluated the national economic and environmental impacts of the drought of 1987-89, including both urban and agricultural losses. They estimated the overall costs at $39 billion. In 1991, the Institute for Water Resources published *The National Study of Water Management During Drought,*[72] which surveys the state of drought preparedness and response at various management levels from the perspectives of geography, economics, and law.

Irrigation

Between 1969 and 1987, the use of groundwater irrigation on the High Plains had expanded substantially in Nebraska, Kansas, and Colorado, while contracting in Texas and New Mexico.[73] Geographers David E. Kromm and Stephen E. White at Kansas State University surveyed 1,750 irrigators (709 responses) in ten High Plains counties to determine the extent of adoption of water conserving practices. The top three among 39 listed measures in terms of extent of usage were to (1) chisel compacted soils, (2) schedule irrigation based on moisture need, and (3) reduce evaporation with stubble mulch. The investigators found the "most common water-saving techniques are management and field practices that rely more on labor than capital." Of the top ten methods that involved redesigning a system, none required substantial investment. Although underutilized measures would presumably benefit fellow irrigators if adopted, irrigators generally favored voluntary adoption rather than the use of government incentives or regulation to promote additional measures.[74]

The Columbia River Basin also experienced rapid expansion of irrigated land after 1970 using center pivot wells and distribution systems. Muckleston and Highsmith of Oregon State University examined some of the socioeconomic implications of this new technology in terms of electrical energy demand, institutional change, and the character of small towns in the region affected.[75]

Rapid expansion has been followed by rapid contraction of irrigation-based agriculture on the Southern High Plains as groundwater levels have declined. Roberts and Emel[76] reject the conventional model of the "Tragedy of the Commons" to explain the destabilization of the farming economy in that region. They found that irrigators in fact have accepted well-spacing requirements and have otherwise cooperated to reduce overpumping. The authors instead draw upon the neomarxist literature of "uneven development" to attribute the region's distress to exogenous socioeconomic factors such as the price of crops, energy costs, credit, and governmental tax and price support policies.

James L. Wescoat, Jr., provides a longer term interpretation of the rise and fall of irrigation schemes in the arid Southwest.[77] Drawing on the experience of four eras of desert reclamation—prehistoric, colonial Hispanic, Mormon, and federal reclamation programs in the twentieth century—Wescoat concludes that "one cannot point to a major settlement that has self-consciously sought a 'sustainable' mode of desert occupance."[78] Adjustments to climatic limitations over time, however, may be identified in, for instance, the evolution of urban landscaping in Tucson, Arizona, from "ersatz humid suburban" to "cactus chic" (my terms inspired by observations of the Canadian landscape architect Michael Hough[79]).

Geography and Water Law

Several geographers, some of whom also hold law degrees, have addressed the interaction of geography and law with particular reference to water issues of the arid West. Olen Matthews has traced the influence of geography in the evolution of certain water law concepts and institutions, e.g. riparian vs. prior appropriation allocation doctrines.[80] Otis Templer, another geographer-lawyer, concurs that water law is a geographic variable serving as "an absolute constraint on the way in which water and related land are used,"[81] and thus as a determinant of the cultural landscape, especially in areas of water scarcity. He cautions against overexpansive generalizations by nonlawyers that ignore nuances and jurisidictional variation in the content and interpretation of water law doctrines.[82] But he urges social scientists to examine the spatial and economic impacts of legal doctrines to assist policy makers (e.g., legislatures, administrative agencies, courts) in revising inefficient or obsolete laws and doctrines.

Emel and Brooks of Clark University have examined the evolution of legal institutions regarding groundwater allocation in Nebraska, Kansas, and Oklahoma.[83] They found a transition in each state from earlier reliance upon the common law standard of "reasonable use," as applied judicially on a case by case basis, to a permit system in which administrative agencies apply preestablished numerical rules. (This is consistent with the evolution of other areas of resource management law including land use zoning and water pollution discharge regulation.) They found that while the "normative content" of each system was similar, the new form of social intervention represented a crystallization of security of property rights and investment at the expense of equity and flexibility (and perhaps efficiency) in the use of groundwater resources.

F. Andrew Schoolmaster has studied water markets as a redistributive mechanism.[84] Focusing his work on the Lower Rio Grande Valley in Texas, he found that the establishment of a regional "water master" under state law facilitates the transfer and administration of water rights between agricultural and municipal users. This office also contributes to the maintenance of adequate instream flows. Larger issues of water management along the Rio Grande in light of climatic uncertainty is the subject of current research by Marvin Waterstone of the University of Arizona under the sponsorship of the Institute for Water Resources.

James Wescoat of the University of Colorado is probably the preeminent American geographer to navigate the rapids, shoals, and eddies of western water law. In a 1985 article in *Economic Geography,* he addressed "the most important water policy problem facing the American West, namely how to reconcile the Colorado doctrine of prior appropriation (the nation's strongest of its type) with newly emerging concerns for conservation, instream uses, and 'maximum beneficial use.'"[85] Western Colorado and much of the rest of the West "suffers from historically excessive diversion rates, loose administration, and an absence of regional water markets."[86] Based on extensive review of the applicable statutes and case law, Wescoat proposed three avenues of improvement: (1) better definition of legal terms of art such as "waste" and "beneficial use," (2) improved public administration, and (3) organizational adjustments to increase the propensity to conserve water through economies of scale. In a sequel article, Wescoat explored the implications of water conservation through federal salinity control projects for the administration of appropriative water rights in the Colorado River Basin.[87]

Conclusion

American water resource geography at the end of the twentieth century is thriving but increasingly specialized. Compared with the classic river basin studies of the 1930s and 1950s, geographical research on water issues today is less holistic, less prescriptive, and less visionary. The gospel of "economic efficiency" of earlier times has been supplanted by "environmental sustainability" with an accompanying sense of limits and distrust of grand technical solutions. Like their peers in other disciplines, geographers have been swept up in the popular notions of the time. These include the "wise use" principle of the progressive conservation movement in the 1920s and 1930s, "multiple use" (including recreation) in the 1960s, and finally "non-use" in the 1970s and 1980s. Geographers have actively encouraged the transition from structural to non-structural methods as primary responses to flood hazards, and they have helped to broaden the range of societal choice applicable to other water management issues such as drought and water pollution abatement. Still, they, like others, are perplexed by the nation's rejection of regulatory law to better society and, instead, its embrace of the same sort of selfish laissez faire policy that spawned Progressivism a century ago.

Geographers are nevertheless optimistically contributing to water resources management in many ways. As researchers, they are broadly engaged in studying water issues in both a physical and social sense, and they are publishing widely beyond their own field (as indicated in the references cited in this paper). In a technical sense, geographers have contributed fundamentally to the spectacular advances in the collection, storage, display, and analysis of water resource data through remote sensing, computer mapping, and geographic information systems. In a philosophical sense, they are formulating new perspectives on the legal and economic nature of water rights as common goods and as property. In a practical sense, they continue to apply their spatial and integrative perspective to the assessment and remediation of regional, national, and global water problems.

Notes

1. Gilbert F. White, *Strategies of American Water Managemen*, (Ann Arbor, MI, 1969).
2. For a recent overview of water resources geography, see Gary L. Gaile and Cort J. Willmott, eds., *Geography in America*, (Columbus, OH, 1989).
3. George Perkins Marsh, *Man and Nature: Or Physical Geography as Modified by Human Action*, ed. David Lowenthal, (Cambridge, MA, 1965).
4. Ibid., ix.
5. Ibid., Ch. 4.
6. William L. Thomas, Jr., *Man's Role in Changing the Face of the Earth* (Chicago, 1956).
7. Wallace Stegner, *Beyond the Hundredth Meridian: John Wesley Powell and the Second Opening of the West*, (Lincoln, NE, 1954), 204.
8. John Wesley Powell, *Report on the Lands of the Arid Region of the United States with a More Detailed Account of the Lands of Utah* (1878), 45th Cong., 2d sess., H. Doc. 73.
9. Theodore M. Schad, "Water Resources Planning—Historical Development," *Journal of the The Water Resources Planning and Management Division, American Society of Civil Engineers* 105 (March, 1979): 9-25.
10. U.S. Congress, *Estimate of Cost of Examinations, Etc., of Streams Where Water Power Appears Feasible*, (1926), 69th Cong., 1st sess., H. Doc. 308,.
11. Harlan H. Barrows, "Geography as Human Ecology," *Annals of the Association of American Geographers* 13 (March 1923): 1-14.
12. Quoted in Rutherford H. Platt, "Floods and Man: A Geographer's Agenda" in *Geography, Resources, and Environment*, II, eds., Robert W. Kates and Ian Burton, (Chicago, 1986), 28-68, 33.
13. Gilbert White has been compared with John Dewey who preceded him at the University of Chicago in his belief in pragmatism, learning from experience, and the value of discourse in democratic society according to James L Wescoat, "Common Themes in the Work of Gilbert White and John Dewey: A Pragmatic Appraisal," *Annals of the Association of American Geographers* 82 (December 1992), 587-607.

14. The Tennessee Valley Authority (TVA) was established in 1933 as a federal agency empowered to "improve" the depressed region drained by the Tennessee River through hydropower, navigation, flood control, and economic development. The "blueprint" for TVA was a "308 report" prepared for the basin by the Army Corps of Engineers in the late 1920s.
15. Gilbert F. White, "A Perspective of River Basin Development," *Law and Contemporary Problems* 22 (Spring 1957): 157-84.
16. The President's Water Resources Policy Commission, *Report, Vol. II: Ten Rivers in America's Future*, (Washington, D.C., 1950).
17. Keith W. Muckleston, "Integrated Water Management in the United States" in *Integrated Water Management: International Experiences and Perspectives*, ed., Bruce Mitchell, 22-44 (London and New York, 1990), 26.
18. Rutherford H. Platt and William Nechamen, *Flood Loss Reduction Through Interstate Compacts: An Under-Utilized Approach*, Water Resources Research Center, University of Massachusetts, pub. no. 137, (Amherst, MA, 1983).
19. U.S. Senate, *Report of the Select Committee on National Water Resources.* Report No. 29, 87th Cong., 1st sess., (Washington, D.C., 1961).
20. U.S. Water Resources Council, *The Nation's Water Resources* (Washington, D.C.,1968); *The Nation's Water Resources: 1975-2000,* (Washington, D.C., 1978).
21. U.S. Water Resources Council, *A Unified Program for Flood Plain Management* (Washington, D.C., 1976). This document was prepared at the direction of Secion 1302(c) of the National Flood Insurance Act of 1968, which in turn was based on Executive Order 11296 issued by President Johnson in 1966 at the suggestion of the Task Force on Federal Flood Control. The "Unified Program" document was reissued in revised form in 1979 to reflect Executive Orders 11988 and 11990 issued by President Carter in 1977. With the demise of the Water Resources Council in 1981, responsibility for the "Unified Program" was moved to the Federal Emergency Management Agency where it was further revised and reissued in 1986 under the direction of geographer Frank Thomas.
22. Muckleston, "Integrated Water Management," 35.
23. Gilbert F. White, "Comparative Analysis of Complex River Development" in *Environmental Effects of Complex River Development*, ed. Gilbert F. White, 1-21 (Boulder, CO, 1977).
24. John C. Day, *Managing the Lower Rio Grande: An Experience in International River Development*, University of Chicago, res. paper no. 125, (Chicago, 1970).
25. Keith W. Muckleston, "The Columbia River" in *Environmental Effects of Complex River Development*, ed. Gilbert F. White, 1-21 (Boulder, CO, 1977).
26. W. R. Derrick Sewell, "Changing Approaches to Water Management in the Fraser River Basin" in *Environmental Effects of Complex River Development*, ed. Gilbert F. White, 1-21 (Boulder, CO, 1977).
27. Gilbert F. White, "The Environmental Effects of the High Dam at Aswan," *Environment* 30 (September, 1988): 4-11; 34-40.
28. Philip P. Micklin, *The Water Management Crisis in Soviet Central Asia,* The Carl Beck Papers in Russian and East European Studies (University of Pittsburgh), Paper no. 905, (Pittsburgh, 1991).

29. Session on "International River Basin Development in a Changing Global Climate" at the 88th Annual Meeting of the Association of American Geographers, San Diego, California, 20 April 1992.

30. National Water Commission, *Water Policies for the Future*, (Washington, D.C., 1973).

31. Theodore M. Schad, "The National Water Commission Revisited," *Water Resources Bulletin* 14 (April, 1978): 302-12.

32. Ibid., 306.

33. National Water Commission, App. III.

34. Robert W. Kates, *Hazard and Choice Perception in Flood Hazard Management,* University of Chicago, res. paper no. 78, (Chicago, 1962); *Industrial Flood Losses: Damage Estimation in the Lehigh Valley,* University of Chicago, res. paper no. 98, (Chicago: 1965).

35. Ian Burton, *Types of Agricultural Occupance of Flood Plains in the United States,* University of Chicago, res. paper no. 75, (Chicago, 1962).

36. John R. Sheaffer, *Flood Proofing: An Element in a Flood Damage Reduction Program,* University of Chicago, res. paper no. 65, (Chicago, 1960).

37. Thomas F. Saarinen, *Perception of the Drought Hazard on the Great Plains,* University of Chicago, res. paper no. 106 (Chicago, 1966).

38. Duane D. Baumann, *The Recreation Use of Domestic Water Supply Reservoirs: Perceptions and Choice,* University of Chicago, res. paper no. 121, (Chicago, 1969).

39. Shue Tuck Wong, *Perception of Choice and Factors Affecting Industrial Water Supply Decisions in Northeastern Illinois,* University of Chicago, res. paper no. 117, (Chicago, 1968).

40. Day, "Managing the Lower Rio Grande."

41. James F. Johnson, *Renovated Waste Water: An Alternative Source of Municipal Water Supply in the United States,* University of Chicago, res. paper no. 135, (Chicago, 1971).

42. James K. Mitchell, *Community Response to Coastal Erosion: Individual and Collective Adjustments to Hazard on the Atlantic Shore,* res. paper no. 156, (Chicago, 1974).

43. For a later case study of this phenomenon, see Rutherford H. Platt, " The Jackson Flood of 1979: A Public Policy Disaster," *Journal of the American Planning Association* 48 (Spring 1982): 219-31.

44. U.S. Congress, *A Unified National Program for Managing Flood Losses,* (1966), 89th Cong., 2d sess., H. Doc. 465.

45. James L. Wescoat, Jr., "Expanding the Range of Choice in Water Management: An Evaluation of Policy Approaches," *United Nations Natural Resources Forum* 10 (1986): 239-54; James L.Wescoat, Jr., "The 'Practical Range of Choice' in Water Resources Geography," *Progress in Human Geography* (1987): 41-59.

46. For example, Burrell Montz and Eve C. Gruntfest, "Changes in American Urban Floodplain Occupancy Since 1958: The Experiences of Nine Cities," *Applied Geography* 6 (1986): 325-38.

47. Eve C. Gruntfest, ed., *What We Have Learned Since the Big Thompson Flood: Proceedings of the Tenth Anniversary Conference,* Special pub. no. 16. (Boulder, CO, 1987).

48. Keith W. Muckleston, "The Impact of Floodplain Regulations on Residential Land Values in Oregon," *Water Resources Bulletin*, 19 (1983): 1-7; Burrell E. Montz, "Floodplain Delineation and Housing Submarkets," *The Professional Geographer* 39 (1987): 59-61; Burrell E. Montz and Graham A. Tobin, "The Spatial and Temporal Variability of Residential Real Estate Values in Response to Flooding," *Disasters* 12, no. 4 (1988): 345-55; Graham A. Tobin and Burrell E. Montz, "Catastrophic Flooding and the Response of the Real Estate Market," *The Social Science Journal* 25, no. 2 (1988): 167-77.
49. Rutherford H. Platt, et al., *Intergovernmental Management of Floodplains*, Monograph no. 30, (Boulder: 1980); Platt, "Metropolitan Flood Loss Reduction Through Regional Special Districts," *Journal of the American Planning Association* 52 (Autumn 1986): 467-79; Rutherford H. Platt, ed., *Regional Management of Metropolitan Floodplains*, Monograph no. 45, (Boulder, CO, 1987).
50. M. Gordon Wolman, "The Nation's Rivers," *Science* 174 (November 1971): 905-18. Richard A. Smith, Richard B. Alexander, and M. Gordon Wolman, "Water Quality Trends in the Nation's Rivers," *Science* 235 (27 March 1987): 1607-15.
51. Wolman, "The Nation's Rivers," 916.
52. Smith, et al., "Water Quality Trends in the Nation's Rivers."
53. James M. Omernik, "Ecoregions of the Conterminous United States," *Annals of the Association of American Geographers* 77, no. 1 (1987): 118-29.
54. Robert M. Hughes and David P. Larsen, "Ecoregions: An Approach to Surface Water Protection," *Journal of the Water Pollution Control Federation* 60, no. 4 (April 1988): 486-93; James E. Omernik and Glenn E. Griffith, "Ecological Regions Versus Hydrologic Units: Frameworks for Managing Water Quality," *Journal of Soil and Water Conservation* 46, no. 5 (Sept.-Oct. 1991): 334-40.
55. Christopher L. Lant and Jo Beth Mullens, "Lake and River Quality for Recreation Management and Contingent Valuation," *Water Resources Bulletin* 27, no. 3 (June 1991): 453-60.
56. Christopher L. Lant and Rebecca S. Roberts, "Greenbelts in the Cornbelt: Riparian Wetlands, Intrinsic Values, and Market Failure," *Environmental and Planning A* 22 (1990): 1375-88.
57. Ibid., 1386.
58. Geoge H. Nieswand, Robert M. Hordon, Theodore B. Shelton, Budd B. Chavooshian, and Steven Blarr, "Buffer Strips to Protect Water Supply Reservoirs: A Model and Recommendations," *Water Resources Bulletin* 26, no. 6 (December 1990): 959-66.
59. W. Andrew Marcus, "Regulating Contaminated Sediments in Aquatic Environments: A Hydrologic Perspective," *Environmental Management* 13, no. 6 (1989): 703-13.
60. W. Andrew Marcus, "Managing Contaminated Sediments in Aquatic Environments: Identification, Regulation, and Remediation," *Environmental Law Reporter: News and Analysis* 21 (1991): 10020-32.
61. W. Andrew Marcus and Michael S. Kearney, "Upland and Coastal Sediment Sources in a Chesapeake Bay Estuary," *Annals of the Association of American Geographers* 81, no. 3 (1991): 408-24.
62. Ibid., 422.

63. Clifford S. Russell, David G. Arey, and Robert W. Kates, *Drought and Water Supply: Implications of the Massachusetts Experience for Municipal Planning,* (Baltimore, 1970),

64. Duane Baumann, John J. Boland and John H. Sims, "Water Conservation: The Struggle over Definition," *Water Resources Research* 20 (1984): 428-34; Benedykt Dziegielewski and Duane D. Baumann, "Tapping Alternatives: The Benefits of Managing Urban Water Demands," *Environment* 34 (November 1992): 6-11, 35-41.

65. Planning and Management Consultants, Ltd., *The IWR-MAIN Water Use Forecasting System,* (Carbondale, IL, nd).

66. Planning and Management Consultants, Ltd., *Evaluation of Urban Water Conservation Programs: A Procedures Manual,* (Carbondale, IL, 1991).

67. Christopher J. Woltemade, "Environmental Impact Mitigation Under the Clean Water Act and the National Environmental Policy Act: The Case of the Two Forks Dam," *Water Resources Bulletin* 27, no. 2 (April 1991): 293-2.

68. Jacque (Jody) Emel, "Resource Instrumentalism, Privitization, and Commodification," *Urban Geography* 11, no. 6 (1990): 527-47.

69. Rutherford H. Platt, "The 2020 Water Supply Study for Metropolitan Boston: The Demise of Diversion," *Canadian Water Resources Journal,* forthcoming.

70. Saarinen, *Perception of the Drought Hazard.*

71. William E. Reibsame, Stanley A. Changnon, and T. R. Karl, *Drought and Natural Resources Management in the United States: Impacts and Implications of the 1987-1989 Drought* (Boulder, CO, 1990).

72. Benedykt Dziegielewski, Gary D. Lynne, Donald A. Wilhite, and Daniel P. Sheer, *The National Study of Water Management During Drought: A Research Assessment,* IWR Report 91-NDS-3, (Fort Belvoir, VA, 1991).

73. David E. Kromm and Stephen E. White, "Adoption of Water-Saving Practices by Irrigators in the High Plains," *Water Resources Bulletin* 26, no. 6 (December, 1990): 999-1012.

74. Ibid.

75. Keith W. Muckleston and Richard M. Highsmith, Jr., "Center Pivot Irrigation in The Columbia Basin of Washington and Oregon: Dynamics and Implications," *Water Resources Bulletin* 14, no. 5 (October, 1978): 1121-28.

76. Rebecca S. Roberts and Jacque Emel, "Uneven Development and the Tragedy of the Commons: Competing Images for Nature-Society Analysis," *Economic Geography,* forthcoming.

77. James L. Wescoat, Jr., "Challenging the Desert" in *The Making of the American Landscape,* ed. Michael P. Conzen, 186-203 (Chicago, 1990).

78. Ibid., 202-3.

79. Michael Hough, *Out of Place: Restoring Identity to the Regional Landscape,* (New Haven, 1990), Ch. 4.

80. Olen Paul Matthews, *Water Resources: Geography and Law,* Resource Publications in Geography, Assoc. of American Geographers (Washington, D.C. 1984).

81. Otis W. Templer, "Water Rights Issues," *The Role of Social and Behavioral Sciences in Water Resources Planning and Management,* eds. Duane Baumann and Yacov Y. Haimes, 216-37 (New York, 1988).

82. Ibid., 228.

83. Jacque L. Emel and Elizabeth Brooks, "Changes in Form and Function of Property Rights Institutions Under Threatened Resource Scarcity," *Annals of the Association of American Geographers* 78, no. 2 (1988): 241-52.
84. F. Andrew Schoolmaster, "Water Marketing and Water Rights Transfers in the Lower Rio Grande Valley, Texas." *Professional Geographer* 43, no. 3 (1991): 292-304.
85. James L. Wescoat, Jr., "On Water Conservation and Reform of the Prior Appropriation Doctrine in Colorado," *Economic Geography* 61, no. 1 (January 1985): 3-24
86. Ibid., 5.
87. James L. Wescoat, Jr., "Impacts of Federal Salinity Control on Water Rights Allocation Patterns in the Colorado River Basin," *Annals of the Association of American Geographers* 76, no. 2 (1986): 157-74. See also, Wescoat, Integrated Water Development: Water Use and Conservation Practice in Western Colorado. University of Chicago, res. paper no. 210. (Chicago, 1986).

Political Science: The Past and Future of Water Resources Policy and Management

Dean E. Mann

Political scientists come in all shapes and sizes and in 57 varieties with respect to their concern for science, values and policy advocacy. Moreover, the domain of political science is as expansive as the vision and competence of the individual investigator, appropriating to itself the work of sister disciplines without apology and finding itself being invaded by similarly imperialistic investigators from the same sister disciplines for whom "politics" is common sense, venality, or a transactionnal cost that has to be understood and dealt with.

Political scientists also vary in the extent to which they pretend to present objective evidence with respect to the workings of the political system or act as passionate exponents of one or another view with regard to how the system should or should not work. I suspect that many, if not most, political scientists combine both empirical analysis and theory testing with prescription in their research on water resources management.

Politics, and therefore political science, is concerned with collective choice, i.e., the decisions of the polity with respect to the constitutional distribution of power and constraints upon those who exercise that power as well as the more quotidian decisions made by the public's representatives with respect to issues that are legitimately on the public agenda. The classical definition of politics as the authoritative allocation of values appropriately describes the role of the state in sorting out values—material or symbolic—over which there are policy disputes and that are constitutionally subject to its will.

Politics is often seen as having instrumental value only, i.e., a means by which society can achieve goals that it cannot achieve by private transactions or a means by which individuals and groups seek to achieve goals through public processes. While those instrumental values are clearly present in water politics, it must be recognized that politics in general, and the politics of water, are also vehicles of self-actualization. From Aristotle to the National

Environmental Policy Act, the political processes and participation in them may be seen as a meaningful way by which citizens can both achieve private and public goals as well as express themselves as thoughtful contributors to the policymaking process. It may be argued that water politics in the last several decades have vastly improved along this dimension with numerous groups that were formerly excluded from the process or perceived no opportunity to participate now regularly making their influence felt in a more open and accessible policy process.[1]

Character of the Political System and Water Policies

For most political scientists, the term "polyarchy" probably best describes the nature of the American political system.[2] It is a political system in which there are multiple centers of power, each competing for control and dominance with respect to policy issues of concern to them. In this conceptualization, there is no single dominant elite or even close-knit coalitions of elites, but rather numerous power centers concerned about different public issues and having different internal processes. Some are highly concentrated in their decision-making structures while others are characterized by a broad sharing of power.

A leading student of American politics described the prevailing system as "triadic power" in which there is a dynamic process that reflects the character of specific policy issues, the organized power of producer and countervailing groups, administrative agencies with considerable automony in pursuit of their goals, and complicating roles played by the presidency and the judiciary.[3] The dynamic quality is found in the changing and variable relationships among these actors and the distribution of benefits and costs, both of which may be either concentrated or diffuse.

The differences in theoretical orientation may be seen in three books on water policy, two of which I reviewed for the *Los Angeles Times*.[4] In his study *Rivers of Empire*, Donald Worster takes his cue from Karl Wittfogel's view of hydraulic society and conceptualizes the water business historically as largely an unarticulated conspiracy of large corporate, agricultural and municipal interests which have dominated water politics.[5] They have set the agenda, the terms of conflict, and dictated the unfortunate results. Others talk of the "water industry," meaning public and private officials in positions of public power, such as in the Metropolitan Water District of Southern California, who quietly, behind closed doors, make sweeping decisions concerning water development that reflect the interests of the business community and others in water development.[6] On the other hand, Marc Reisner, in *Cadillac Desert*, sees the water picture in far more variegated and pluralistic patterns, reflecting a wide variety of conflicting interests which engage in political interplay that results in crazy-quilt decisions and illogical compromises.[7]

56

Patterns in Water Policy Decision Making

U.S. water policy has often been characterized as the quintessential example of distributive or pork-barrel politics: politics in which individual members of Congress trade votes on water projects included in omnibus legislation or anticipated in future omnibus legislation.[8] Working with bureaucratic agencies and local groups, congressional committees put together these legislative packages that are seen as virtually costless because they depend largely on the federal treasury for their funding.[9] This pattern of political behavior has been so consistent that it was given the title "iron triangle."[10] It was a relatively closed system in which even the president was a non-actor because of the overwhelming incentives for mutual accommodation among the principal actors in the triangular relationship.

There is little question that this traditional pattern of politics with respect to water projects, especially rivers and harbors and reclamation projects, has been altered. The question is the extent to which this system has been fundamentally changed, given the changed circumstances in which all public policy must be made and the rise of new policy issues and new interest groups. One of the circumstances is the growth of the federal budget and the budget deficit. No longer can water projects be viewed as minor additions to a budget that is itself a minor fraction of the gross national product. Water projects must compete with other programs and projects that have expanded enormously, have higher priority, and are often framed in terms of entitlements rather than discretionary expenditures. New starts have virtually ceased and cost-sharing with states and local interest has become the norm, in theory if not always in practice.

This has meant that the iron triangle has been modified to make the president and his chief budget aide, the Office of Management and Budget, important actors. Whereas presidents have previously interfered with the traditional process at their peril—witness President Carter's hit list—now they play important roles, largely resisting water projects on budgetary grounds. This appears to be a permanent alteration and will inevitably modify the roles of other actors in the process.

The new interests and issues are largely environmental in character. No longer can local groups promoting water development depend on public consensus or at least acquiescence in their proposed projects. Both local as well as national environmental groups are energized to oppose or substantially modify water projects that have high environmental costs and are often dubious on economic grounds as well.[11] Not only do they effectively oppose projects, but they also urge more efficient practices with respect to the management of existing projects and water supply systems.

In effect, it may be argued that the iron triangles have been permanently altered so that the notion of a triangular relationship no longer applies.[12] The issues are more complex and multifaceted, the revenue source has diminished, and the incentives to support water projects has been substantially reduced at both the local and congressional levels.[13] Issue networks now predominate in which manifold interests and interrelated issues are negotiated on a much broader basis.

Even this broad generalization is subject to some reservations, however. Issue networks bring in other interests and issues, but this greater inclusiveness may simply expand the coalitions that are necessary for water projects to proceed. Promoters of water projects in the West, for example, who have often ignored or bypassed Indian water interests and projects, now find that inclusion of these projects or programs enhances the possibilities for successful action.[14] Moreover, Indian water rights claims are sufficiently weighty to induce other water interests to include them in the coalition. The question of whether Indian-Anglo projects make any more sense economically or even in terms of the long-term future of the Indian reservations, may never be raised, let alone answered.

Similarly, the concern over water quality and industrial and municipal pollution has brought environmentalists and those promoting municipal pollution control projects together in support of federal financial support of the construction of sewage treatment plants.[15] There is clearly no political rule that says that only water developers can join coalitions that seek and gain access to the federal treasury as a means of achieving their goals.

Politics of Implementation

The pluralistic character of American politics extends far beyond the legislative venue where major policy decisions are made. Not surprisingly, the bargaining mode fits the bureaucratic process as well. Even the authoritative and seemingly ironclad water pollution statutes with their systems of permits, timetables, enforcement measures, and penalties are for the most part opportunities for negotiations between polluters, the EPA, and state agencies over the extent and timing of compliance with deadlines and standards. The entire process is built on a mutual recognition by public authorities and industries that companies and municipalities will not be forced to shut down in order to meet rigidly applied deadlines.[16] Inspections, notices, warnings, compliance schedules, and enforcement actions all require extended periods of time. Delays are often reinforced by lawsuits brought by regulators, the regulated, and interested third parties such as environmental groups.[17] These actions are complex disputes not only over laws and regulations but also over the evidential base upon which government agencies proceed.

Problems of implementation have played a large part in the study of the politics of public policy and this certainly includes water policy. Recently, emphasis has been placed on the discovery of the appropriate tools for achieving the goals of public policy. Rather than relying on regulation alone—the setting and enforcement of standards—consideration has been given to alternative strategies for achieving those goals. These strategies include—for water policy—the use of effluent charges, tradeable effluent permits, taxes on the use of substances that threaten water quality, judicial strategies that emphasize changes in water rights definitions, subsidies or cost-sharing, introduction of market-like arrangements for transferring water from use to another, expanding or contracting the scope of public participation, and even privatization of water rights.[18] These strategies, alone or combined in various ways, provide alternative courses of action, reflecting both the nature of the resource and the goals of the policies themselves. This kind of analysis places attention on the incentive structures for the actors—both bureaucrats and the public—the costs of administration, the problems of the complexity of joint action, and the necessity of foresight in making such choices with their long-term consequences.

An important perspective that political scientists as well as others have brought to the understanding of both water and other forms of politics is the extent to which there are various kinds of regimes operating with respect to decision making. Not all are of the formal kind, depending on laws, rights, legal obligations, contracts, and judicial decisions. Agreement on water matters are often worked out in fairly informal and transitory agreements among parties with common interests.[19] The extent to which informal and commonly understood practices are often operative was displayed in case studies of water districts in Spain and Northern Colorado and the Central Valley of California.[20] These informal arrangements also present formidable obstacles to rules by centralized managers who want to impose them on reluctant water agencies.

Voluntary transfers of water within irrigation districts is reportedly a fairly common practice on a year-to-year basis although few of these are accounted for in the literature. Yet, informal to informal arrangements on a temporary basis, often in crisis situations, have become increasingly the norm. Although hardly a case of total informality, the steps taken by the Department of Water Resources of the State of California are illustrative of a major effort to cope with drought through voluntary exchanges and purchases.[21] Standards were developed and contracts for water purchases and sales were rapidly developed on a one-time basis and these agreements clearly had an impact on critical situations many water users were facing. Similarly, both voluntary and involuntary measures to adjust water rights to new and emerging values in the Truckee-Carson River basins included changes in federal law, purchases of water rights by recreational and fish and wildlife interests, and state legislative allocation of funds for water rights purchases.[22]

The Value of Water

The definition of the value of water has been one of the important sources of controversy with respect to water policy. For economists, the definition of the value of water tends to be expressed in monetary terms, like that of any other resource or commodity. The price reflects what individuals and other interests are willing to pay for water of a given quality and in a given amount relative to the price of other commodities for which they also have a demand structure. The criticisms by economists of much water policy in the United States have focused on the distortions of price by means of subsidies offered to special groups of beneficiaries of water development: federal assumption of interest on construction of reclamation projects, assumption of construction costs on rivers and harbors projects, charges based on slippery formulas such as ability to pay, allocation of costs to other beneficiaries as electrical users, and basin-wide accounting systems.[23]

Defense of these subsidies has largely relied on arguments about the national interest, equity, prior commitments, and regional and local development. Governmental interference in the private market through various forms of direct and indirect benefits given to other interests have justified both particular and general programs and projects in water development for the benefit of those who are disadvantaged by those interventions. Government water projects persist on the basis of historical practice because of individual and group expectations regarding those benefits. Governmental actions are also arguably required to stimulate economic development through water projects in less prosperous areas of the nation.

The argument that water should be treated as a commodity is in partial reaction to what has been called the "water is different" syndrome.[24] Water is variously considered as "basic" to an economy, it is "priceless" because it is necessary, and it provides a "fundamental" resource on which society must build. For the critics of this conceptualization, water is a resource, different in some respects because of its flow nature, but a resource nevertheless, subject to capture, management, legal definition as to ownership and use, and pricing. For the most part, "shortages" of water are comparable to shortages of $500 Cadillacs.[25]

The remedy for policies based on notions of "water as different" are several: improved definitions of water rights, including rights to groundwater and to instream uses; withdrawal of the federal and state governments from financing and construction of water projects; and the creation of markets through which exchanges of water could be encouraged through the medium of price. The role of government, especially state government, would be to perfect these water rights, relax impediments to water transfers and encourage the creation of true markets in water resources.

This kind of argument has met resistance from some political scientists and others who are persuaded that water, after all, is a fundamental and distinctive element in the creation and maintenance of social organizations, especially small towns, rural communities, and ethnic societies. Markets for water arguably threaten and inevitably will lead to the decline of communities generally, and particularly will work to the disadvantage of minority and impoverished communities.[26] They emphasize the community value of water; its symbolic and emotional meaning, the traditional public character of water supply and management, the stress on the equitable distribution of water to all members of society, and the opportunity for social control that water management provides for local groups.[27]

Equally important is the concern that some groups in society will be materially disadvantaged in any bargaining process through which markets will function. Any advantage accruing to those who give up their water rights—already in a weak bargaining position because of their impoverished circumstances—will be dissipated in a piecemeal process or taken up by a relative few. The fundamental structures of communities arguably will be altered as they move away from water-related activities on which their traditional societies have been built.[28]

The value question extends for some political scientists to the matter of environmental ethics and justice.[29] Deriving principles from philosophical analysis, political theory, and public choice arguments, they espouse a broad planning and environmental framework in which water issues are examined from a standpoint far broader than a benefit-cost calculus. They are concerned about ultimate consequences that include consideration of both human and nonhuman welfare, equitable distribution of costs, alignment of water management with the character of bioregions, and the adoption of a criterion of reasonable fallibility in evaluating water resource projects.[30] This criterion places emphasis on small projects with less intrusive impacts in light of the uncertainty associated with disturbances to the environment.

The Federal System and Water Policy

One of the most durable and pervasive issues of the American constitutional order is the distribution of powers geographically. The federal system affects nearly every policy issue in America, ranging from issues such as national defense and medical care to the management of natural and therefore water resources. Despite the secular trend in the twentieth century toward an increasing role for the national government in public policy generally and water policy in particular, recent enactments with respect to water pollution control and air pollution control clearly demonstrate that resource policy will continue to be a shared responsibility between the national government and the states.

The states have always claimed extensive jurisdiction over water development owing to their administration of water law and water rights. Even here, the states have to share authority, given the complications of reclamation projects and reclamation law in the West, the interstate nature of both surface and underground water, and the reserved rights of public land and Indian tribes. Undoubtedly, the national government and the states will continue to sort out their responsibilities through laws and litigation well into the future.

The states have responded in a variety of ways to the increased responsibility for water development and management and pollution control. While all these responses indicate the need for change, they suggest priorities and answers that reflect an incongruous mix of perceptions and constraints: (1) whether the principal water problem is scarcity or pollution, (2) the availability of financial resources, (3) the interest group structure within each state, (4) the institutional capacity to deal with water problems, and (5) the economic and political culture of each state.[31] States have become increasingly reluctant to approve financing of large development projects, have in some cases established very restrictive conditions on groundwater management, and have varied in their willingness to create integrated management structures and to engage in the research on water management improvements. They have also varied in their willingness to alter water law to ensure the protection of the interests of emerging claimants on water and to increase the law's flexibility in terms of allowing transfers of uses. Inevitably, changes that have taken place in state water management have led to consideration of changes in other policy areas such as population and land-use management.

This variability in state responses to increased but shared responsibilities with respect to water policy is illustrated by the roles they have played with respect to controls of point and non-point sources of pollution. The federal presence is greatest regarding point sources of water pollution, with EPA specifying standards, means of achieving them, time tables, and compliance. With respect to non-point sources, the federal presence is considerably less, setting attainment goals but leaving the methods and procedures up to the states. State investments in water pollution control do not vary uniformly with the recognition of need but respond to such factors as threats by polluting industries to leave the area or state (the exit option) in the face of tough regulation of, for instance, non-point source pollution. Moreover, federal involvement affects the extent to which the federal government can coordinate efforts among states and the extent to which states share their experience with each other.[32]

Clearly, one of the most controversial issues concerning the sharing of responsibility for water management concerns the regulation of groundwater. Various federal statutes affect groundwater management, but states generally retain broad authority over groundwater. The extent to which the states have adopted effective regulation of groundwater in the absence of national regulation with respect to quality and quantity varies substantially. But the general picture, at least in the West, is in a positive direction.[33]

The situation with respect to federal-state relations on groundwater is complicated by the fact that tougher federal regulations have considerable implications for control over water rights, an area of state authority. Reviewing the record of federal and state regulation of groundwater, the variable benefits achieved, the fragmented picture of regulation, and the potential crisis in groundwater quality, one political scientist sees an important role for the adoption of a national groundwater code.[34]

The delicate interrelationship of national and state government is further illustrated in the matter of water transfers from agriculture to municipal and industrial uses. Largely considered a state matter, the introduction of environmental, instream and third-party interests protected by both federal and state laws has threatened the basic appropriation doctrines that largely prevail in western states. Decisions protecting those interests on a basin-wide basis threaten to substitute riparian rights and at the same time limit the capacity of states to undertake water transfers that are facilitated by appropriative systems.[35]

Lessons from the Past and Implications for the Future

The simple answer to questions that political scientists are supposed to be able to answer is one of political feasibility. But this answer is deceptively simple because it masks questions that have to do with values, strategy, and processes. Political feasibility depends on the analysis of goals and values of public policy, the benefits and costs of alternative strategies, and the extent to which the process itself accommodates the multiple values of society.

In this context, I offer a modest list of lessons that have been learned and might be kept in mind by decision makers in the future:

- The political system is decidedly more open with respect to water policy and therefore more amenable to a variety of interests that are concerned with its character. Even if coalitions are simply broader in their nature, their greater broadness reflects a susceptibility to influence by a multiplicity of groups and particularly to a new and more inclusive ethic corresponding to a greater emphasis on the protection of the environment. Thus, large water projects and programs that are narrowly drawn and reflect the inputs of single interests are not likely to gain political favor.
- Greater emphasis should be placed on policy tools—alternative strategies for accomplishing water policy goals. Strategies should be examined in terms of the nature of the resource, the history of its management or mismanagement, the configuration of interests arrayed in support of, or in opposition to, policy alternatives, the administrative costs, and the extent to which and the manner in which these alternatives may be helped or hindered by greater openness to public participation.
- Incorporation of federal and state roles in public policymaking is virtually a *sine qua non* of water policymaking. Discovering the appropriate roles of each level of government is a work of art, requiring careful examination of the nature of the hierarchical relationships and the consequences for behavior of state and private interests at the state level and among the states. Efforts to develop regional instruments of governance require special sensitivity to the interests of state-level officialdom and private interests.

• Greater research, philosophical speculation, or logical analysis should be devoted to the varying conceptions of the value of water. Conflicting conceptions of its value clearly lead to divergent conceptions of how water should be treated in policy and in law. How is it different from other resouces? Why and how is it more basic than trees, food, land or other resources?

Notes

1. Dean E. Mann, "Democratic Politics and Environmental Policy," in *Controversies in Environmental Policy,* eds. S. Kamieniecki, R. O'Brien and M. Clarke (Albany, NY, 1985).
2. Robert A. Dahl, *Polyarchy: Participation and Opposition* (New Haven, CT, 1971).
3. Andrew S. McFarland, "Interest Groups and Theories of Power in America," *British Journal of Political Science,* 17 (April 1987): 129-47.
4. Dean E. Mann, *Los Angeles Times,* Book review section, 21 July 1986, 1.
5. Donald Worster, *Rivers of Empire: Water, Aridity and Growth of the American West* (New York, 1985).
6. Robert Gottlieb and Margaret Fitzsimmons, *Thirst for Growth: Water Agencies as Hidden Governments in California* (Tucson, 1991).
7. Marc Reisner, *Cadillac Desert: The American West and Its Disappearing Water* (New York, 1986).
8. Arthur Maass, *Muddy Waters: The Army Engineers and the Nation's Rivers* (Cambridge, 1951).
9. Helen M. Ingram, *Water Politics: Continuity and Change* (Albuquerque: 1990).
10. J. Leiper Freeman, *The Political Process* (New York 1965).
11. Robert Gottlieb, *A Life of Its Own: The Politics and Power of Water* (San Diego, New York and London, 1988).
12. Hugh Heclo, "Issue Networks and the Executive Establishment," in *The New American Political System,* ed. Anthony King (Washington, D.C., 1978).
13. See, for example, Thomas J. Schoenbaum, *The New River Controversy* (Winston-Salem, NC, 1979).
14. Daniel McCool, *Command of the Waters: Federal Water Development and Indian Water* (Berkeley, 1987).
15. Dean E. Mann, "Political Incentives in U.S. Water Policy: Relationships between Distributive and Regulatory Politics" in *What Government Does,* eds. Matthew Holden, Jr. and Donald Dresang (Beverly Hills, 1975).
16. Susan Hunter and Richard W. Waterman, "Determining and Agency's Regulatory Style: How Does the EPA Water Office Enforce the Law?" *Western Political Quarterly* 45, no. 2 (June 1992): 403-18.
17. David Vogel, *National Styles of Regulation: Environmental Policy in Great Britain and the United States* (Ithaca, 1986).
18. Terry L. Anderson, *Water Crisis: Ending the Policy Drought* (Baltimore and London, 1983).
19. Oran Young, *Resource Regimes* (Berkeley, 1982).
20. Arthur Maass and Raymond Anderson, *...and the Desert Shall Rejoice: Conflict, Growth, and Justice in Arid Environments* (Cambridge, MA, 1977).

21. California, Department of Water Resources, *The 1991 Drought Water Bank* (Sacramento, 1992).
22. Bonnie G. Colby, Mark A. McGinnis and Ken A. Rait, "Mitigating Environmental Externalities through Voluntary and Involuntary Water Reallocation: Nevada's Trickee-Carson River Basin," *Natural Resources Journal* 31 (Fall 1991): 757-84.
23. For a summary, see the *Final Report, National Water Commission* (Washington, D.C., 1973).
24. M. Kelso, "The Water is Different Syndrome or What is Wrong with the Water Industry," Proceedings of the Third Annual Conference of the American Water Works Association (Urbana, IL, 1967).
25. See generally, J. Hirshleiter, J. DeHaven, and J. Milliman, *Water Supply, Economics, Technology, and Policy* (Chicago, 1960).
26. F. Lee Brown and Helen M. Ingram, *Water and Poverty in the Southwest* (Tuscon, 1987).
27. Ibid.
28. Ibid.; see also Helen M. Ingram, "Politics, Markets, Society and Water Resources," *Halcyon/1992* 14 (Reno, 1992).
29. John Dryzek, *Rational Ecology, Environment and Political Economy* (New York, 1987).
30. David Lewis Feldman, *Water Resource Management: In Search of an Environmental Ethic* (Balitmore and London, 1991).
31. Jurgen Schmandt, Ernest T. Smerdon and Judith Clarkson, *State Water Policies: A Study of Six States* (New York, 1988).
32. William R. Lowry, *The Dimensions of Federalism: State Governments and Pollution Control Policy* (Durham and London, 1992).
33. Lawrence J. McDonnell and David J. Guy, "Approaches to Groundwater Quality Protection in the Western States, *Water Resources Research* 27, no. 3 (March 1991): 259-65.
34. Henry C. Kenski, *Saving the Hidden Treasure* (Claremont, CA, 1990).
35. A. Dan Tarlock, "New Water Transfer Restrictions: The West Returns to Riparianism," *Water Resources Research* 27, no. 6 (June 1991): 987-94.

Engineering Perspectives on Water Management Issues

Neil S. Grigg

Introduction

This article presents an engineering perspective on needed water policy initiatives. In the panel discussion, two principal questions are raised: what does the discipline bring to water resources management, and how can we increase the application of the discipline to the management of water resources?

Other disciplinary views to be expressed here include history, economics, geography, and political science. We should not neglect the natural and life science disciplines because engineering's base is science and because of the current concern with environmental issues. For this reason, some of the roles of natural and life science disciplines in water resources management will be discussed, though the focus of this paper will be on engineering.

Engineering is a changing discipline, one that includes many diverse and advancing bodies of knowledge. Three trends are especially apparent: the unfolding of technologies, with a high-tech emphasis on areas such as materials, biotechnology, microelectronics, and information sciences; diversification, with engineers finding new fields in which to apply technology; and the broadening of engineering, with engineers utilizing other branches of knowledge in the service of society. These trends do not easily lead to a single unified view of engineering. In fact, even within the practice of water resources management, at least six different types of engineering can be identified. They will be listed in a later section.

In a narrow sense engineering and science usually deal more with technical issues than with policy. Nevertheless, today engineers and scientists ignore policy and management issues at their peril. Past policy forums have concluded that technical tools have outpaced our ability to apply them in current institutional settings. Theodore Schad states this well: "The greatest need is for implementation of the institutional changes that will be needed to put our scientific and technical knowledge to use in the service of mankind."[1] Taken this as a given, if engineering and science cannot offer new contributions to solving institutional issues in water resources management, they will take back seats in the policy debates; in today's difficult and fractious water policy environment, the same statement could be made about the other disciplines represented here. Schad's comment is on the mark: institutional changes are needed to enable us to put to work knowledge from all disciplines.

If there is anything important to discuss at this Forum it is how to implement institutional change to improve water resources management. If the disciplines discussed here take back seats in the policy debate, it is because of our failure to make the requisite institutional changes. Who will take the front seats? I will suggest ways to put engineering and science at the front of the debate over improving water resources management. There will always be political issues to work out, and boundary problems between disciplines, but we must find ways to increase the contributions of engineering and science to water resources management if complexity and conflict are to be overcome.

Policy Issues

We know in general what the policy needs are; they repeat themselves in policy discussions. Some recent reviews of policy issues include: a review by Schad[2] of four decades of policy discussions, an overview paper by Warren Viessman,[3] the Harvard water policy study,[4] a discussion of the National Water Commission report,[5] a conference report by the American Water Resources Association,[6] Marc Reisners and Sara Bates' book,[7] and a state government policy study.[8]

Viessman's review provides a useful list of policy issues. Those dealing with institutions include providing information, modernizing institutions, providing national and regional perspectives, paying for water management, uniting technology and society, improving state planning/management capability, modifying agency roles, and defining beneficial use. His list of resource issues embraces global climate change, non-point discharges, solid waste management, water for natural systems, allocating water resources, dealing with extreme events, water renovation and reuse, protecting and enhancing water quality, restoring water-related attributes, transboundary water management, groundwater protection and management, and land-water management.[9]

In policy studies, the institutional issue that most frequently appears is uncoordinated federal and state water policies and programs. The oft-proposed solution is a federal government coordinating body, something to replace the Water Resources Council. Another frequently cited problem is the mismatch between water regions and political districts. One answer is to establish regional water management councils, something like the river basin commissions authorized by the Water Resources Planning Act. There has been a flurry of proposals to deal with inadequate and uncoordinated research, data, and education. Suggested solutions include a national water information program, a clearinghouse of information and policy analysis, a renewal of the national water resources research program, a national water extension service, better educational efforts at all levels to raise awareness, and launching new policy studies. Many of the problems are ascribed to ineffective water pricing. To the extent this is true, these problems might be ameliorated by the introduction of modern pricing and water marketing for all federally produced water, and by undertaking other needed pricing reforms, such as using conservation rates for urban water.

These policy issues occur mainly in national studies. For the West, Reisner and Bates[10] suggest policies for water transfers, solving environmental problems, and improving water use efficiency. One proposal is for federal and state governments to enhance possibilities for water transfers. The authors also recommend reducing subsidies, tackling special environmental problems, protecting basins of origin, enhancing instream flows, introducing the public trust doctrine, and improving water use efficiency.

While most visible policy issues clearly focus on institutions, technical matters cannot be ignored. Engineers and scientists must not only investigate technical issues in an effort to improve our knowledge, but must also work to resolve them.

Water Resources Management: Definition and Tasks

It is difficult to draw boundaries between disciplines involved in water. William Whipple stated the point well: "Water resources management is becoming a broad and complex field, increasingly difficult to characterize by reference to a single discipline."[11] If we are to find ways for the disciplines to work together in water resources management, we should work from compatible definitions.

A narrow definition of water resources management is preferable: the application of structural and nonstructural measures to control natural and man-made water resources systems. The key words are "measures," "control," and "systems," and each of these is loaded with implications for engineers. Measures, both structural and nonstructural, include the full range of tools and techniques: technologies, laws and regulations, finance and pricing, and management programs. Control refers to all actions that result in water allocation, use, treatment, and conveyance. Water resources systems include a combination of water control facilities and environmental elements working together to achieve water management purposes. Water control facilities for water quantity and quality are man-made structural systems including water supply and wastewater management systems for cities, industries, and farms; systems for drainage of land and control of floods; and systems for water control in rivers, reservoirs, and aquifers. Examples of water control facilities are conveyance systems, diversion structures, dams and storage facilities, treatment plants, pumping stations, wells, aquifers, and appurtenances. Environmental elements involved in water resources management embrace the atmosphere, catchments, stream channels, aquifers and groundwater systems, lakes, estuaries, seas, and the ocean. Our definition suggests the need for institutions to provide guidelines for water management control systems, for engineers and scientists to develop and manage them, and for systems of accountability to make sure engineers and scientists fulfill their goals.

The Engineering Perspective

What does the engineering discipline bring to water resources management? From the point of view of some, engineers wear the black hat in the water development saga. What is the truth? Should engineers wear black hats or white? Are engineers uncreative, insensitive bullies interested only in pouring concrete? Are they techno-nerds interested only in computers and numbers, or are they sensitive, creative professionals who really want to do what is best for society and the environment?

Engineering is usually defined as the application of mathematics and science to solving practical problems such as designing, constructing, and operating economical and efficient structures, systems, and equipment. You might say that the distinction between engineering and its science base is the engineering focus on practical problems.

Scientists have not been assigned the black hat. If anything, science has been mostly left out of the jokes about black and white hatters in water management. Sciences such as biology, chemistry, and geology are important in water resources management, and we can cite many examples of their contributions. Still, with politics and finances the driving forces of water resources management, science may sometimes be forced out of the equation—except if environmental or health issues dominate; then science may bring engineering, politics and financial interests to a standstill.

Blending science and engineering to find integrated solutions to water management problems is the key to solving problems both of hydrodiplomacy and sustainable natural systems. Hydrodiplomacy, a term coined by Professor Evan Vlachos of Colorado State University, refers to finding solutions to transboundary water conflicts. Sustainable water systems are those that provide for human uses of water, sustain natural ecological systems, and answer questions of intergenerational equity.

A broad view of engineering is suggested, one that seeks to represent fully what is going on in engineering today. Engineering is an evolving discipline that uses, although hardly exclusively, math and science. It also uses management tools (which may themselves use math and science) and social science, including economic and policy studies that are critical to success in water management. In this sense, engineering is an integrative discipline. Engineers blend knowledge from other disciplines, and they lead problem-solving teams. This has been a characteristic of engineers for many years. One of the fathers of the management discipline, Frederick Taylor, made important contributions to scientific management from an engineering base.

Here there is a question about vertical stratification of disciplines: where does engineering stop and management start? The term "management" does not fully describe the challenges of water resources. These include complicated coordination among many public and private institutions, addressing critical social issues, and responding to complex ecological systems. This complexity is evident in other management challenges facing civil engineers who deal with public works. Donald Stone, writing about public works management challenges, described the problem this way:

> Engineering capability alone is insufficient for these multidimensional purposes. Engineering and other specialized skills must be complemented by public affairs and managerial competencies. These include capacity to deal with the gamut of social, economic, environmental and political factors inherent in planning, policy resolution and program implementation. Practitioners are needed who can integrate public works systems and subsystems into urban and national development programs.[12]

To address this problem, the American Society of Civil Engineers (ASCE) created a technical division devoted to focusing on water resources planning and management issues. This division's purpose emphasizes interdisciplinary approaches to planning and management of water resources and embraces social, economic, environmental, and administrative aspects of water management.[13]

One can discern several different types of engineering that are practiced within the broad field of water resources management. At the risk of oversimplification, I have identified six types: the engineer-manager, the engineer-scientist, the engineer-planner, the systems/operation engineer, the systems/design engineer and the environmental engineer. Each of these engineer types makes a contribution, but each contribution is decidedly different. There may be as much difference between the views of the engineer-manager and the engineer-scientist as between a political scientist and a systems engineer.

Given this diversity, what are the engineer's contributions to the problem-solving team? I suggest two important roles, one unique and the other shared with other disciplines. The unique role is technical expert. It involves planning and designing facilities, operating systems, and providing expertise in dispute resolution and regulatory forums. This role demands innovation, finding new solutions to complex technology-based problems, adapting

70

computers to management, and engineering research. It can embrace most of the work of the engineer-scientist, the engineer-planner, the systems/operation engineer, the systems/design engineer and the environmental engineer. The shared role is integrator and problem solver, serving as the leader of interdisciplinary teams to reduce complexity and mitigate conflict in water management. This higher level management role is often assumed by engineers, but it can be assumed by those from other disciplines as well. If these two roles, technical expert and integrator, are filled well, engineers can be key players in providing for hydrodiplomacy and sustainable systems.

My answer to the white hat or black hat question is that some engineers should get the white one and some, the black one. Engineering, especially civil engineering, has shifted its priorities, and what would be a white hat in the past might be black today. In 1990, *Civil Engineering* magazine stated that 60 years before proponents of cheap electricity were planning to dam the Colorado River, the Empire State Building was about to claim the title of the world's largest, and a $35 million bond issue was enabling the construction of Golden Gate Bridge.[14] These were all big, structural projects, but in contemporary water management what is not so visible are the solutions produced by engineers through nonstructural programs. *Civil Engineering* magazine predicted that future civil engineers will tackle less grandiose water projects, but infinitely more complex water problems. The complexities will include such areas as hazardous waste, groundwater cleanup, rising sea levels, recycling, conservation, and disaster mitigation. These will often require solutions based on management approaches rather than structures alone.

Engineers bring science and technology-based solutions to management. A few examples include systems analysis, computerized water accounting, sustainable systems, and monitoring systems for accountability. The management of complex water systems requires systems analysis—defining water resources systems and finding mathematical functions to simulate them and derive optimal solutions. The systems characterization can be quite complex, for example, an entire river basin with all water users. The requisite math and science are imposing. To deal with this complexity, engineers utilize decision support system (DSS) nomenclature. DSS involves models, geographic information systems, data, and the dialog between system and decision maker. Some of the best advances in DSS result from cooperative efforts of engineers and computer scientists, especially in providing the graphics interface to take into account the human factors in decision making.

Systems analysis should also involve social scientists. The uncertainty of data must be considered. Complexity is often not directly quantifiable, or it might change with time and with the players. However, systems analysis provides the best hope we have to deal with complexity using quantitative analysis. The foundation for hydrodiplomacy should be the social science contribution to systems analysis.

Another important aspect of water management is computerized water accounting using hydrologic balances. Water accounting for river basins, aquifers, urban water systems, and other hydrologic accounting units is the object of simulation models. It is the tool needed to deal with water allocation issues. Interstate compacts and water rights systems require water accounting, and instream flow management systems increasingly need it. Water accounting involves solving problems of hydrologic science such as rainfall-runoff, infiltration, return flow, seepage, evaporation, and all other hydrologic processes. In the future, it will require more biological data, and the biological sciences will be considered an essential tool for engineers to use in water management. Sustaining a water system's ecology means nourishing and sustaining its natural ecology. Therefore, water managers must understand all of the system's ecological aspects from the smallest component of the food chain up to the largest.

Monitoring for accountability brings all of these science issues together. It involves everything from streamflow gaging, needed for water allocation, to biological monitoring that might include a diverse menu of species. Effective and economical monitoring requires users to determine in advance the ways in which the information to be obtained will be used. Once this question is decided, the appropriate monitoring system can be designed carefully and scientifically. Accountability systems can provide some of the trust needed to overcome the inherent conflict in water resources management.

Engineers and scientists reduce complexity through research and systems analysis. They blend science and engineering to find integrated solutions to water management problems, including the design of sustainable natural systems. They serve as technical experts, finding new solutions to complex technology-based problems, and they provide for accountability through effective monitoring systems. If all of the above is successful, they can contribute to hydrodiplomacy. The next question is how can we increase the capabilities of the disciplines to do these things?

Complexity, Conflict, and Integration and Water Management

The chief impediments to progress in water resources management are complexity and conflict. These arise from scientific uncertainties, apparently irreconcilable values, and from water programs operated by diverse government and nongovernmental organizations to serve diverse groups in diverse regions.

To overcome complexity we need competence in each discipline and in the overarching management roles. Prescriptions for conflict include cooperation, coordination, and communication. I suggest this as a "six C" model for water resources management: competence to overcome complexity; cooperation, coordination and communication to overcome conflict. While this model is interdisciplinary, engineers are usually on the firing line, being required to put together the whole picture and make it work.

Integrated water management requires reconciling different viewpoints, regardless of whether their frames of reference are geographical, political, ecological, or functional. This is a formidable task. The geographic perspective refers to scale and accounting unit: global, river basin, country, water body, locale, region, etc. Political analysis is important because government water management agencies (who may disagree among themselves) must respond to divergent constituencies and interest groups. Not only may political issues divide agencies, constituencies, and interest groups horizontally, but vertically, i.e., federal, state, and local agencies may disagree. The ecological perspective addresses hydrologic and biological issues such as "conjunctive use of water," a term describing the combined and joint use of surface and groundwaters. To resolve ecological problems in a river basin requires an integrated analysis of water, plant, biological, and wildlife issues. Functional issues focus on water use applications, such as urban water supply, wastewater management, navigation, and irrigation.

The diversity of these viewpoints, reflecting far more than disciplinary concerns, illustrates the task of the integrator in water management. The engineer is as well-suited as any water resources professional to be the integrator, but this task is not bound to any single discipline. Preparing professionals of whatever discipline for this task—especially for the problem of sustaining natural systems—is a principal challenge to water resources management.

The future decision-making environment for water resources managers will be filled with conflict. The most promising approaches will improve institutions and will provide for integrated problem-solving utilizing disciplinary and interdisciplinary knowledge about water management.

Conclusion

Engineers and scientists can make unique and essential contributions to improving water resources management, but they need to be better prepared. Probably the most critical need is leadership, but, leaving this issue aside, engineers and scientists can help improve water management if they enjoy better research opportunities, obtain professional education, and can clearly identify issues and win-win solution scenarios.

Education issues must be addressed at a time when education at all levels—including the question of technological illiteracy—is one of the nation's most critical policy issues. Will we be able to manage the increasingly complex society that is emerging? We have problems today with preparing students for college, especially minority groups who will be the majority of Americans in the next century. Can we expect the United States to continue to have superior engineers? We will need more competent technical personnel to analyze and operate the complex systems described in this article. Education policy is a major concern for water policy even at the lower technical and management levels.

The educational debate comes at a time when our approach to water mangement requires greater sophistication. Today's engineers must seemingly be Renaissance men (or women). Using the systems approach, they must integrate the contributions of each discipline on the problem-solving team—engineering, economics, law, ecology, business, and politics—to find the needed win-win solution. Systems analysis illuminates complex, interacting systems. Solutions will depend on showing the relationships between natural and man-made systems.

To help solve problems, engineers must not only be equipped with the best systems analysis tools, but also be familiar with Altenative Dispute Resolution (ADR) techniques. They must combine technical expertise with in-depth knowledge of policy, planning, communications, finance, and public involvement. If they are prepared, engineers can bridge technology and policy, a new role for them. Of course, they cannot, by themselves, stop the inevitable conflicts in water management, because conflict resolution is basically a function of the political process rather than of science and engineering. However, engineers can help to reduce the conflicts to those that require policy debate and political action by providing information, reducing complexity, and pointing out how to reach integrated decisions.

In the *Civil Engineering* magazine 60th anniversary issue, David Marks stated that there will be an acrimonious education battle in the next decade; the new curriculum must focus on preparing for lifelong learning, with the four year degree stressing fundamentals and societal context. He also noted that environmental and infrastructure issues will be priorities.[15] The four year engineering degree itself is a policy issue. How can we squeeze what is needed for water management into a four year degree? Is a water manager's academy needed? Can other disciplines fill the gap? Should a new engineer, the water resources engineer, be produced in four years? Can environmental engineers fill the gap? How do we produce engineers to recognize and solve infrastructure problems? Other issues include continuing education and special training for water managers in integrative problem solving.

What about water resources research and the exchange of scientific information? Complexity requires research and more focus on integration issues. Yet research has languished, the Water Resources Research Act has been neglected at the federal level, and the states have not picked up the ball. Engineers respond to financial incentives, but it is not clear that the marketplace will supply them. Without them, we will not have the technological innovations we need in areas such as point-of-use treatment, recycling, dual water systems, water pricing and conservation. Returns can be very high, but the research (and policy) initiatives must be organized and financed? Something is needed in the policy arena to stimulate research incentives for technological innovations at all levels.

Indeed, many policies need attention in the water management arena, but finding policies that work will be a challenge in tomorrow's complex and

competitive world. Policies are needed to enable us to make the nation's infrastructure more responsive to economic and social development and to
demands for environmental enhancement. Clearly, institutional issues will
continue to dominate the policy agenda. The clash of values between groups
and issues surrounding property rights in water seem sure to prevent the
visionary dreams of planners from coming true. Water conflicts will not be
resolved in reasoned, negotiated sessions between interest groups; they will be
resolved in elections, court battles, agency rule making and decision making,
and in water right purchases. This is the policy arena for water managers in the
future. For engineers and scientists to fit into that arena requires changes in
our education and science policy.

Notes

1. Theodore M. Schad, "Past, Present, and Future of Water Resources Management
   in the United States," in *Water Management in the 21st Century*, American Water
   Resources Association, (Bethesda, MD, September 1989), 1-8.
2. Ibid., 8.
3. Warren Viessman, Jr., "Water Management: Challenge and Opportunity," *Journal
   of the Water Resources Planning and Management Division, ASCE* 116, no. 2
   (March/April 1990): 155-69.
4. Charles H.W. Foster and Peter P. Rogers, *Federal Water Policy: Toward an
   Agenda for Action*, (Harvard University, Energy and Environmental Policy Center, John F. Kennedy School of Government, August 1988).
5. "Whither Federal Water Policy," *California Water*, 3 (Summer 1989).
6. Stephen M. Born, ed., "Redefining National Water Policy: New Roles and Directions," American Water Resources Association (AWRA) special pub. 89-1
   (Bethesda, MD, 1989).
7. Marc Reisner and Sara Bates, *Overtapped Oasis: Reform or Revolution for Western Water* (Washington, D.C., 1990).
8. Leonard U. Wilson, Council of State Governments, State Water Policy Issues,
   (Lexington, KY, 1978).
9. Viessman, "Water Management," 155.
10. Reisner and Bates, *Overtapped Oasis*.
11. William Whipple, Jr., "Future Directions for Water Resources," in *Water Man-
    agement in the 21st Century*, (Bethesda, MD, September 1989), 9-13.
12. Donald C. Stone, *Professional Education in Public Works/Environmental Engi-
    neering and Administration*, (Chicago, 1974), 8.
13. American Society of Civil Engineers, *ASCE Official Register 1991*, (New York),
    44.
14. *Civil Engineering*, "From the Editors" 60, no. 10 (October 1990): 6.
15. David Marks, "The Challenge of the 90's," *Civil Engineering* 60, no. 10 (October
    1990): 45.

Comment

Theodore M. Schad

For this session, the program committee asked experts in five different disciplines to address the questions of what their discipline brought to water resources management and how can we increase the application of their discipline to the management of water resources. Recognizing that some disciplines might have been overused in the past, a better word would have been "improve." After reading the papers, I realize what we are really looking for is an interdisciplinary approach because the last thing we want to encourage is competition among the disciplines.

The five papers are remarkably good and make a substantial contribution to the growing mass of literature on water resources policy. Whether the papers or this meeting will lead to improvement in national water policy I do not know. All we can hope to do is try to influence what will probably happen anyway in ways that will contribute to the well-being of the American people.

I will refrain from detailed comment on the individual papers except as needed as a framework for my own remarks. Professor Grigg's paper has already identified that no one discipline can provide all of the expertise needed for sound water resources management. He points out that engineers trained in systems analysis are well-qualified to meld the contributions of all disciplines into an integrated program, but the task is not exclusively that of the engineer.

What is needed is the ability to provide sensitive leadership, a quality that I do not think we know how to develop. Since engineers are frequently called on for this role, we certainly need to expand the engineering education curriculum to include more courses in the humanities and the behavioral sciences, a position I have long espoused. Whether this will really produce better leaders, I do not know, but it should produce more well-rounded citizens with a better basis for decision making.

Professor Mann made the point that political scientists come in all shapes and sizes and in fifty-seven varieties as well. The same is abundantly true of engineers and all other professions. The reasons that engineers took the lead in water resources development and management for the first fifty years or so after the principles of comprehensive development were advanced early in this century is that they were there, and no one else seemed to be interested.

The engineers, having the job of meeting human needs for water and water-related services, moved into the vacuum. I do not think they can be blamed for the mistakes that were made. Maybe in a century or so we will be able to apply enough perspective to discern whether we did the right thing by establishing the age of dam building. This may be a good subject for debate, but it would not be a very productive debate. The results are there and they will be there for a long time: Hoover Dam, Shasta, Grand Coulee, Fort Peck, Glen Canyon, the TVA, and myriad lesser dams. They were built to produce benefits and no one can deny their accomplishments, even though all the costs may not yet be known. We probably could not build them now, but who can tell whether there were other alternatives that should have been pursued at the time they were built?

Professor Grigg also pointed out that the work of all disciplines needs to be soundly based on the basic physical and life sciences. He should have included the social and behavioral sciences, and I am sure he meant to. At the risk of sounding like a broken record, I must again express my view in support of both basic and applied research in the social and behavioral sciences as well as in the physical and life sciences. Management of research, like water management, needs good leadership, a quality that we have trouble developing. Perhaps more research in the behavioral sciences might develop criteria that would help in developing leadership ability.

The premise in Professor Kelly's paper that water development has been peculiarly marked by effective power being close-held in a few hands in a way that is essentially undemocratic in nature may be true in the California example cited, but it seems to be in conflict with his statement later on that the peoples' representatives in the Congress have exercised an "iron grip" over their policymaking prerogatives over water.

It is nice to know that historians have discovered what water resources professionals have long known—that national water resources policies are controlled by Congress and not by any "water management elite." In fact, history shows that development of rational water policies that would benefit all people of the United States has suffered from that "iron grip" exercised by members of Congress who have placed parochial interests above the national interest. Well-stated by Professor Platt, river basin development has been driven by the political geography of congressional politics. And members of Congress just love to dedicate dams.

Water policy as practiced by members of the Congress continues to suffer today from its origins in the first half of the nineteenth century. The Supreme Court decision in 1824 that established control of the Congress over navigable waters opened the door to the pork-barrel philosophy of "if you vote for my project, I'll vote for yours." This philosophy completely dominated the nation's approach to water resources development until the turn of the century. If there were any rationale for the policy, it was along the lines of the statement attributed to "Engine Charlie" Wilson, who said, "What's good for General Motors is good for the country" many years later.

It was not until 1902, with the enactment of the Federal Reclamation Act and the creation of the Board of Engineers for Rivers and Harbors in the Army Corps of Engineers, that economic analysis became a part of project formulation. Both actions were the product of legislation stemming from cooperation between water management professionals in the executive branch of the federal government (I would hesitate calling them an "elite") and the Congress. Most federal water policy is formulated in this way. The experts have been trying to use economic analysis to gain control over policy ever since, without notable success, except possibly in the Tennessee Valley, where the water resources were more or less turned over to the experts for management, with very few strings attached.

Elsewhere, "Engine Charlie's" philosophy still permeates the entire field on the grounds that development of resources of one section of the country is good for the whole country, regardless of who pays the costs and who reaps the benefits. I am not aware that anyone has ever tried to repeal those famous words in the Flood Control Act of 1936 to the effect that federal cost-sharing for flood control is justified whenever the benefits "to whomsoever they may accrue" exceed the costs.

Of course, Congress has almost always stated in water resources legislation that it recognizes the rights and responsibilities of the states, but the statement is usually followed by ironclad rules that must be followed, regardless of state wishes, if the states and localities want to participate in the federal programs. As long as the federal money flowed liberally, few objections were raised, and there was little incentive to rationalize national water policy. In recent years, the expansion of federally financed programs into wide-ranging areas, tax cuts without accompanying program reductions, and the resulting budget deficits are doing more to rationalize water resources management than the efforts of the experts in all of the professional disciplines.

The appetites of the American people for government services are far greater than their apparent willingness to pay for them, and no one in either the executive or legislative branches of government seems to have the political "guts" to tell them that they are going to have to pay for any services that are provided. In spite of the well-stated division of responsibilities in the Constitution, there is no real agreement as to what should be done by the federal government, what should be done by the states, and what should be left to localities and the private sector in the water resources field.

Professor Mann dismisses extensive discussion of this subject, suggesting that the national government and the states will continue to sort out their responsibilities through laws and litigation well into the future. I do not think we can dismiss the problem this lightly. As Professor Grigg says, "Water conflicts will not be resolved in reasoned negotiation sessions between interest groups: they will be resolved in elections, court battles, agency rule-making and decision making and in water right purchases." He forgot to mention vote-swapping and political trade-offs.

Yet, the reason we are holding this water management policy forum is not to accept the status quo, but to try to develop a basis for evolving better, more rational policies that will lead to improvements in water management in the future. There has been a great deal of progress in the last few decades, but we have a long way to go. Let us see what we can do.

Trends in Water
Resource Management

The Trend Toward Judicial Integration of Water Quality and Quantity Management: Facing the New Century

William Goldfarb

It has long been recognized that effective, efficient, equitable, and environmentally protective water resources management requires an integration of water quality and quantity management.[1] The Water Quality 2000 group's recent report, entitled *Challenges for the Future,*[2] states the problem as follows:

> Water quantity is important to water quality in many areas of the U.S., yet the quantity aspects of water resources are almost always regulated and managed separately from the quality aspects. Water withdrawal for all types of consumptive uses can have profound effects on aquatic habitat downstream. To the effect that water is withdrawn from streams and not returned, less in-stream flow is available for fish and wildlife habitat, inputs to wetlands and other aquatic resources, and mixing in estuaries to preserve critical freshwater/saltwater balances and prevent saltwater intrusion into coastal aquifers. Water used, degraded, and returned to waterbodies can have equally significant effects on water quality. Irrigation return flows often have high concentrations of salts and metals, for example. In addition, excess water use places a burden on overloaded sewage treatment plants.

We have all encountered other examples of suboptimal management of surface water and groundwater that are reflections of this disjunction of water quantity and quality management. The United States has failed to adequately coordinate these two major aspects of water resources management. The reasons for this failure and recommendations for improvement will be explored in a later section.

The Trend Toward Judicial Solutions

Courts are the institutions of last resort in American society because they are dedicated to rendering justice and available to all comers without the need for political intermediaries. The judicial system acts as a legal and moral safety valve where our political system has failed to satisfactorily resolve acrimonious and significant public disputes.

There are significant disadvantages, however, to judicial resolution of conflicts involving the allocation of natural resources. First, judges are generalists who are, in most cases, dependent on the testimony presented before them. Modern water resources management justifiably places a premium on expertise, planning, and active investigation. Because judges are untrained in managing particular resources, they cannot respond as quickly as expert administrators to emergency situations involving those resources. The judicial process, moreover, with its manifold procedural safeguards, is too slow for effective natural resources management.

Second, judicial decrees are retrospective, geographically limited, and quite fact-specific. Unlike administrative agencies, courts are incapable of issuing prospective, uniform regulations of general applicability. Judges are adept at applying vague principles embodying both empirical and normative elements—for example "reasonable use"—to unique sets of facts. Judicial decisions tend to be sporadic, "one shot" affairs that do not establish general principles or plans on which regulators or the private sector can confidently rely. Courts also lack the ability to consistently monitor and evaluate solutions that they have devised.

Third, water is a public trust resource that should primarily be managed by institutions that are politically responsible to the public. Like most judges, administrators are not directly elected, but, unlike judges, they are directly responsible to elected legislatures that enact their enabling legislation, approve their appointed leaders, control their budgets, and exercise oversight over their activities.

This is not to say that courts should be completely removed from the water resources management process. They should continue to act as inhibitors of extreme agency behavior, guardians and interpreters of legislative intent, advocates of procedural due process of law, and protectors of fundamental constitutional and public trust rights. Still, these are secondary rather than primary management functions.

It is the thesis of this essay that because the American political and water resource management communities have failed to integrate water quantity and quality management, courts are being forced to perform this synthesis, to the detriment of optimal water resources management. Ironically, this trend is occurring simultaneously with the displacement of courts from primary management roles with regard to water quantity and quality allocation as they are separately implemented. For example, many eastern states have replaced the riparian system of water quantity allocation—in which courts determine "reasonable use" with regard to water diversions—with administrative permit systems.[3] In the water quality area, the federal Clean Water Act has virtually supplanted the previous system in which courts resolved water quality controversies based either on common law causes of action such as private or public nuisance, or on doctrines of riparian rights. On the one hand we have recognized that courts cannot adequately perform water resources management; on the other hand we are deferring to them by default.

The following four court cases—two from the West and two from the East—illustrate this thesis. In each case, a court was forced to integrate water quantity and quality concerns because a state or local government was unwilling or unable to perform this synthesis in a comprehensive manner.

United States v. State Water Resources Control Board[4]

This set of lawsuits arose out of efforts by the California State Water Resources Control Board (the Board) to set new water quality standards for the Sacramento-San Joaquin Delta in order to take account of the combined effects on the delta of the state's two massive water projects: the Central Valley Project (CVP) and the State Water Project (SWP), operated by the U.S. Bureau of Reclamation (BUREC) and the California Department of Water Resources (DWR), respectively.

The delta serves as a conduit for the transfer of water by the statewide water projects. Both the CVP and the SWP divert water from the rivers that flow into the delta and store the water in reservoirs. Quantities of this stored water are periodically released into the delta. Pumps situated at the southern edge of the delta eventually lift the water into canals for transport south to the farmers of the Central Valley and the municipalities of Southern California. Water which is neither stored nor exported south passes through the delta where it is used by local farmers, industries, and municipalities. The excess flows out into San Francisco Bay. Fish and wildlife in the delta depend on a delicate balance between fresh and saline water.

BUREC and the DWR hold a combined total of 34 state permits for various units of the CVP and SWP to authorize diversion and use of the delta's waters. These permits were issued by the Board and its predecessors over a period of years prior to 1970.

In 1978 the Board adopted the "Water Quality Control Plan for the Sacramento-San Joaquin delta and Suisun Marsh" (the Plan) and "Water Rights Decision 1485" (the Decision). In the Plan the Board established new water quality standards for salinity control in order to protect fish and wildlife in the delta and Suisun Marsh as well as for agricultural, industrial, and municipal users of delta waters. In the Decision the Board modified the permits held by BUREC and the DWR, compelling the operators of the projects to release enough water into the delta or to reduce their exports from the delta so as to adhere to the water quality standards the plan established. BUREC and numerous out-of-basin users of water from the basin sued to overturn the Board's action. California DWR intervened as an additional plaintiff.

The major factor affecting water quality in the delta is saltwater intrusion. Delta lands, situated at or below sea level, are constantly subject to ocean tidal action. Saltwater entering from San Francisco Bay extends well into the delta, and intrusion of the saline tidal waters is checked only by the natural barrier formed by fresh water flowing out from the delta.

As agricultural, industrial and municipal developers increasingly diverted fresh water from the delta, salinity intrusion intensified, particularly during the dry summer months and in years of low precipitation and runoff into the river systems. In fact, one of the original purposes of the CVP and the SWP was containment of maximum salinity intrusion into the delta by storing water during periods of heavy flow and releasing water during times of low flow, thus maintaining the freshwater barrier at a constant level. Over the years, however, with increases in demand for water in the Central Valley and Southern California, the interests of delta and trans-delta users could not always be reconciled. In this conflict, the enormous combined political power of the Southern California municipalities and Central Valley farmers assured that their water needs would take precedence over the requirements of delta water users, including those "politically impotent" fish and wildlife.

Since saline intrusion is non-point source pollution, it is not controlled by the federal Clean Water Act but is exclusively relegated to state control programs. In California, the Board is both the state water pollution control agency and the issuer of water allocation permits based on the doctrine of prior appropriation. Fundamentally, *U.S. v. SWRCB* was a dispute between two California state agencies: the Board, which was attempting at least partially to integrate existing water quantity allocation permits with recently recognized water quality needs, and the DWR, which, in its responsibility for the SWP, was concentrating only on water supply. BUREC was also a plaintiff, but the most significant quarrel here was intrastate.

The California Court of Appeals overturned the Board's decision and remanded it to the agency for reconsideration, based primarily on the Board's having interpreted its legal authority *too narrowly* (i.e., the Board considered only the effects of the CVP and SWP on *existing* water rights in the delta; it *should* have considered the effects of *all* upstream diversions on *all* delta water uses, including fish and wildlife requirements). More generally, the court upheld the Board's authority to modify allocation permits in order to limit water quality impacts on downstream consumptive uses pursuant to the California Constitution's declaration that all uses of water, including appropriative diversions, must be reasonable. Modification of allocation permits to protect nonconsumptive uses—such as fish and wildlife protection—was upheld under the public trust doctrine as applied in *National Audubon Society v. Superior Court (Mono Lake)*.[5]

The court in *U.S. v. SWRCB* broke the California water policy logjam by validating the Board's authority to integrate water quality and quantity concerns—

in the context of formulating a water use policy predicated on overall reasonableness—without requiring the Board to give preference to particular uses based either on type or temporal priority of use. However, the court concluded that the Board had simply not gone far enough in integrating quality and quantity considerations.

On remand, the Board decided to divide its planning process for water quality control in the delta into separate water quality and water quantity phases. Advocates of this split "contend that requiring water quantity issues to be linked to federally mandated water quality issues gives the federal government too much control over an area traditionally within the SWRCB's sole jurisdiction."[6] Environmental groups have brought a lawsuit challenging the Board's bifurcated planning process.[7]

As the Board reconsiders its decision, the locus of this dispute may be shifting to the federal level. The U.S. Fish and Wildlife Service has proposed listing the Delta Smelt (Hypomesus transpacificus) as a threatened species. Apparently, the freshwater inputs that are necessary for its continued survival in the delta are declining due to the California drought and the upstream withdrawals by the CVP and the SWP.[8] If the Delta Smelt is finally listed as a threatened species, and a particular mixing zone in the delta is listed as its critical habitat, the federal courts may become involved in this water quality-quantity issue, just as they have become involved in the Snail Darter and Northern Spotted Owl controversies and in the following situation.

Carson-Truckee Water Conservancy District v. Watt[9]

The federal Endangered Species Act formed the legal context of this case. The Truckee and Carson Rivers flow from the mountains that lie on the California-Nevada border, south of Reno, toward the northeast.[10] The Truckee River empties into Pyramid Lake, which is surrounded by the Pyramid Lake Paiute Indian Reservation. One purpose of the reservation, which was established in 1859, was to enable the Paiute to take advantage of the Pyramid Lake fishery, which includes a native species of cutthroat trout and the cui-ui fish, which exists nowhere else and is an important social and religious totem for the Pyramid Lake Paiute. The Carson River, approximately 25 miles east of the Truckee, flows into the Stillwater wetlands, part of which has been designated as the Stillwater National Wildlife Refuge because of its importance as a sanctuary for migratory birds.

In 1903, BUREC received congressional authorization for the Newlands Irrigation Project. This project involved the damming and diversion of water from both the Truckee and Carson Rivers in order to irrigate local farms. As a result, the Derby Dam was constructed on the Truckee River to divert Truckee water eastward to the Lahontan Reservoir, which was formed by the construction of the Lahontan Dam on the Carson River. Water from the Lahontan Dam is distributed through irrigation canals operated by the plaintiff Carson-Truckee Water Conservancy District (the District). These irrigation diversions reduced flows to Pyramid Lake and the Stillwater wetlands, both of which increasingly became dependent on irrigation return flows for inputs of water.

By 1938, the level of Pyramid Lake had dropped 40 feet. Soon thereafter the cutthroat trout became extinct. (They have since been restored with genetically similar fish through stocking.) The cui-ui fish barely survived by spawning along the edges of the lake where the cooler Truckee River water entered.

In 1956, Congress appropriated funds to restore the fishery by authorizing the construction of the multipurpose Stampede Dam on the Truckee River below Reno. Water impounded by the Stampede Dam is released to provide the augmented supplies of cool water that the cui-ui fish require in order to spawn successfully. Nevertheless, because the Stampede Dam was not actually constructed until 1970, the cui-ui fish was listed by the United States Department of the Interior as an endangered species in 1967. The Lahontan cutthroat trout was listed as a threatened species in 1975.

The Stillwater wetlands on the Carson River were also deteriorating as a result of the irrigation diversions. The irrigation return flows that now constituted their only water supply contained arsenic, boron, and other heavy metals leached out of the western Nevada soils. Dead birds and fish became a commonplace occurrence. In 1987, an estimated 1,500 birds and seven million fish were found dead on the northeast edge of the refuge.

Carson-Truckee v. Watt involved the rather narrow issue of how the water impounded by the Stampede Dam should be allocated. Plaintiffs (the district, the State of Nevada, and a power company) claimed that the Pyramid Lake fishery was entitled only to sufficient water to avoid jeopardizing the existence of the cui-ui fish and the trout. All additional water, according to the plaintiffs, should be used for irrigation, power generation, and municipal water supply. The defendant Department of the Interior, also representing the Pyramid Lake Paiute, argued that the fishery is entitled to enough water to replenish the species so that they are no longer endangered or threatened with extinction— under certain scenarios a significantly larger quantity of water than that needed for mere species survival.

The court held for the defendants, determining that the Endangered Species Act required the Secretary "to give the Pyramid Lake fishery priority over all other purposes of Stampede until the cui-ui fish and the Lahontan cutthroat trout are no longer classified as endangered or threatened."

Whereas the conflict in *U.S. v. SWRCB* was essentially between agencies of California state government and their constituencies, *Carson-Truckee v. Watt* pitted Nevada state and local governments and their economic development constituencies against the federal and tribal governments, which were concerned with fish and wildlife resources.

In *U.S. v. SWRCB*, the California State Water Resources Control Board, although it had agreed to integrate water quantity and quality management, was unwilling to deal with the system as a whole (it would not consider the impacts of all water diversions on all water users) until ordered to do so by the court. By contrast, the federal district court in *Carson-Truckee v. Watt* was incapable of addressing the adverse impacts of the Newlands Reclamation Project on the Stillwater wetlands—as distinguished from Pyramid Lake— because (1) no endangered or threatened species had been identified as having established a critical habitat there, and (2) the relatively recent establishment of the Stillwater National Wildlife Refuge precluded relief through the asser- tion of federal reserved water rights for the Refuge.[11] Fortunately for the Still- water wetlands ecosystem, the federal government, the Nature Conservancy, and the Nevada Department of Wildlife, have been buying up marginal farm- land—along with its water rights—within the Newlands Project, taking it out of production, and arranging to transport the water saved by retiring the farm- land directly to the Stillwater wetlands.

Hudson River Fishermen's Association v. New York City[12]

At normal times, New York City's need for potable water is adequately served by the city's Delaware, Catskill, and Croton reservoirs. However, New York City has constructed a pumping station at Chelsea on the Hudson River for emergency drought relief. When Chelsea is in use, water is diverted from the Hudson and pumped into the Delaware Aqueduct, through which water from the Delaware watershed flows by gravity into holding reservoirs in the Croton system. Under these circumstances, the Delaware River water already in the Delaware Aqueduct combines with the Hudson River water in a ratio of at least 4:1. This combined flow continues through the Delaware Aqueduct for approximately ten miles to the West Branch Reservoir of the Croton system. Because the quality of Hudson River water is usually inferior to that of the Delaware and Croton systems, the City treats the Hudson River water at Chelsea with chlorine and alum before pumping it into the Delaware Aqueduct.

Plaintiff citizens' group became concerned that the unfiltered alum sludge formed in the Delaware Aqueduct might have damaging effects on the water and fish in the West Branch Reservoir. The result of this concern was a law- suit against the city for discharging pollutants (chlorine and alum) into waters of the United States (West Branch Reservoir) without a state discharge permit as required by the federal Clean Water Act. The city countered with two major arguments: that (1) the federal Safe Drinking Water Act, which requires that potable water be treated to meet federal maximum contaminant levels, preempts the Clean Water Act in this instance; and (2) "beneficial" chemicals such as chlorine and alum are not pollutants under the CWA. The court interpreted the CWA in plaintiff's favor, and ordered New York City to apply for a discharge permit for its Chelsea Pumping Station operations.

In *Hudson River Fishermen's Association* we observe the now familiar pattern of state and local governments refusing to integrate water quality and quantity management until forced by a court. Unlike the situations in *U.S. v. SWRCB* and *Carson-Truckee v. Watt*, however, this was not a stark "either-or" conflict between diversions for human use and instream ecological uses. New York City can probably filter the alum sludge, at a relatively reasonable cost, before discharge. In CWA terms, there may well be a best available technology economically achievable that will result in zero discharge of pollutants.

Village of Tequesta v. Jupiter Inlet Corp.[13]

Jupiter Corporation, a real estate developer, owned property near Tequesta, Florida, on which it planned to build a 120-unit condominium project. This property was located approximately 1,200 feet from Tequesta's well field. Tequesta's wells, which were 75-90 feet deep, pumped in excess of a million gallons of water a day from a shallow aquifer to supply Tequesta's residents with water. As a result of Tequesta's withdrawals, salt water intruded into the shallow aquifer, and Jupiter was forced to drill its well to the Floridian Aquifer located 1,200 feet below the surface. Jupiter sued Tequesta for the difference between Jupiter's drilling costs in tapping the Floridian aquifer and the lesser amount it claimed it would have spent to tap the shallow aquifer had Tequesta not caused saltwater intrusion by its excessive pumping for municipal supply. Jupiter's lawsuit was based on inverse condemnation—Jupiter alleged that Tequesta had taken its property without just compensation.

The Florida Supreme Court decided in favor of Tequesta, holding that Jupiter had no legal right to use the water beneath its land; thus, Jupiter possessed no property that Tequesta could have taken. In the court's view, the Florida Water Resources Act, requiring that diversion permits be obtained from local water management districts, had replaced the system of common law rights that had preceded it. The act provided that a common law water right would terminate unless converted into a permitted water right within two years after the act's passage. Tequesta had perfected its water right by acquiring a permit in timely fashion, while Jupiter had lost its common law right by not filing for a permit within the two year statutory period.

The *Tequesta* v. *Jupiter Corp.* court did not explicitly discuss the integration of water quantity and water quality law because the lawsuit was brought under water rights and constitutional law theories. In addition, as in most states, water quality and quantity law in Florida are administered by different agencies with different statutory mandates.[14] Yet the court did, at least implicitly, integrate water quality and water quantity concerns because it had to in order to resolve the dispute brought before it. Generalist judges are proficient at recognizing holistic and comparatively equitable and cost-effective solutions to problems that legislators, administrators, and litigants have fragmented.[15] However, the fact that judges, by virtue of their roles as dispute resolvers, have been forced to perceive complex technical problems in holistic ways does not mean that they should therefore be in the forefront of water resources management. The court's decision in *Tequesta v. Jupiter Corp.* may be legally correct and favorable to a presumably fiscally burdened municipality at the expense of a presumably wealthy developer, but it is bad water resources management in that it condones the degradation of an aquifer and is inconsistent with the "polluter pays principle."

Conclusions and Recommendations

Although there are some sporadic signs that politicians and water resource managers are beginning to integrate water quality and quantity concerns,[16] there has been no systematic, widespread move in that direction. The author submits the following conclusions as well as recommendations for achieving a new synthesis between water quantity and quality management:

- The current trend toward judicial integration of quality and quantity concerns is counterproductive.
- Integration of water quality and quantity programs is one aspect of, and is inseparable from, comprehensive, coordinated, multipurpose, basinwide water and related resource planning and management (CCMBPM).[17]
- Although CCMBPM is a concept that has been consistently affirmed by Congress and the water resources community, its application has been prevented by "conflicts that have historic roots; are traceable to the diffusion of agency technical assignments and priorities; reflect differences in law, capacities, and will of the members of the federal system; result from interagency competition and that are tied to power struggles inside Congress and between Congress and the executive branch."[18]
- Any attempt to establish at this time new, formal, permanent basinwide institutions with planning or regulatory powers would be naive and futile.[19]
- The goal of CCMBPM should be restated by Congress. The outcome of CCMBPM should be explicitly identified as unitary water-use permitting for any and all water and related land resource uses within a basin. Some of the water and land uses that would be included in this single water use permit system would be surface and groundwater diversion, wastewater discharge, non-point source discharge, flood control, dredging and filling, hydropower production, instream flow allocation, drainage, navigation maintenance, and public recreation.
- Unitary water and related land use permitting does not mean centralized permitting. It does, however, mean coordinated, integrated planning and one-stop permitting for water users in a basin.

- No single type of coordinating institution would be appropriate for all basins in the United States, which exhibit a wide range of existing water resource management institutions: e.g., TVA; federal-interstate compact commissions; river authorities; natural resource districts; groundwater management districts; drainage districts; irrigation districts; regional planning agencies, etc.[20]
- Congress should authorize and direct the federal water resources agencies, under a lead agency, to define appropriate basins and empanel voluntary, temporary, basin-wide working groups to plan for CCMBM. These groups should include representatives from relevant federal, interstate, state, substate regional, and local governments as well as academics, private sector water users and citizens' groups interested in water resource issues. A similar process has already begun in the Great Lakes Basin to formulate Integrated Pollution Control strategies for Areas of Concern.[21]
- Each basinwide working group should be directed to produce, within a particular time period, and submit to Congress a report recommending legislative, institutional, fiscal, administrative or other changes necessary to achieve CCMBPM and unitary water use permitting in its basin.[22]
- Congress should establish a Blue Ribbon Commission to study the basin-wide working group reports and recommend legislative and administrative modifications necessary to implement the reports' recommendations.

The potential success of this decentralized, "bottom-up," voluntary planning process is based on a number of assumptions: (1) that there now exists a nearly universal recognition of natural constraints on human water uses and the impossibility of simultaneously satisfying all human desires relating to water; (2) that the current fiscal situation will continue through the 1990s and stimulate moves toward institutional and economic efficiency; (3) that the trend away from federal water resources development financed from the general federal budget toward state and local development financed by user charges will continue; (4) that the decentralization of water resources management will intensify; and (5) that water resources professionals and concerned citizens will work together, in good faith, to develop improvements to our water resources planning and management system as long as those system modifications do not threaten the institutions or positions of the participants.

I believe this planning process will build a consensus for CCMBPM and elicit innovative, realistic, basin and site-specific ideas for accomplishing CCMBPM in geographically and institutionally unique settings.

Notes

1. For example, see William B. Lord, "Unified River Basin Management In Retrospect And In Prospect," in *Unified River Basin Management—Stage II*, eds. David J. Allee, Leonard B. Dworsky, and Ronald M. North (Minneapolis, 1981), 58; and Leonard B. Dworsky, David J. Allee, and Ronald M. North, "Water Resources

Planning and Management In The United States Federal System: Long Term Assessment And Intergovernmental Issues," *Natural Resources Journal* 31 (Summer 1991): 475, 509, 515.
2. *Water Pollution Control Federation/Water Quality 2000: Challenges for the Future* (Alexandria, VA, 1991), 32.
3. See George W. Sherk, "Eastern Water Law: Trends In State Legislation," *Virginia Environmental Law Journal* 9 (Spring 1990): 287; Robert H. Abrams, "Water Allocation by Comprehensive Permit System in the East: Considering a Move Away From Orthodoxy," *Virginia Environmental Law Journal* 9 (Spring 1990): 268.
4. 182 Cal. App. 3rd 82, 227 Cal. Rptr. 161 (1986), *review denied* 42 Cal. 3rd 192 (1986).
5. 33 Cal. 3d 419, 189 Cal. Rptr. 346, 658 P. 2d 709 (1983). In this decision, the California Supreme Court held that the state may reconsider and modify past allocation permits in light of current public trust needs.
6. American Bar Association, Water Resources Committee, 1991 *Annual Report*, 4.
7. *Golden Gate Audubon v. State Water Resources Control Board*, No. 366984 (Sacramento Superior Court, 1991).
8. *New York Times*, 27 October 1991, 10.
9. 549 F Supp. 704 (D.C. Nev. 1988) *aff'd in part and rev'd in part on other grounds, Carson-Truckee Water Conservancy District v. Clark*, 741 F. 2d 257 (9th Cir. 1984), *cert. denied*. 22 ERC 2120 (1985).
10. These facts were derived from the court's opinion in *Carson-Truckee v. Watt*, and from Don Vetter, "Teeming Oasis or Desert Mirage?" *Nature Conservancy* (September/October 1991): 22; and Bonnie G. Colby, Mark A. McGinnis, and Ken A. Rait, "Mitigating Environmental Externalities Through Voluntary and Involuntary Water Reallocation: Nevada's Truckee-Carson River Basin," *Natural Resources Journal* 31 (Fall 1991): 757.
11. Additionally, it has not been firmly established that federal reserved water rights can be applied to wildlife refugees.
12. 751 F. Supp. 1088 (S.D. N.Y. 1990), *aff'd*. 940 F. 2d 649 (2nd Cir. 1991).
13. 371 So. 2d 663 (1978), *rehearing denied* (1979), *cert. denied* 444 U.S. 965 (1979).
14. The Florida water pollution control program is, in general, administered not by the regional water management districts but by the Florida Department of Environmental Regulation. One commentator has criticized the Florida water management system for its lack of coordination between water use permitting and water quality concerns. See Richard C. Ausness, "The Influence of the Model Water Code on Water Resources Management Policy in Florida," *Journal of Land Use and Environmental Law* 3 (1987): 20-22. On the positive side in Florida, the South Florida Water Management District, through its stormwater permitting program, requires non-point dischargers of stormwater to adopt best management practices to protect water quality and quantity. For a general critique of eastern water allocation permit programs, see Robert H. Abrams, "Water Allocation by Comprehensive Permit Systems in the East: Considering a Move Away From Orthodoxy," *Virginia Environmental Law Journal* 9 (Spring 1990): 268.
15. For a discussion of this role of judges, see Joseph L. Sax, *Defending The Environment*, (New York: 1970), chapter 10. Professor Sax argues for an enhanced judicial presence in resolving disputes over natural resources allocation.

16. For example, the Ohio River Valley Sanitation Commission (ORSANCO) and the Delaware River Basin Commission are integrating quality and quantity management in the context of drought management; more states are conducting comprehensive state water resources planning; EPA is considering watershed-wide supply needs in its industrial stormwater permitting program; Western states are using various devices to adapt their prior appropriation diversion permit systems to assure adequate instream flows for protection of fish and wildlife; the Great Lakes states and Canada are exhibiting cooperation with regard to quantity-quality issues through the medium of the International Joint Commission; and New York State is enforcing its land-use management powers in the Delaware, Catskill, and Croton watersheds in order to protect its water supply from contamination.

17. Dworsky, Allee, and North, "Water Resources Planning and Management," 507, 515.

18. Ibid., 516

19. Ibid., 517. The author's experience with implementation of Section 208 of the Clean Water Act is in accordance with Dworsky, Allee, and North's pessimism about new watershed institutions.

20. Ibid., 536-537.

21. Barry G. Rabe and Janet B. Zimmerman, "Cross-Media Environmental Integration in the Great Lakes Basin," *Environmental Law* 22, no. 1 (1992): 262-63.

22. Ibid., 263. Analogous to the Remedial Action Plans being developed in the Great Lakes Basin.

Bargaining, Markets, and Watershed Restoration: Some Elements of a New National Water Policy

Leonard Shabman

Restoration of aquatic systems can become a new focus for national water policy. However, the specific meaning and scope of restoration has yet to be established. The term "restoration" has been used to describe the return to wetlands status of small prairie potholes that have been drained for agriculture.[1] At the same time, the massive engineering effort of the Corps of Engineers and the South Florida Water Management District to reverse past alterations to the Kissimmee River, Florida, has also been described as restoration.[2] A recently published report of the National Research Council, National Academy of Sciences, reviewed the conceptual meaning of restoration and described techniques for successful restoration.[3] It recommended a national aquatic system restoration strategy based on four elements: national restoration goals for rivers, lakes and wetlands; principles for priority setting and decision making; policy and program design for federal agencies; and innovation in financing and in the use of land and water markets. The objective of this paper is to consider how the restoration theme will influence national water policy in the years ahead and to briefly elaborate on two of the NRC's elements: decision-making protocols and the use of market-like incentives.

Watershed Restoration: A New Agenda for Water Policy

Two centuries of national water policy have resulted in diversion works, storage facilities, and river channel modifications which allow us to move water into and out of watersheds and regulate annual and seasonal patterns of flow. The results of this policy have been impressive: a water transportation network; a renewable source of electric power; reduced flood hazards for agricultural and urban lands; reliable water supply for municipal, industrial and agricultural purposes; and expanded recreational opportunities. At the water's edge, past public policy encouraged clearing, drainage, and cultivation of land for increased food and fiber supplies.

Although these alterations of watersheds have yielded many benefits, the current condition of the nation's estuaries, rivers, lakes, and wetlands has been of increasing public concern. Waste products from human activities are delivered to the aquatic system as chemicals, nutrients, and sediments. Dredge and fill activities, shoreline modifications, and changes in land cover redirect flows, change the quality of the waters, and reduce fish and wildlife habitat. Despite massive investments in wastewater treatment, desired improvements in the chemical conditions of the nation's water have yet to be realized. Meanwhile, there have been declines in fish populations, waterfowl numbers, species diversity, and other indicators of the biological services of watersheds.

Recognition of these trends has made total aquatic system restoration a central concern for the next decade, a concern that may redefine the goals and decision-making processes of water policy. The emerging political support for restoration of watershed landscapes is the next step in the evolution of the environmental movement's separate attention to improving the chemical quality of the nation's water and to maintaining fish and wildlife populations. These were the concerns that displaced more traditional water development problems and opportunities that were the focus of water policy until the 1990s.

In the execution of a water policy for watershed restoration the conceptual goal is the return of the system to some pre-disturbance condition, rehabilitating the hydrologic and ecologic functions which give rise to services people value: clean water for recreation, flood storage, and fish and wildlife populations are examples. Watershed restoration is intended to reestablish a matrix of chemical, hydrologic and biological processes which have been compromised by human modifications to the aquatic system. Restoration means returning to patterns and timing of water flows which more closely mimic some historical condition. Restoration means reestablishing and rehabilitating wetlands and riparian areas while also reducing the delivery of sediments and chemical contaminants to the waters. Restoration also means that the biological resources of the waters are integrated back into the watershed by revegetating upland and riparian areas and reintroducing native species.[4]

Restoration in a Watershed Context: Designing for Success

Watersheds cover both large and small areas. However, watershed restoration is about the smaller spaces on the landscape where self-maintaining, evolving ecosystems would be expected to function.[5] Restoration is not a goal for every watershed, no matter its location or size. However, where restoration is attempted, there needs to be a spatial and temporal scale to the design of the restoration project which reflects a watershed perspective; that is, the design must emphasize the interdependence of hydrologic, biologic and chemical processes within uplands, rivers and wetlands. Simply put, *the attention to a spatial and temporal scale larger than the restoration site itself is required to assure the success of the restoration project.*[6]

Restoration in a Watershed Context: A Planning Challenge

When restoration means manipulation of the existing hydrologic regime and structural features of the landscape, it is an "engineering" problem. When restoration means discouraging further alterations of the watershed it is a regulatory problem, emphasizing protection of existing resources. Yet fundamentally, restoration means redesign of a watershed around engineering and regulatory decisions directed toward the future. In that sense restoration is planning for change. A restoration focus sheds, for example, a different light on wetlands management, shifting the attention from protection of a point in the landscape to integrating these points, called wetlands, into a larger context. Wetlands per se are not the concern. Concern is for the role that wetlands play in the support of watershed functions and the services that follow.

Because restoration is a landscape design problem, watershed restoration is about making tradeoffs between alternative actions that can be taken to achieve desired watershed services. Tradeoffs may be needed to be made within watershed features, for example when making a decision on which wetlands might be permitted for development and where, in turn, restoration of wetlands-uplands complex might be initiated. Another tradeoff may weigh, on one hand, the most effective non-point source pollution control approach to restore riparian zone wetlands against, on the other hand, requiring non-point source best management practices on the uplands. And, of course, tradeoffs will always be about the desirable degree of landscape restoration in relation to the opportunity costs of foregone services from past watershed alterations.

Integrating Negotiation and Technical Analysis for Watershed Restoration

The restoration planning and design challenge is to evaluate tradeoffs, not only between restoration and the current state of the aquatic system, but also between alternative restorations. No computational procedure by itself will establish either how far restoration should proceed or the relative priority for funding of alternative restoration efforts. The choice to restore is a choice to select one set of values over another.

Computation of values is often associated with economics, and more specifically benefit-cost analysis. For the benefit-cost analyst, value is appropriately expressed through individual preferences which are measured in money equivalent terms. Success in measuring the value of environmental services has been achieved in specific instances, but widespread application of the measurement approaches to environmental services has not occurred, despite the presence of a rich and growing literature. In part, this represents the experimental nature of the valuation approaches and in part this represents a lack of agreement on the philosophical bases upon which such values are based.[7]

In lieu of benefit-cost analysis, an opportunity cost decision-making approach might be used. Within the opportunity cost framework, the correct answer to the question "how much restoration is enough?" emerges from legitimate social choice processes which will determine the degree of restoration that is desirable. Confronting participants in the decision process with cost information elicits "values" from that process by continually focusing the restoration question on whether an action is worth its cost. Costs include direct (life cycle) financial outlays by government and individuals. Costs also include services derived from the existing state of the watershed which would be foregone with the restoration. These foregone services may be described in monetary or nonmonetary terms. An example of an opportunity cost approach is the way the Corps of Engineers determines the extent of justifiable mitigation for environmental damages done by a water development project. The Corps' mitigation analysis prohibits the use of solely monetary measures of environmental values. Instead the process requires the establishment of alternative mitigation goals and approaches to achieve these goals. A justifiable level of mitigation is chosen in recognition of the incremental monetary and nonmonetary costs of increasing mitigation levels, and as part of a negotiation process with affected interests and other federal agencies.

The adoption of the opportunity cost decision-making model requires a fundamental policy shift toward increased design and acceptance of group bargaining as a tool to make tradeoffs among ends and means over time. It is these bargaining processes, informed by opportunity cost analysis, which will establish whether a restoration might be warranted. Such a shift will diminish the reliance on agency experts to lead and guide choice making. For most of this century, a political ideology rooted in the Progressive conservation movement promoted the view that sound public decisions would arise only from scientific (expert based) public policy analysis. Therefore, when progressive ideals began to be translated to water policy and programs, the programs were to be administered by an expert agency. Neither political leaders nor the courts would substitute their judgment on the merits of an action for the expert in agencies such as the TVA, the Corps of Engineers, the Bureau of Reclamation, and Soil Conservation Service. It was in this context that the advocacy and development of evaluation tools such as benefit-cost analysis advanced.[8]

Still, a call for reliance on group negotiation is not a call to abandon expert analysis. What is required is that analysis inform participants in the decision process and not define the "best" course of action. Analysis should be in the service of the parties to the negotiation by providing "neutral" impacts assessments to help parties discover possible gains. For example, groups may have different perceptions of the effect of increased water withdrawals upon lake levels or there may be disagreements about how a water transfer will affect a region's economic activity. These disagreements may be resolved by sound technical analysis of the impacts. With such analysis, negotiators can focus on the values gained and lost by changes in water quality and quantity. Today, there is an enhanced interest in using structured forms of group inter-action such as Alternative Dispute Resolution (ADR)[9] and negotiated water rights transfers to discover the value of water in alternative uses.[10]

In what sense can negotiation in the face of opportunity costs direct "opti-mal" restoration? In negotiation those who bear the costs of a restoration often will be compensated. With the assurance of compensation for losses from a change, that change might be deemed equitable. If agreement-with-compensation is reached, the change might be deemed economically effi-cient, much as we presume voluntary exchange relationships in markets yield efficiency. Some take exception to this "public interest" interpretation of the bargained outcome, expressing concern that negotiated solutions may not achieve equity and economic efficiency if the interests who are party to the bargain are not the only ones affected by a decision. The concern about who is represented at the negotiation is a concern about a new pork barrel.[11] To discourage this possibility, beneficiaries must bear the costs of an action. Otherwise the potential for costs shifting to others will make the outcomes of the negotiation optimal for the parties to the negotiation, but at a cost to soci-ety at large.

For example, environmental interests have a limited ability to pay com-pensation for water rights reallocations necessary to restore aquatic systems. However, the federal government can. For instance, it purchased water rights for the restoration of the wetlands in the Truckee-Carson River, Nevada.[12] Such federal spending might be viewed as an effort to make bargaining work better. An alternative perspective is that tapping the federal treasury to buy water rights raises the risk of a new pork barrel, like that which developed around the funding of storage projects in the past. As a result, it may be desir-able again to review intergovernmental cost sharing, as well as financing and repayment provisions for restoration, as part of the evolving water policy. Even though cost sharing was only recently addressed in the Water Resources Development Act of 1986, intergovernmental cost-sharing for restoration projects was not a focus of concern. Massive subsidies from the general trea-sury to particular beneficiaries can produce questionable government pro-jects, whether for the development of flood control, hydropower navigation, or for the restoration of wetlands. To illustrate, the Kissimmee River restora-tion proposal is impressive, but the project is expensive. As a technical mat-ter, the restoration is an exciting possibility which will be substantially financed by federal funds. However, the money might be better allocated to protect what now exists or for restoration elsewhere in the region. As our national watershed restoration policy matures, this type of question can be at the forefront only if there is a cost-discipline in the decision-making process.

Market-Like Tools for Aquatic System Restoration

There is growing recognition of the potential of market exchange to achieve water policy goals. Especially western water users have witnessed an increasing reliance on markets to reallocate water rights. Only a few decades ago, the public generally rejected the buying and selling of water use rights, but times have changed. In 1992 all of the presidential candidates stressed a "market-based" environmental policy. Such statements suggest support for water rights markets. More than that, they seem to embrace emission fees and transferable pollution rights (TPR) in water quality, mitigation banking for wetlands, and removal of public subsidies which may encourage water and land use patterns that work against restoration. An example of the last point was the removal, in the 1985 farm bill, of price and income support eligibility for farmers who drained wetlands, the so-called swampbuster provision. Today market forces determine the feasibility of drainage, and the rate of agricultural wetlands drainage has slowed to a halt.[13]

Examples of how two market-based tools, environmental damage fees and transferable pollution rights, might be employed for watershed restoration are described here, although other possibilities can be imagined. The general institutional design for these tools is found in the applied environmental economics literature.[14] In using a fee system for water quality, for example, an ambient water quality goal is established for a watershed, river segment, or lake. The ambient goal is, in turn, translated into a maximum allowable waste discharge to the area. Once the ambient goal is established, an institution must be designed to allocate waste reduction requirements among all pollution sources. To accomplish this allocation, a fee on each unit of pollution discharge is administratively established. Pollution sources can avoid paying the fee by reducing their waste discharge. If the cost of waste reduction exceeds the tax, then they will choose to pay the tax and discharge their waste. Without attempting to prove the point here, it can be analytically demonstrated that such a system will (1) minimize the cost to the economy of achieving the watershed water quality goal, and (2) create powerful incentives for pollution prevention behavior on the part of the waste generator. Offsetting these benefits is the possibility of increased administrative costs in government.

A TPR system lets market sales of pollution discharge rights establish the fee structure. In this case rights to pollute are allocated to waste dischargers in a watershed and these rights may be bought and sold. This market establishes a price for a waste disposal right. The number of pollution rights are limited to an amount consistent with achieving watershed water quality goals.

99

An Application to Wetlands and Watershed Restoration

Wetlands programs can serve the larger purpose of watershed restoration. Wetlands management would begin by initiating a process of "watershed design" for determining wetlands and uplands complexes within the watershed that have the potential for long term survival as functioning ecosystems. This design can only follow from evaluating existing wetlands as well as land parcels that have been altered but which might be successfully returned to wetlands status. Once some understanding of the place of wetlands in watershed restoration is established, the public can acquire existing wetlands, public projects can restore wetlands, private landowners can be paid for wetlands restoration (for example under the wetlands reserve program), and a wetlands development permit program can proceed.

The case of permitting offers the opportunity for application of market-based policy. Under the existing wetlands programs, often based on Section 404 of the 1972 Clean Water Act, whenever a permit is granted, compensation is required in-kind and on-site. Replacement may be by purchase and preservation of wetlands that otherwise would be lost to development or by restoration of another wetlands area. Advanced compensation might be required, as in mitigation banking, where wetlands areas are restored prior to an action, and credits for wetlands restoration are drawn upon as wetlands are destroyed by commercial development. However, no matter how degraded the wetlands proposed for filling, and no matter how isolated those wetlands are from a watershed complex, the current regulatory program insists on avoidance of those wetlands for all activities deemed to be not water dependent.[15]

A more market-oriented approach to wetlands policy would increase the contribution of wetlands to watershed restoration. Any recipient of a wetlands development permit would need to pay the permitting agency, i.e., for a pollution fee. The agency would use the funds to restore wetlands within a watershed area and would consider both upland, contiguous land uses and river flows. The agency could collect wetlands conversion fees and, when revenues were sufficient, initiate restoration projects or engage in the purchase of restoration sites from private entrepreneurs. Alternatively, the agency could finance restoration and then collect fees to recover costs. Engaging some of the traditional water development agencies in such "restoration for sale" might be a new mission for those agencies. The fee system may be especially attractive if scale economies exist in restoration which can be realized only by the management agency, or if the scientific expertise available at the management agency and in specialized restoration firms enhance the probability of success. Ultimately, it may be possible to establish a true market where private restoration firms might offer their services directly to developers. The amount of restoration that the developer would be required to purchase from the firms would be established by the permit process.[16]

100

Once goals are established, the regulatory problem is to insure that payments are made whenever a wetlands is developed, rather than trying to assess the water dependency of each individual permit prior to making a decision. In effect this relaxes the current requirement to always avoid wetlands without regard to the cost of avoidance or the functional value of the wetlands site. Indeed, it is often the case that the emphasis on avoidance results in fragmentation of the landscape and the isolation of the "saved" wetlands from the watershed. The result is that the saved wetlands are no longer of significant functional value. In such cases, collection of fees to support more carefully planned watershed restoration may have greater ecological value than preservation of a wetlands site that becomes isolated from the watershed.

Nevertheless, it would be a mistake to assert that there is professional consensus about the possibility for successful wetlands restoration, which, after all, is the key to this market-based approach. Much of this skepticism is attributable to a failure to conceive of this approach in the context of watershed restoration. Often it is argued that it is physically impossible to recreate certain wetlands types at certain geographic locations. This possibility renders it necessary to design a management system that classifies wetlands into three classes: Class I, wetlands of exceptionally high ecological value to the watershed—development rarely would be permitted for those "wetlands wilderness areas"; Class II, wetlands of moderate functional value to the watershed or where development which avoids the wetlands would compromise its functional values—development might be permitted here when the development value is exceptionally high and a wetlands development fee is paid; Class III, wetlands could be developed with modest permit review, as long as a fee is paid.

In all cases, the fee payment should generate sufficient revenues to replace, and then enhance, wetlands functions. This system of permitting, which if done in the context of solid restoration science and an overall watershed restoration plan, would allow highly valued development to proceed on some wetlands, while capturing from this development the revenues needed to make significant watershed restoration. For the development sector, this fee system increases the regulatory certainty for the applicant. And, as with the effluent fee, the applicants face a cost for environmental damage. They can make individual adjustments in their development plans which are most appropriate to their own situation.

An Application to Water Quality and Watershed Restoration

In most watersheds point source (PS) pollution control to achieve ambient water quality standards has been the primary focus of water quality management efforts. Although plans for addressing the problem of non-point source (NPS) pollution have been developed in many areas, plans have been infrequently implemented. Still the attention to NPS control remains, with particular focus on the control of the nutrients nitrogen and phosphorus.

In many areas nutrient loads from NPSs are greater than from PS discharges. It is possible that NPS controls might be implemented at a lower marginal cost per unit of control, especially where PS controls are already at a technologically advanced stage. Watershed quality can be improved to a certain standard at a minimum cost if an appropriate combination of point and non-point controls is used. However, this requires coordination of the point and non-point source pollution control programs.

Here is where the market logic applies. Pollution control responsibility is fixed with some initial pollution source. Then that source (a factory, for instance) has a choice either to reduce the polluting effects of its own loadings at some cost or to pay another source to control its pollution. When an increase in NPS control has been used to reduce requirements for PS control the term pollution reduction trading (PRT) has been used.[17] PRT is an application of the general market-based tool of transferable pollution rights. Based upon the implementation of a PRT program at the Dillon Reservoir in Colorado and experiments in the Tar-Pamlico basin in North Carolina, the possible application of PRT at other sites in the nation has been under consideration. Some congressmen are considering the insertion of specific language in the Clean Water Act reauthorization to encourage use of this tool.[18]

The PRT concept can be expanded to incorporate wetlands restoration to achieve a watershed water quality target, thereby establishing a cross link between water quality and wetlands programs. In some cases, it may be cost-effective for municipalities operating sewage treatment plants to pay landowners to implement best management practices. However, even more cost-effective programs may be those that make payments for restoration of riparian wooded wetlands instead of emphasizing changes in land use practices. Former wetlands adjacent to rivers, lakes, or estuaries that are restored as wetlands can reduce nutrient loadings by capturing nutrients in tree and plant biomass. In addition, other restoration benefits, such as habitat and water temperature control, are provided by the increased tree canopy at the water's edge.

One could get quite expansive in thinking about use of markets. In terms of reducing loadings of carbon dioxide to the atmosphere, new utility or industrial sources of carbon dioxide might be allowed to offset their emissions by paying for replanting forests which can act as carbon sinks. This also has a positive watershed restoration effect, especially if the restoration was to forested wetlands from agricultural land that originally had wetlands status.

Conclusion

The emerging interest in watershed restoration as a focus of water policy should be complemented by an interest in, and development of, negotiation and market-like tools as decision-making aids. Watershed restoration is a radical departure in water policy objectives. It requires a new openness to bargaining and to the use of water markets that will permit the innovation necessary to assure the best chances of success.

Notes

1. Jon A. Kusler and Mary E. Kentula, *Wetlands Creation and Restoration* (Washington, D.C., 1990).
2. M. Kent Loftin, Louis A. Toth, and Jayantha T. B. Obeysekera, *Kissimmee River Restoration* (West Palm Beach, FL, June 1990).
3. National Research Council, *Restoration of Aquatic Ecosystems* (Washington, D.C., 1992). For a clear statement on the need for a national ecosystem (watershed) restoration program, see: U.S. Environmental Protection Agency, Science Advisory Board. *Reducing Risk: Setting Priorities and Strategies for Environmental Protection.* SAB-EC-90-021 (Washington, DC, 1992).
4. National Research Council, 55-70.
5. Daniel E. Willard and John E. Klarquist, "Mitigation Banks: A Strategy for Sustainable Ecosystem Function" (Bloomington, IN, 1992).
6. National Research Council, 55-70.
7. For a concise review of nonmarket evaluation methods, see: Organization for Economic Cooperation and Development, *Environmental Policy Benefits: Monetary Valuation* (Paris, 1989).
8. For a complete discussion of this history see, Leonard Shabman, "Water Resources Management: Policy Economics for an Era of Transitions," *Southern Journal of Agricultural Economics* 16 (July 1984): 153-65.
9. Gail Bingham, *Resolving Environmental Disputes* (Washington, D.C.: The Conservation Foundation, 1986).
10. Bonnie G. Colby, Mark A. McGinnis, and Ken A. Rait, "Mitigating Environmental Externalities Through Voluntary and Involuntary Water Reallocation: Nevada's Truckee-Carson River Basin," *Natural Resources Journal,* 31 (1991): 757-85.
11. In associating negotiated outcomes with equity and efficiency, some also express concern about the imbalances in the relative power of those who negotiate. Others might question the nature of the negotiated outcomes themselves, especially if the values they favor are not advanced by the accepted solution.
12. Colby, et al.
13. Randall Kramer and Leonard Shabman, "The Effects of Agricultural and Tax Policy Reform on the Economic Return to Wetland Drainage in the Mississippi Delta Region," *Land Economics,* (in press).
14. For a concise survey of this literature, see Tom Tietenberg, *Environmental and Resource Economics,* 3rd ed. (New York, 1992).

15. David Salvesen, *Wetlands: Mitigating and Regulating Development Impacts* (Washington, D.C., 1990).

16. At present, the state of Maryland's nontidal wetlands program includes a semblance of this fee-based system. In the past, a simple approach to such a fee system has been put in place by the California Coastal Conservancy. Other states are moving in this direction (for example, Lousiana) for small wetlands alterations.

17 Apogee Research, Inc., *Incentive Analysis for CWA Reauthorization: Point Source/Non-point Source Trading for Nutrient Discharge Reductions.* Draft report for USEPA/Office of Water, October 1991.

18. Ibid.

Perspectives on the Role of the Citizen in Chesapeake Bay Restoration

Ellen L. Fraites and Frances H. Flanigan

Introduction

The Chesapeake Bay—the nation's largest estuary—is a system under threat. This reflects the situation for most enclosed coastal waters where population growth and development, habitat loss, discharge of pollutants, overharvesting of fisheries, and disease have resulted in degraded environmental quality and productivity. Human impacts on the Chesapeake Bay have reached levels of complexity and severity that threaten the assimilative and life support capabilities of the Bay.

At the same time, the past twenty years have seen an impressive series of significant institutional and legislative reforms for the governance of the Chesapeake Bay. Signatories to the Chesapeake Bay Agreement of 1983 agreed to develop and implement coordinated plans to improve and protect the water quality and living resources. The Bay Agreement of 1987 expanded the scope of action in terms of more substantive commitments for pollution control, resource management, population growth and development, education and public participation, public access, and governance. Among the more noteworthy legislative initiatives were, the phosphate ban, stricter point and non-point source pollution controls, a striped bass moratorium, critical areas protection, nontidal wetlands and forest lands preservation, and growth management. Collectively, this body of law and institutional agreements constitutes the Chesapeake Bay governance regime, a continuing process of resource management, policy reform, institution building and interjurisdictional political negotiation.

Throughout the Bay region, citizens have participated in and helped to establish the programs and policies for the Chesapeake Bay resources. This paper examines the role of citizen action in Maryland, specifically, the expansion of citizen interest and participation in Chesapeake Bay policymaking and program development that occurred in the late 1970s and 1980s when restoration and protection of the Chesapeake Bay acquired a new urgency.

We focus primarily on those citizens representing conservation and environmental concerns as well as educational and civic associations. Government officials, resource managers, political leaders, business representatives, scientists, resource user interest groups, and the media participate in and have helped to create the Chesapeake Bay program. Nevertheless, the efforts of Maryland's citizens and citizen groups to affect the future of the Chesapeake Bay is the topic of this essay.

Considering the diverse interests, organizations, programs, objectives, and goals that encompass citizen action, we believe that citizens may perform six roles on behalf of Chesapeake Bay restoration: (1) influence public policy, (2) achieve governmental accountability, (3) build political consensus, (4) participate in hands-on restoration, (5) educate citizens, and (6) preserve and protect watershed and special resource areas. We will examine examples of how individual citizen groups have played one or more of these roles or worked together.

Citizen groups have played an important role in building public support for Chesapeake Bay restoration strategies and translating Chesapeake Bay science into policy. We will consider the potential for citizen restoration initiatives, land preservation efforts, environmental education activities and political action to instill new values and provide important social learning. At the same time, we must be mindful of the limitations of citizen action in terms of fragmented environmental decision making, shortsightedness of environmental policy, and harmful polarization. Finally, we address the challenges posed by an ecosystem approach to Chesapeake Bay management that looks at the Bay system as a complex ecological system with subtle interdependencies among land, water, air and biota. This approach recognizes the Bay as an integrated ecosystem, not clusters of isolated problems. Inherent in this approach is the view that management for the Bay should evolve in response to new information that sheds greater understanding of Bay processes and conditions. We believe the ecosystem approach has important implications in terms of the challenges of informing the public as well as the citizen activists themselves, and engaging public support for new approaches and initiatives.

A Brief History of the Bay Effort

By the early 1970s, Chesapeake Bay was experiencing rapid declines in Bay grasses and fishery resources. A broad coalition of informed citizens, spearheaded by the Citizens Program for the Chesapeake Bay, sought to publicize the problems of the Bay and to obtain more information on its health. Responding to this publicized concern, Congress directed EPA to make a comprehensive evaluation of the estuary. At the conclusion of this six-year, $27 million study in 1983, EPA recommended a series of management actions. Ultimately, the EPA study opened the way for the Chesapeake Bay Restoration program, a comprehensive regional, intergovernmental cooperative program that takes an integrated, baywide ecosystem approach to management.

The EPA study brought together a regional panel of pollution control and resource management officials to translate the scientific findings into management strategies for government action. Working with Bay ecosystem scientists and a citizen advisory group, the panel developed a management agenda. Concurrent with this effort, a political strategy developed.

At the outset of his second term, Maryland Governor Harry Hughes stated that restoration of the Chesapeake Bay would be a high priority for his administration. Accordingly, he created a cabinet-level working group to develop a comprehensive Bay restoration program to address pollution control, land-use, resource restoration and management, environmental education, and institutional capacity. In addition, he worked with the governors of Virginia and Pennsylvania, the mayor of Washington, D.C., the administrator of EPA, and members of Congress and state legislatures from the three jurisdictions to organize a regional, federal-state Chesapeake Bay program. The culmination of these efforts was an executive agreement to restore the Chesapeake Bay, accompanied by the announcement at a major conference in Fairfax, Virginia, of a comprehensive program of federal-state initiatives to implement the agreement.

Following the Fairfax conference, the Maryland General Assembly passed an ambitious program of Chesapeake Bay initiatives, and the regional partnership established a governing body to oversee progress and coordinate science and management activities. Within each jurisdiction, the emphasis shifted to the implementation of Bay initiatives by various government agencies.

In 1987, the successor to Hughes, Governor William Donald Schaefer and his fellow governors, the mayor of Washington, and the EPA administrator, again meeting in Virginia, formally adopted a series of agreements which set specific pollution-control targets in the areas of toxics, nutrients, and other sources as well as programmatic goals for land-use and resource-management strategies. These agreements and regulatory strategies, together with the institutional enhancements for science, technology, and citizen education, comprise the Chesapeake Bay restoration program as it exists today.

Shaping Public Policy—Setting the Agenda

There is substantial evidence of the significant role that citizen action has played in the Chesapeake Bay effort. Government reports, organization newsletters and newspaper articles record activities and events extending as far back as the 1960s that involved numerous individuals and citizen organizations with varying interests, objectives, ideologies, and skills. While activities occurred on a number of fronts during the 1970s and early 1980s, they were not strategically linked or coordinated. Collectively, however, they focused attention on the environmental problems facing the Bay and mobilized support for government action.

During this early period, most efforts primarily aimed to influence the public policy agenda and educate the public. Examples of citizen committees and conferences included the Chesapeake Bay Interagency Planning Committee, which presented "a comprehensive inventory of the present and anticipated problems plaguing the Bay"; the 1968 Governor's Chesapeake Bay Conference; the 1971 Citizens Conference that developed the citizens' agenda; and the Bi-State Conference on the Bay. There were also a number of Bay restoration campaigns for single tributaries, such as the celebrated Potomac River tours and Patuxent River study, and a consensus-building exercise which developed a river basin restoration strategy. Finally, numerous citizen-oriented environmental organizations emerged. These included the Chesapeake Bay Foundation, which popularized "Save the Bay" and grew from an education and policy nonprofit organization to a combined education, advocacy, research, and land-conservation organization with strong policy expertise; Citizens' Program for the Chesapeake Bay, an information clearinghouse; Save Our Streams, a grassroots activist organization that focused on stream restoration and organizational development; and Clean Water Action, a volunteer grassroots activist organization that addressed water quality issues and political organizing.[1]

In addition, contemporary news accounts reflected the concerns of Bay scientists, ecologists and citizen activists over the decline in Bay grasses and fish and the pollution of water resources. Also, an abundance of public events celebrated the Bay heritage and its natural beauty and warned about the declining health of the Bay. The emphasis on the cultural aspects of resources—along with grassroots environmental education efforts, citizens conferences, activist advocacy campaigns and the growing nationwide public interest in the environment—gave the Bay effort a strong populist spirit.

The continuous communication among citizen groups during this early period, their increasing science and policy expertise, and the interaction of diverse environmental interests and perspectives were sufficient to build a strong consensus for governmental reform and legislative action and to mobilize broad-based public support. While each entity's contribution is worthy of discussion, the unique role of the Citizens' Program for the Chesapeake Bay in blending science, government, and environmental perspectives to build a consensus for management strategies deserves special mention.

Citizens' Program for the Chesapeake Bay/Alliance for the Chesapeake Bay

Organized in 1971 as an outgrowth of a citizens conference concerning the future of the Chesapeake Bay, the Citizens' Program for the Chesapeake Bay was created on the premise that a comprehensive approach to the Bay's ecosystem management was necessary. Serving as a clearinghouse and public policy forum, the Citizens' Program's coalition of Chesapeake Bay interests and user groups was an effective framework for balancing the competing demands on the Bay's resources and for understanding complex interrelationships within the Chesapeake Bay system. The Citizens' Program provided a "neutral forum" for discussion of water quality goals, economic impacts of environmental policies, institutional arrangements for Bay management and science, and technological issues related to restoration of the Bay.

Utilizing scientific data and research, the Citizens' Program focused on the Bay as an ecosystem and assisted in the translation of the scientific and technological aspects of ecosystem management into a comprehensive policy agenda. In this way, its efforts helped to establish an integrated water quality and resource management approach and to provide citizen activists and the public with scientific knowledge of the Bay's ecosystem.

The Citizens' Program, however, was not the typical environmental advocacy organization, and there were tensions concerning its role. During the early years, it was hindered somewhat by difficulty in reaching consensus on the focus and mission of the organization.[2] However, it succeeded in educating a diverse constituency of Chesapeake Bay interests and in emphasizing the various ways that citizens could participate in the public policymaking process. Today, its successor organization, the Alliance for the Chesapeake Bay, is nationally recognized for its contributions in estuarine policy development and analysis, citizen information programs, and for its creative ability to reconcile diverse interests.

Translating Science Into Policy

The role played by the Citizens' Program during the early period (and in later years by the Alliance, the Chesapeake Bay Foundation, Environmental Policy Institute, Nature Conservancy, and other environmental organizations) in bringing science into the policy arena is significant and frequently overlooked. In the history of the Bay restoration effort as well as in other environmental causes, the environmental community has been instrumental in informing policymakers of scientific debate, advancing new science and technology, and popularizing scientific issues.

For example, during the 1970s government officials stressed the Bay's "resilience" and resisted the notion of the Bay's poor health. Believing that the dwindling numbers of fish and other species were merely temporary fluctuations of the Bay system, they stressed the ability of the Bay to "flush" itself. Environmental activists countered with scientific arguments that the Bay system was in decline and that the losses of Bay grasses, species of fish and shellfish, and other living resources were indicative of this decline. Later, they challenged governmental nutrient strategies that relied heavily on reducing phosphorus, arguing that this approach was insufficient for certain tributaries. Additionally, they advocated the removal of nitrogen.

Environmental organizations have raised scientific questions concerning the effect of air transport of nitrogen on the Bay, the effects of acid deposition on fish, the disposal of dredged spoil material in the deep trough, the effect of sea level rise on wetlands and coastal areas, and the impacts of certain forestry practices on habitat and water quality. In the area of toxic and hazardous waste, they have educated citizens about medical and ecological risks and issues associated with testing procedures, site selection criteria, and risk- management assumptions.

Some individuals think the relationship between the environmental and scientific communities has lessened in recent years because of tensions that are inherent in differing perspectives and objectives. Some also strongly believe that the level of comprehensive policy analysis and research applied to solving environmental problems is inadequate. There is no doubt, however, that the environmental community was instrumental in moving science into the policy realm and popularizing science.

Shaping Public Policy—Lobbying Government Officials

The majority of the legislative and regulatory initiatives that comprise Maryland's Chesapeake Bay program were developed during the early 1980s. While government and state legislative leaders developed many of the initiatives, environmental and citizen activist organizations played a significant role in helping to define the problems and propose alternatives.

Eight environmental organizations took an active role in lobbying for the initial package of Chesapeake Bay legislation: Chesapeake Bay Foundation, Sierra Club, Clean Water Action, Save Our Streams, Maryland Waste Coalition, Environmental Policy Institute, League of Women Voters, and the Maryland Conservation Council. They provided different levels and types of expertise and served a variety of roles within the policymaking arena. For example, both the Chesapeake Bay Foundation and the Environmental Policy Institute provided policy specialists in water quality, land use and habitat issues. They were the primary organizations with policy development capabilities. Several other organizations, particularly the Sierra Club and Clean Water Action, utilized the policy expertise and resources of the national affiliates. While all of the organizations lobbied legislative and government officials, there were significant differences in their expertise, political philosophies and availability of resources. Some organizations were more effective in providing expert testimony, others in generating constituent calls or conducting media campaigns. As these groups became collectively focused on the Chesapeake Bay issues, they were extremely effective in popularizing an issue and generating a strong expression of public support.[3]

The Importance of Teamwork

The strong degree of cooperation among organizations, specifically, splitting the workload and using diverse tactical skills, was particularly evident in several legislative campaigns. The most notable campaigns led to the passage of the phosphate ban and the nontidal wetlands bill and to the enactment of the critical areas law and regulations.

For example, a coalition of environmental organizations, legislators, and government officials orchestrated the legislative strategy utilized to secure both legislation establishing the Critical Areas Commission and the endorsement of the commission's criteria. Collectively, the environmental community used the skills and networks of different organizations to play the key role in mobilizing grassroots support. The Chesapeake Bay Foundation provided information analyses of technical issues and tapped its extensive Baywatchers grassroots membership organization for letters of support and local citizen testimony at hearings. It also provided scientific and legal expertise to the coalition. Clean Water Action used its grassroots canvass to target particular legislative districts to lobby for support. Sierra Club and Save Our Streams informed their members and provided citizen and special-interest witnesses for committee hearings. The Maryland Conservation Council also helped to communicate legislative developments through the *Legislative Report*. The Environmental Policy Institute's Chesapeake Bay Project provided lobbying support as did all of the other organizations. The teamwork widened and strengthened support for the program.

This kind of teamwork, which optimizes the skills, talents, and respective interests of the organizations, has been a significant factor in other legislative and nonlegislative campaigns such as the removal of the cap on funding for the state land conservation program, Program Open Space, forest preservation legislation, opposition to stream channelization within the Chester River watershed, preservation of special natural resource areas, the local land-trust movement, the anti-incinerator movement, and the recent push for recycling.[4]

Citizen action has helped create an extensive arsenal of laws, policies, and programs and the institutional framework for Bay management. In no small measure, this results from the rich diversity of interests, skills, and expertise within Maryland's environmental community. The smaller, grassroots-based advocacy groups, who constitute the majority of the environmental organizations, provide the energy and political momentum by using media and constituent communication strategies to popularize environmental issues and mobilize public support. The larger Annapolis-oriented statewide organizations use a variety of strategies, such as lobbying, information campaigns, formal participation in agency proceedings, and litigation, in an attempt to intervene at strategic points to influence changes in the formulation of public policy.

Comprehensive Environmental Decision Making

This diversity within Maryland's environmental community generates sufficient synergistic representation and advocacy across a broad range of Bay related issues. Nevertheless, many individuals have criticized what they believe is an overemphasis on narrowly focused legislative remedies to environmental problems. They question the lack of attention to underlying economic forces—transportation, energy, and development policies. Legislative initiatives are too focused on pollution and resource management, and less oriented toward pollution prevention, economic incentives and promoting nonlegislative solutions such as long range planning and cooperative environmental dispute resolution. Still others question whether legislative strategies are deliberately more to escalate political momentum and polarize debate than to gain legitimacy for clearly defined objectives and to build a political consensus to achieve environmental goals over a longer period of time.[5]

The persistent theme underlying these criticisms is that environmental activists do not stress comprehensive environmental decision making and long-range planning. A related theme is the adversarial nature of the relationship between citizen activists and government officials. Environmental policy and resource management issues are often difficult and contentious. Frequently, the conflicts between the citizen activists and government officials (and other interest groups) revolve around varying concepts of governance and differing ideological perspectives. While it may be impossible to reconcile differences in political views and moral judgments about environmental problems, improved communication could correct mistaken preconceptions which characterize much of the dialogue between the environmental community and governmental policymakers. Along with better communication, more effort toward cooperative strategies and negotiated solutions might enhance environmental governance.

Developing Political Support and Government Accountability

A significant consequence of the Chesapeake Bay restoration effort was the expansion of the environmental community and recognition of the need for a strong political base. There was considerable growth in both the number and size of environmental organizations during this period. In 1974, the Chesapeake Bay Center for Environmental Studies of the Smithsonian Institution released a study of Maryland-based Chesapeake Bay watershed citizen organizations which identified 19 environmental citizen organizations working on environmental issues within the Chesapeake Bay area. Today, the *Chesapeake Bay Citizens' Directory*, a comprehensive directory published by the Alliance for the Chesapeake Bay, identifies 76 Maryland environmental/resource conservation organizations.

112

With the advent of new organizations and the heightened level of environmental interest and activity across the state, new beliefs arose concerning community-action strategies and environmental political action. The increased level of environmental interest and activism and the successes of the environmental community in the legislature accelerated organized political action. Initially, the political activity was limited to lobbying and canvassing activities in local districts to assure passage of Bay legislation. Gradually these efforts expanded as environmental activists desired more access to political decision makers and more political influence.

While the number of activists and organizations involved in political action strategies was modest during the development of the Chesapeake Bay program, the strategy has continued to grow in importance. Activity has evolved since 1978, when the Maryland League of Conservation Voters was established. The Maryland League evaluates and publishes the voting record of public officeholders at the state level and supports those with outstanding environmental records. It actively campaigned for environmental candidates in the early 1980s and played a significant role in statewide elections with its endorsement of candidates. Over the years, the League has compiled an impressive success record. In 1986, 68 of the 75 candidates it endorsed were elected, of whom 18 were new members replacing non-environmental incumbents.

The League is not the only environmental political action group in Maryland. Organizations such as Citizen Action, Clean Water Action, and Sierra Club are also actively involved in electoral politics. In addition, a number of local citizen groups have recently formed local political action committees in the belief that political action at the local level is the only means to achieve influence over local decision making. Citizen leaders envision that greater local political activity will increase recruitment of environmental candidates and ultimately lead to greater participation in electoral politics and in political party politics.

Monitoring Government

Monitoring government and industry compliance with pollution control and resource management requirements is an important role for citizen action. So, too, is the monitoring of state and local regulatory programs. The complexity of Chesapeake Bay environmental and resource management prompted extensive bureaucratic policymaking and formal rulemaking. To participate in these deliberations, citizen activists had to be knowledgeable about the process and the opportunities for involvement. A primary way citizens, particularly those located a considerable distance from the state capital, could participate in governmental agency decision making was by joining a citizen advisory committee. They also could stay abreast of state administration programs through ongoing conversations with government officials and other policymakers and through using communication networks.

Another way of assuring government accountability is through litigation. Whether through intervening in agency decision making, suing government agencies to obtain compliance with environmental laws, or taking polluters to court, a number of Maryland organizations and individuals have pursued legal action. The majority of the organizations have relied upon public-spirited attorneys who are willing to take on environmental cases on a *pro bono* or reduced-fee basis. Only the Chesapeake Bay Foundation has had professional legal staff, although a number of organizations have members who are attorneys and may be called upon for assistance or advice.

A number of organizations have played the "watchdog" role in monitoring permit-issuance procedures and government enforcement of permits. The Chesapeake Bay Foundation challenged state enforcement of water quality permits for Bethlehem Steel and ultimately sued to force compliance. The Maryland Waste Coalition, a coalition of grassroots organizations concerned about waste management and toxics regulation, joined with community organizations to protest pollution control violations at several industrial facilities. These and other organizations played a "watchdog" role in monitoring permit issuance procedures and government enforcement of permits. Further, they successfully sought legislation imposing stricter government regulation on industrial facilities, tougher penalties for noncompliance, strict liability for harm caused by pollution, and clean-up requirements for abandoned waste sites.

Educating The Public

Education is an important component of Maryland's Chesapeake Bay program. The importance of being able to arouse public concern and support for the Chesapeake Bay—which depends on a basic understanding of the Bay's ecology—and the desire to keep each other informed of important developments in public policy help to explain the strong educational emphasis of Maryland's citizen and environmental organizations, the private sector, and Maryland government. Their collective contribution to environmental education probably exceeds well over $20-25 million annually. While the environmental community and private sector have been strong contributors, the core commitment by Maryland state and local government is substantial. This commitment involves both formal environmental education programs as well as state and local government programs that support such activities as youth conservation corps, nature appreciation and environmental education services, museum programs, and specific initiatives providing assistance for instruction materials, outdoor education experiences, curriculum development, and teacher training.

In short, Maryland's government institutions, the private sector, and civic and environmental organizations have funded an extraordinary variety of environmental education programs and projects that explore ecological principles and the relationship of these principles to human society. For example, the Chesapeake Bay Foundation sponsors fifteen education programs on the Bay's ecology and related environmental concerns. The programs are tailored to different school populations and learning experiences, but all are designed to get students out on the Bay or to some natural environment away from their community. Another example is Hard Bargain Farm. This project is administered by the Alice Ferguson Foundation and is a working demonstration farmstead in Accokeek, Prince George's County, on 330 acres within the Potomac River corridor. In cooperation with the National Park Service, the Farm provides environmental learning experiences for school children and overnight and day camping for organized groups to explore the natural world. Active involvement in farm chores and nature study are featured. These and other projects go well beyond nature appreciation and principles of ecology. There is a strong orientation toward understanding the environmental impacts of human activities and cumulative impacts of development activities on habitat loss, pollution, and resource depletion. Environmental values, life-styles, and behaviors are also examined. In addition, many of the projects emphasize environmental citizenship, government responsibility, and political empowerment.[6]

Ecosystem Management

The desire to save the Bay galvanized the public, the political establishment, and government bureaucracies into action. At the same time, the collective efforts of numerous organizations, agencies, and individuals also educated the public about the environmental problems within the watershed and the need for action. During this period, many civic, watershed and environmental organizations, interest groups, and businesses joined in the desire to clean up the Bay.

This collective identity with the Bay and environmental spiritedness was evident in many local restoration projects, increased participation in environmental activities, and support for environmental organizations. The Alliance for the Chesapeake Bay and Save our Streams initiated projects using citizens to collect water quality and biological data to augment government monitoring on smaller tributaries not being monitored. Furthermore, the Chesapeake Bay Trust, a nonprofit foundation established by the state, funded a variety of hands-on projects to instill stewardship and teach citizens and students about the importance of ecology, environmental values, and the ways in which lifestyle choices have an impact on the environment.[7]

In addition to restoring streams and participating in recycling programs, citizens have helped preserve land and Bay habitat areas. The dramatic demographic changes that have occurred over the past three decades leave no doubt that land development has far outstripped land preservation throughout the state. Therefore, on one level it is difficult to regard the limited number of protected public land areas, conservation easements, and wilderness holdings as a success. Yet, in view of the tremendous pressure for economic growth and the pro-development attitudes of business and public leaders during this period, preserving certain land and wilderness areas and enlisting more people in the cause are viewed by many as an impressive feat of the environmental community.

A citizens group, the Maryland Wildlands Committee has protected 13,733 acres of wilderness area. Their work has received praise from both environmental activists and government officials. The Maryland Environmental Trust (MET) continues as a state-supported, nonprofit, land trust established to accept and solicit conservation land easements. Further, it provides technical and financial assistance to local land trusts and serves as a clearinghouse for all land conservation groups. In addition to MET, Chesapeake Bay Foundation, Nature Conservancy, National Lands Trust, and others have land-conservation easement programs for varying purposes ranging from scenic enhancement and protection of natural heritage areas to preservation of biodiversity.

The land-trust movement in Maryland has undergone significant growth in the number of local land trusts that have recently been created. In the past two years alone, 24 local land trusts have been created. All together, 29 local land trusts and 10 state and national organizations have put conservation easements on approximately 75,000 acres.

This review of the citizen's role in Maryland's Chesapeake Bay restoration effort cannot give the full picture of issues, protests, politics, consensus building efforts, and direct-action campaigns which have occurred or are continuing. Nor can it properly analyze the underlying resource conservation and development conflicts or questions of governance and environmental ethics. It does suggest certain lessons. They include: the importance of coalition-building in influencing public policy, the need to build a political base, and the need for science and long-range policy research and development.

The Challenge of Ecosystem Management

The ecosystem management approach to Chesapeake Bay restoration poses several challenges to citizens who desire to influence policymaking and participate in decision making. The premise of an ecosystem approach to Chesapeake Bay management is that since land, water, air and biota interact and influence one another, traditional pollution control and resource management programs that partition the environment into separate components tend to produce shortsighted strategies that solve one environmental problem at the expense of another. Inherent in this approach is the view that management for the Bay should evolve in response to new information that sheds greater understanding of the Bay processes and conditions.[8]

Ecosystem bay management encompasses a variety of regional jurisdictions, resource users, conservation interests, and other stakeholders who are concerned about a wide range of issues, policies, and projects in areas such as water quality control, habitat protection, stream restoration, sewage treatment, pollution control facilities, forestland preservation, fisheries management, new fish species, sustainable agriculture, shore erosion, disposal of dredged material, cleanup of toxic dumps, growth management, and environmental education. The success of the Bay restoration program is measured in terms of the environmental health and living resources of the ecosystem rather than by administrative program measurements. Therefore, the ecosystem approach to Chesapeake Bay restoration poses significant challenges to citizen involvement:

- The comprehensiveness and complexity of the approach requires a high level of information, organizational skill, and political strategy.
- The diversity of stakeholders requires more attention be given to coordination and collaborative efforts as well as greater emphasis upon consensus building techniques.
- There is a need for individual actors and organizations with policy analysis capabilities who are able to take a systemic view, keep a long-range perspective, and be willing to learn.

In defining the citizens' role in the Chesapeake Bay program, the citizen and environmental organizations recognized the importance of effective communication and the need for building public support. The early history of the Bay restoration effort includes examples of media strategies, citizen forums, and environmental education centers. Citizens were brought into the public policy process through citizen advisory programs, public hearings and community-based volunteer activities.

Early environmental successes diagnosed the Bay's problems, built consensus for action strategies, and taught people that the Bay's problems are interconnected with no quick fixes or isolated individual solutions. Today, the challenge is to deal with problems conclusively, something that is nearly impossible because of the complex, variable, and stressed nature of coastal seas and because many problems originate beyond jurisdictional boundaries and extend beyond the planning horizons of current state and local administrations. As new information unfolds, the problems become layered with complexity, involving more clusters of interests and stakeholders.

This underscores the need for more emphasis on negotiation techniques and structured policy forums that attempt to bring various interests and stakeholders together to create consensus. Long-range planning and comprehensive decision making that looks at all the parameters of an issue, including root causes, needs to be emphasized. Yet, as noted previously, there has been less emphasis on these techniques.

Finally, perhaps the ultimate challenge is defining success. The ecosystem management approach to Chesapeake Bay restoration necessitates that this be a dynamic, evolving program that will respond to new data about the Bay as it becomes known. It requires more flexibility for learning and adapting and places greater emphasis on monitoring and planning. The challenge confronting citizen activists and policymakers alike is to define and continually redefine the ecological health of the Bay and to create a governance regime that can maintain its credibility operating in progressive stages.

For this reason, a program as massive as the Chesapeake Bay restoration must have ongoing citizen interest, involvement, and support to assure the necessary constancy of commitment. Chesapeake Bay restoration and protection cannot be achieved solely through science, technology, and legislative and administrative reforms. Chesapeake Bay management is inherently social and political. Effective governance requires social learning and citizen participation in the articulation of public policy choices. Without citizen involvement, the protection of the common future of the Chesapeake Bay's economic and environmental resources is at risk.

Notes

1. Marjorie Beane, "Environmental Organizations in the Chesapeake Bay Area," Study by the Chesapeake Bay Center for Environmental Studies, Smithsonian Institution, Maryland, 1974.
2. Governor's Conference on Chesapeake Bay, Proceedings, September 12-13, 1968.
3. Ellen Fraites, *Environmental Leadership Report: Environmental Activism in Maryland*, Coastal and Environmental Policy Program, University of Maryland, 1991, 61-69.
4. Ibid., 27.
5. Ibid., 65-69.
6. Gary Heath, Maryland Department of Education memorandum, "Describing Environmental Education in Maryland Public Schools: Summary of Non-governmental Organizations' Involvement in Environmental Education," Baltimore, MD, November, 1988. See also Maryland Department of Education, *Status Report of Environmental Education, 1988*.
7. Citizens' Program for the Chesapeake Bay, *Chesapeake Bay Citizen Report*. 1984-1986.
8. George R. Francis, "Great Lakes Governance and the Ecosystem Approach: Where Next?" in *Perspectives on Ecosystem Management for the Great Lakes*, ed. Lynton N. Caldwell (Albany, NY, 1988), 319-37.

Sustainable Development

The Role of Technology in Sustainable Development

Arthur E. Williams

The relationship between humans and the natural world is changing, and with it the notions of our duties, obligations, and responsibilities with regard to the environment. Borrowing Russell Peterson's term, we speak of an "Earth Ethic" that commits us to preserving our biosphere while enhancing our present and future quality of life.[1] Our objective must be sustainable development. Part philosophy, part practical guidance, the notion of sustainable development provides a thoughtful blueprint for engineers engaged in public service. No public works project should be constructed that causes irreparable environmental degradation, for over the long run such a project can neither improve nor even maintain quality of life.

Simply put, sustainable development means meeting "the needs of the present without compromising our ability to meet those of the future."[2] The United Nations Brundtland Commission report, *Our Common Future*, notes that we must not live "beyond the world's ecological means" but we must promote consumption standards that can reasonably be within everyone's reach.[3] Long-range planning is necessary. Nothing we do should mortgage the hopes and welfare of future generations. The challenge is enormous. Means must be found to improve the quality of human existence without harming fragile ecosystems.

The Environmental Crisis

If the challenge is enormous, the alternative—the status quo—is unacceptable. The world is faced with many problems today. Underlying many of these problems is human population growth. It is estimated that, barring some unforeseen circumstance, the world's population will double sometime in the next century. By the year 2000, the developing countries will represent about 75 percent of the world's population, and the large urban areas of these countries will feel this increase most acutely. Today, we have the what some have

120

called "environmental refugees," i.e., victims of drought in Ethiopia or defor- estation in Haiti.[4] As Jessica Tuchman Mathews suggested, the mixture of scarce resources and growing population can lead to "frustration, resentment, domestic unrest or even civil war."[5] It also can lead to ecological crisis, espe- cially in those countries afflicted by overpopulation. In poor regions of the world, long-term environmental and political stability must always be sacri- ficed to short-term survival. Jim MacNeill, the secretary general of the World Commission on Environment and Development, concluded that developing countries require a minimum three percent growth in per capita income to enable the transition to sustainable development.[6] Under such circumstances, it is unreasonable for wealthy countries to assume that developing countries can solve their problems without outside aid.

Of course, wealthy nations have their own problems too. In the United States, urbanization, ranching, and agricultural development have turned mar- ginal lands to desert in the West. Human activity has caused massive erosion problems and the loss of valuable topsoil throughout the country. Meanwhile, wetlands are disappearing at alarming rates. The United States has now lost over half of the wetlands that existed when the Pilgrims landed at Plymouth Rock, and we continue to lose nearly half a million acres a year.[7] Other prob- lems include air and water pollution and the disposal of toxic, nuclear, and solid wastes.

Modern life also produces unanticipated environmental modifications. The obvious example is the "greenhouse effect," half of which is caused by carbon dioxide and half by a mixture of methane, nitrous oxide, ozone, and man-made chlorofluorocarbons. Some experts now predict that the effect will cause global temperatures to increase from five to nine degrees Fahrenheit in the next 50- 100 years (it took nature 18,000 years to accomplish this), sea levels to rise and precipitation and soil moisture to change, with important effects on land-use and agricultural production.[8] If so, the protection of U.S. coastal areas could cost anywhere from $32 billion to $309 billion and would inevitably result in more loss of wetlands. Inland areas would also be affected. Reduced river flows would force increased reliance on irrigation. Pine forests in Texas could be reduced by as much as 90 percent as the habitat moves northward. There would be significant changes in crop patterns.[9] Major social consequences could result from these changes in the natural regimen. Sustainable development offers us the opportunity of reducing, if not eliminating, the effects.

Sustainable Development

Sustainable development is about finding new ways to do business. It demands change. It requires doing more with less—less resources used and less waste generated. Its implementation means new manufacturing processes, more use of recyclable materials, and the development of regenerative or recyclable output components. Sustainable development also necessitates consideration of the life-cycle consequences of production. It requires an approach that imitates natural or biological processes. It seeks new solutions to old problems and far more efficient use of natural resources in meeting human needs and developing or redesigning products. It also calls for new ways to market, deliver, and dispose of those products. It may require the development of new infrastructures or services. Technology will play a key role.

The concept is simple, but its implementation is not. What works for wealthy nations may not work for developing countries. Many factors shape the possible options for each country. These can include social elements such as religion, market mechanisms, environmental resources, population, industrial structure, labor force, urban hierarchy, and infrastructure. They will also reflect historical and geographical circumstances. Certainly, misapplied technology may be worse than no technology at all. For example, large-scale dams have led to inundation of productive land, massive displacement of people, and increased disease in some parts of the world. Also, downstream productivity is sometimes adversely affected because of salt intrusion, erosion, and dried-up lakes. A major engineering and political mistake is to confuse river basin development with water resource management. In Africa, for instance, river basin development generally has focused on hydropower and irrigation and not on badly needed facilities for community water distribution and supply.[10] While a large-scale project may produce major national economic benefits, its degradation of the environment and harmful effects on local populations have not always been appreciated.

So, how will sustainable development happen? We do not know all the answers, but in a general sense we know that engineers will play a key role and that properly applied technology will be critical. To be successful, sustainable development requires a "process" for change. First, there must be knowledge, awareness, and understanding of the conditions for development, and then there must be a commitment to act. Effective decisions to invest in the essential social, physical and institutional infrastructure require understanding. Effective decisions to develop or adapt technologies require that same understanding. Critical to the process are the knowledge bases that describe the gamut of interactive physical, chemical, biological and human processes that shape what is sustainable and what is not.

Creative application of technology encompasses the responsibility to plan, design, and construct systems that will not only solve the immediate problems, but will be sensitive to long-term interactions that sustain affected natural resources. Thoughtful development does not need to affect the environment adversely. Development can be long-term, efficient, effective and ecologically beneficial—in a word, sustainable. How do we move toward that goal?

Concepts

Over the last year, the U.S. Army Corps of Engineers has developed nine concepts which serve as the foundation—the framework—for sustainable engineering. The Corps has used many of these concepts for years, but now the challenge is to use them to the optimum level to facilitate sustainable development.

The first concept is *education*. As facilitators of sustainable development, engineers must have the skills, knowledge, and information which are the stepping stones to a sustainable future. Whatever their specialty, engineers need to understand environmental and economic issues and problems, especially the risks and potential impacts of engineering actions.

The second concept is *"ecosystems" thinking*. Engineers are traditionally taught linear problem-solving techniques: they break each problem into its simplest pieces, study each piece, and then move on to the next challenge. Ecosystems thinking, on the other hand, calls for synthesis—the combining of separate elements to form an integrated and coherent whole. If we are to approach sustainable development (as we must) in a manner that imitates the natural processes around us, then engineering must become a unifying, not a partitioning, discipline.

The third concept, which is related to the second, is to *emphasize the aggregate consequences* of what we are recommending. Practicing "ecosystems" thinking requires that engineers begin to examine more carefully the aggregate long term consequences of decisions in terms of both time and space. We must understand the net contribution of individual impacts or decisions. This approach moves well beyond what we refer to as "environmental protection," which is not synonymous with sustainable development.

The fourth concept is to *acquire environmental economic tools* to integrate the environment and social conditions into market economics. History has taught us that, for all its shortcomings and inequities, a market economy based on a free enterprise system affords the best opportunity to achieve the level of global economic development necessary to support growing populations and achieve sustainable development. It is not a questions of either/or; it must be both. Within the context of market economics, we must grapple with the need to develop and practice "environmental economics."

The fifth concept is the *search for sustainable alternatives*. The engineer as a project team leader or member bears much of the responsibility for recommending the technical alternative solutions. We should not be satisfied with engineering studies that have not considered alternatives.

The sixth concept is to *develop and apply technology* to serve sustainability. We need new technologies—new materials, and manufacturing processes that meet and then surpass today's dreams. Technology focused on sustainable development is the key to solving problems created in the past and preventing new ones in the future. The engineering and scientific communities must advance technology to let us use our resources more efficiently, reduce waste, and minimize environmental impacts.

The seventh concept is *listening to those we serve*. We must consider sustainable development as a dynamic process which responds to the continually changing needs and expanded knowledge base of the specific society, culture, and community we serve. Unless we can be truly relevant to societal needs, we will doom even the best engineering efforts leading us towards sustainable development.

The eighth concept is to *cultivate a multidisciplinary team approach*. The approach is not new. We have been doing it for a long time, but "multidisciplinary" in this concept goes well beyond getting the electrical and the mechanical engineers together. It goes beyond the array of engineering disciplines to include many others. We must bring together the knowledge, skills, and insights of the natural, social, and physical sciences and firmly integrate them into the engineering process.

The ninth and last concept goes back to the first—education—except it addresses external education. We must continually *educate those we serve* and promote the adoption of a sustainable development ethic among all elements of society. Perhaps special efforts should be directed toward private and public sector decision makers; investors; and local, regional, national, and even international governing bodies.

Technology

We think of areas without technology as pristine. We see unspoiled rivers, green fields, and snowy mountains in a vision of a world untouched by human activity. In the process we sometimes lose sight of what technology has provided us, or what our quality of life would be in the absence of technology. Consider the poor in developing countries who bathe and wash their clothes in non-potable water, or the human waste that contaminates streams because developing governments are too poor to treat the sewage. Likewise, in the absence of technology, people in these countries must sustain themselves on sickly crops, grown in soil stripped of nutrients. The point need not be belabored. While undeniably technology can cause major problems, it has been, and remains, a critical component not only for the resolution of present and future problems, but for the prevention of problems.

The fact is that we live in an increasingly unstable natural environment, mainly the result of human intrusion and manipulation of natural forces. Huge factories, large-scale transportation and power systems, and urbanization may offer the promise of better quality of life; but when things go wrong, they can go very wrong, with enormous environmental consequences.[11] To cope with these dangers, both institutional and technological solutions are needed. Fortunately, advances are being made. New technology holds out the promise of making wastewater not only reusable for agricultural and industrial use but for human consumption too. More stress is being placed on eliminating or reducing waste and pollution at the source, especially in industrial plants.[12] Engineers are also designing more energy efficient buildings and using non-structural approaches, such as zoning, to solve flood control problems. Work continues on developing the technology that will allow a more complete analysis of the Earth's biosphere. The technology includes space satellites, communications systems, and computers. Still in all, the basic challenge remains: to reconcile the demands of an increasingly complex and technological society with the need to preserve and protect our natural environment.

In the ongoing search for appropriate technological solutions, the U.S. Army Corps of Engineers has an important role to play. Although the Corps of Engineers has been involved with water resources developments since 1824, it has been mainly in the last 20 or 30 years that the organization has systematically collected data about the impacts of its projects and programs on ecological systems within the affected areas. Consequently, whether dredging harbors to enable ships to enter the nation's ports, providing flood control through levee building, or operating hydropower dams, the Corps has become increasingly aware of the effects of its activities on the adjacent resources. Increasingly sophisticated technology partially accounts for this new awareness. Today we not only detect changes in the ecological systems surrounding our projects, but predict the impacts of planned or future activities.

Many of the water resource-related activities of the Corps affect wetland resources, so the agency has been conducting research into wetlands and their ecological functions since the 1970s. In 1991, the Corps began a new, $22 million Wetlands Research Program. The program's central purpose is to combine the environmental and engineering disciplines—the eighth of our nine concepts—in order to provide the best technical and cost-effective tools and methods for wetlands management. The initiative involves a partnership with other federal agencies such as the Environmental Protection Agency, the U.S. Department of Interior, the Department of Agriculture, the Department of Transportation, and the National Oceanic and Atmospheric Administration, as well as with state and local agencies and private conservation groups.

The Wetlands Research Program addresses four important areas: critical processes in wetlands, stewardship and management, delineation and evaluation, and restoration and establishment of wetlands. Understanding the critical processes that occur in wetlands and developing more effective management tools will increase significantly the Corps' ability to sustain wetland areas. The program emphasizes technology transfer and public information. Its technological innovations will be widely shared with other federal and state agencies through technical notes and workshops, and with others through educational packages, newsletters and magazine articles.

Closely tied with the Wetlands Research Program is Corps research on wetlands mitigation banking. While the Corps of Engineers continues to proceed under the sequencing concept—first, avoiding all possible wetland damage; next, minimizing damage which is unavoidable; and finally, compensating for damage—there has been an increasing interest in applying the concept of banking to environmental mitigation. Rather than managing small, separate pockets of habitat required for individual projects, it may often be wiser to focus on other areas which provide more of an opportunity to manage ecosystems and substantially increase the values of many resources. The Corps' two-year study will investigate mitigation banking—how it works, the successes and failures—and examine case studies.

The coexistence of productive and healthy natural systems alongside man-made systems requires increasingly sophisticated and complex technology. Remote sensing and geographic information systems (GIS) are just two examples of technology that can aid in finding the point of coexistence. Remote sensing—the use of satellite imagery—can be used to track water quality, aquatic plants, timber and general fish and wildlife habitat conditions. The U.S. Fish and Wildlife Service has a GIS lab at LaCroix, Wisconsin, to monitor environmental conditions on the Upper Mississippi. The staff at the remote sensing/GIS center at the U.S. Army Corps of Engineers Cold Regions Research and Engineering Laboratory in Hanover, New Hampshire, constantly examines the newest advances in sensor and analysis systems to ensure that they are made available to our field offices. Two technologies currently under study involve the use of airborne gamma radiation to determine the water equivalent of snow and the remote measurement of wavefields for coastal erosion studies. These technologies will be critical to designing and operating projects in a sustainable manner.

An understanding of the ecological systems we are modifying or attempting to coexist with and the ability to foresee consequences of our actions are essential requirements for sustainable growth. Only by having a valid assessment of current conditions, an understanding of processes that are responsible for change, and a means to track changes over time can we determine trends and evaluate the effectiveness of our actions. GIS provides the means, in tandem with remotely sensed data, to track trends, identify changes over time, and model environmental processes.

Data obtained from remote sensing can be entered into a GIS for three-dimensional modeling, which can portray a variety of attributes about a given geographic area. Archeological sites, biological resources, hydrologic data, and the presence, diversity and productivity of particular vegetative types are just a few of the attributes which can be built into the model. This technology has been invaluable to engineers as well as to natural resource scientists. It should greatly improve our understanding of the human impact on natural systems and, hence, lead to policies supportive of sustainable development. River systems such as the Mississippi-Missouri and the Columbia-Snake directly benefit from data we receive through GIS technology. These rivers and their adjacent lands provide opportunities for a variety of uses such as water supply, recreation, transportation, and fish and wildlife habitat, including protection of endangered species. The Corps is also doing some exploratory work in "environmental economic tools," the fourth of our nine concepts. Determining the return on environmental investments has been a problem for many years. Engineers use traditional economic measurements to evaluate the benefits and costs of proposed projects. Various effective analytic models exist, but there is no consensus methodology for assessing the efficiency and effectiveness of investments in environmental restoration work. Until we can improve existing techniques or develop new ones, our ability to make sound decisions about allocating resources for environmental restoration will continue to be limited. We are developing methodologies that assess the long term public benefit and provide a basis for identifying the optimum measures for accomplishing environmental objectives.

The Corps has proposed a three-year research program, entitled the Valuation of Environmental Investments Research Program. It will draw on the talents and insights of our field engineers and scientists; the academic and consultant communities; other federal agencies such as the Environmental Protection Agency, U.S. Fish and Wildlife Service, U.S. Forest Service, Soil Conservation Service, Bureau of Reclamation and Tennessee Valley Authority; state agencies; industry; and environmental groups. The study will produce a valuation framework for both monetary and nonmonetary measures. It will develop procedures and techniques for determining the cost effectiveness and efficiency of alternative environmental projects and programs, provide a common basis for comparing environmental projects, and include case study demonstrations of the valuation procedure and techniques. The final report will include a users' manual and will be available for agency-wide testing.

Evolving technologies, both in the Corps of Engineers and in the engineering and scientific communities, are providing new answers to old questions, such as the best way to protect property and lives against flooding and the beneficial uses of dredged material. Can we bioengineer for erosion control, e.g. use willow bundles (as we did in the nineteenth century) instead of concrete or riprap? Research and demonstration projects have shown us that new answers do exist; history provides us with answers we may have forgotten. In any case, we must employ them more often so that the public and the nation benefit.

Technology also offers opportunities for us to get the maximum benefit for the dollars and resources spent. During the Corps' last Repair, Evaluation, Maintenance, and Rehabilitation (REMR) Program, which was completed in 1989, the Corps developed technology which will save over $200 million by 1994. The current $35 million REMR II program will focus on concrete and steel structures, geo-technical issues, hydraulics, coastal concerns, electrical and mechanical issues, and operations management. Many of the new techniques developed use fewer resources. Expertise gained from this program is not only transmitted to Corps field offices, but to other federal agencies and to thousands of other individuals, public entities, professional societies, and private organizations.

The goal of sustainable development is not easily reached. It requires negotiation, good faith, and an accurate assessment of needs and impacts involving both human and natural systems. In 1988, the Corps established the Alternate Dispute Resolution (ADR) program, which helps to create an atmosphere in which the clash of alternative viewpoints can be synergized into creative solutions. A neutral, third party mediator helps find a middle ground to facilitate decisions which are acceptable to all parties.

ADR can be used to regulate waterways and wetlands, plan water development projects, design engineering solutions, construct projects, and manage completed ones. The Corps has used it very successfully in hazardous waste clean up and improving government contracting.

Technology, grounded in a multidisciplinary approach, is critical for a sustainable future, but it is not the total answer. Many other factors are necessary to achieve sustainable development and wise resource use. In addition to the willingness to develop technology, a society must have the capacity—and wisdom—to use it effectively. Planning is necessary. The economist Kenneth Boulding wrote, "a society which loses its identity with posterity and which loses its positive image of the future loses also its capacity to deal with present problems, and soon falls apart."[13] If we wish to leave a better environment, not for tomorrow or the day after, but for the indefinite future, then we will avoid waste and manage our resources more efficiently. We must not short-change future generations, both for their sakes and for ours.

Environmental protection and economic development are not mutually exclusive terms. Indeed, just the opposite is true. If we do not sustain the environment, we lose the resources we need to develop the economy. If we do not find the means to lift people out of poverty and increase the capital and economic capacity of developing nations, we face continued environmental devastation and social upheaval. Sustainable development is the key, and engineering skill is essential. Now is the time to use our engineering capacity to develop and apply the technology that advances both economic and environmental goals. For its part, the Corps of Engineers fully recognizes that sustaining the environment is an important part of building the nation.

Notes

1. Russell W. Peterson, "An Earth Ethic: Our Choices," in National Geographic Society, *Earth '88: Changing Geographic Perspectives* (Washington, D.C., 1988), 360-75. Peterson is president emeritus of the National Audubon Society.

2. Gregory G. Lebel and Hal Kane, *Sustainable Development: A Guide to Our Common Future* (Washington, D.C., 1989), 2.

3. World Commission on Environment and Development, *Our Common Future* (Oxford, 1987), 44.

4. Jessica Tuchman Mathews, "Redefining Security," *Foreign Affairs* 68, no. 2 (Spring 1989): 167-68.

5. Mathews, "Redefining Security," 168.

6. Jim MacNeill, "Strategies for Sustainable Economic Development," *Scientific American* 261, no.3 (September 1989): 256.

7. David Rains Wallace, "Wetlands in America: Labyrinth and Temple," *Wilderness* 49, no. 171 (Winter 1985): 16.

8. Jill Jaeger, "Anticipating Climatic Change," *Environment* 30, no. 7 (September 1988): 14-15; Glenn Nolan Lewis, "Warmer Climate May Make State Drier and Wetter," *The Houston Post*, 2 July 1989, E-1.

9. Lewis, "Warmer Climate," E-1, E-5.

10. On problems with river basin development in Africa, see Thayer Scudder, "River Basin Projects in Africa," *Environment* 31, no. 2 (March 1989): 4-9, 27-39.

11 Gilbert F. White, "Stewardship of the Earth," in Robert W. Kates and Ian Burton, eds., *Geography, Resources, and Environment: Selected Writings of Gilbert F. White* (Chicago, 1986), I, 399-400.

12. Burt Nydes, "Drinking Wastewater," *American City & County* 100, 9 (September 1985): 52; Sheldon K. Friedlander, "Pollution Prevention: Implications for Engineering Design, Research, and Education," *Environment* 31, no. 4 (May 1989): 13-14.

13. Cited in Robert C. Paehlke, *Environmentalism and the Future of Progressive Politics* (New Haven, 1989), 164.

Sustainable Development: An Environmental Protection Challenge

LaJuana S. Wilcher

The topic of sustainable development is as timely as it is important. Conserving and managing our nation's water resources will increasingly engage us as we recognize that water, which sustains all life on this Earth, is not in limitless supply. We see that the way we use water affects, not only its quality, but its quantity. This new vision demands new ways of thinking about water. How can we get the water we need without drastically changing the fabric of our lives, or the fabric of nature? The paradigm which best describes that way of thinking is sustainable development.

General Williams cited a classic definition of sustainable development from the Brundtland Commission, which pretty much invented the term. A former EPA Administrator, William Ruckleshaus, shortens the definition. He says, "nature provides a free lunch, but only if we control our appetites . . . ."[1] Not only must we refrain from gorging at nature's table, but we must think long and hard before we change the menu.

On the Island of Borneo during the 1950s, the Dayak tribe suffered an outbreak of malaria. An international committee of experts met to determine what to do. They decided to spray the island with DDT to kill the mosquitoes. They did so, and the DDT did its job. It also killed wasps that fed on the islands's thatch-eating caterpillars. Without the wasps, the caterpillars bred and ate until all of the roofs of all of the huts on the island fell in. Worse yet, the island's lizards ate the DDT, and the cats on the island ate the lizards, and the cats died. Soon there was nothing to keep the rats in check. Before long, plague swept the island.

The international committee met again. What to do? They decided to airlift live cats to the island and parachute them down to eat the rats. They did so, and the cure worked. Yet, nobody would ever pick that as a good example of long-term planning, let alone sustainable development.

My goal in this paper is to present some ideas about how sustainable development can and should guide federal agencies as they write environmental regulations, and how we should change the way we "keep score" of economic progress in order to allow the concept of sustainable development a chance to work for us.

Environmental Successes

The people of this country care deeply about the environment, and they relate to the idea of living in harmony with it. Mass communications make palpable the connections between us and the Earth. Every day, our televisions show the indignities we have heaped upon our home—pictures of burning Kuwaiti oil fields and the Exxon Valdez spill, for instance. More Americans call themselves environmentalists now than ever have before—90 percent, according to one survey taken last year.[2]

People place value in a clean environment. In the fall of 1992, *Money* magazine made a survey of the qualities Americans look for in a place to live. Clean water ranked highest of all.[3] An "ABC News"-*Washington Post* poll released in November 1991, shows the quality of the environment ranks sixth among the 51 things Americans worry about most.[4] America's leaders have translated that interest into political support and have made record progress in improving the health of the U.S. environment. As President Bush said, "We must manage the Earth's natural resources in ways that assure the sustainability of humanity on this planet, and in ways that maximize the potential for growth and opportunity for all."[5]

The Bush administration put that policy into action by:

- Increasing spending for wetlands acquisition, enhancement and restoration to record levels. If Congress approves Bush's request for $812 million in fiscal year 1993, wetlands funding will have increased 175 percent since 1989.
- Putting a halt to the dumping of solid waste and sewage sludge into the ocean.
- Exceeding Montreal Protocol requirements for phase-out of chloroflourocarbons.
- Doubling funds for parks, wildlife and outdoor recreation, and tripling money to states to acquire national parks and wildlife refuges.
- Nearly doubling worldwide forestry assistance.
- Placing large coastal areas off-limits to oil and gas development for at least a decade to allow time for environmental studies.

Sometimes we forget how much we have accomplished and are accomplishing, and it is useful to compare the way we think and act today with our past thoughts and actions.

Environmental Mistreatment

There are plenty of examples of past environmental abuse. American rivers used to catch on fire, and Lake Erie was once on its deathbed. For the sake of development, taxpayers spent millions of dollars draining land north of the Florida Everglades. It opened more crop land and made room for a growing population, but the resulting hydrologic flow changes and increased nutrients moving down the rivers are big reasons why today the Everglades has 93 percent fewer wading birds than they did in the 1930s. Meanwhile, thanks to damming and diking and channelling, the Mississippi River now sends 30 or 40 square miles of Louisiana to the Gulf of Mexico each year. We have tied up Old Man River so that he can no longer replenish the soil as he once did.

Consider the nation's wetlands. From the 1950s through the mid-1970s our country was bleeding away these natural filters and wildlife breeding grounds at the rate of 450,000 acres a year, for a total loss of more than one-half of the original wetlands in the contiguous 48 states! Our losses continue, although they have been greatly slowed.

The United States has made mistakes, and we are working to correct them. But the history of much of the rest of the developed world is much worse. In the former Communist bloc, the environmental degradation is almost beyond belief. These countries live in the dark shadow of catastrophe created when they chose to forgo environmental controls in their headlong pursuit of industrial strength. In Poland, two-thirds of the rivers are too dirty even for industrial use—the Vistula River is so corrosive as it flows through Krakow that it cannot be used even to cool machinery. Poland's environment minister has estimated that the country's pollution problems are a 15 percent drag on gross national product. In Bulgaria, 80 percent of the farmland is threatened by erosion, and 25 percent of animal and plant species are threatened. A Czechoslovakian environmental consultant estimates the life span in his country has dropped by ten years since the end of World War II because of environmental pollution.

The Aral Sea, in the Central Asian part of the former Soviet Union, has lost 75 percent of its volume in the last 30 years because the rivers which used to feed it are diverted to irrigate 18 million thirsty acres of cotton, rice, and fruit. Massive salt and sand storms from the exposed sea bed poison the crops and make life miserable for the people. The extra fertilizer they spread to fight the salt contaminates the groundwater and wells. The fishing industry of the Aral Sea and the jobs it once supported are no more, and canneries must bring fish from two thousand miles away to keep working.

That is the legacy of communism. It is the legacy of irresponsibility and bungled planning. It is the legacy of development without heed to sustainability. Vaclav Havel, the president of Czechoslovakia, called these results of Marxist ideology, "the consequences of the arrogance of modern man, who believes he understands everything and knows everything, who names himself master of nature and the world. . . ."[6]

Contrasting Legacies of Environmental Policy

When some in this country try to link environmental protection with Communism, the Communist legacy shows us the fallacy of their arguments. Such false comparisons cannot stand. Yet, German Environment Minister Klaus Topfer warns that he sees, "emerging in the United States. . . something like ecologism—fear of a new Communism hidden behind ecology."[7]

In this country, environmental regulations combined with free-market mechanisms have worked to keep the environment relatively clean, and they are working right now. America will spend more than $115 billion dollars in 1992 on environmental protection of all kinds—more than any other country—and we have bought significant successes and created a legacy of our own with that money.

• We have cut lead levels in the air by 97 percent.
• We have cut our emissions of sulphur dioxide in half.
• We have invested more than $75 billion in federal, state and local money in waste water treatment facilities, and we have increased the number of people served by "secondary treatment" or better, to $144 million—a 69 percent increase in less than 20 years.
• We have beaten back point source pollution so effectively that today, about two-thirds of the nation's assessed surface waters meet their statutory goals, based on current water quality standards.

All of our rivers and streams may not be fishable and swimmable yet but, as former EPA administrator Bill Ruckelshaus once remarked, at least they are no longer flammable.

Environmental Stress and the Challenge for Future Policy

Still, there is a great deal left for us to do. The world around us is showing evidence of damage from abuse and overuse. Our oceans cry out. The waters which once teemed with fish have met their matches in technology. Bigger commercial fishing ships armed with sonar can find and harvest fish any time of the day or night, in any weather. In May 1992, *The New York Times* sketched this vivid picture:

> In 1954, the world's annual fish catch was 21,600,000 tons. In 1983 the amount had more than trebled, and the figure by last year was well over 100,000,000 tons. There is a limit to fish in the sea. . . if Ahab sought the White Whale today, he would almost certainly find a frail Leviathan, defiant still, but riddled with ailments.[8]

133

You have read about and heard General Williams talk about the now-endangered Snake River sockeye salmon; the annual migration of all salmon on the Columbia River is an eighth of what it once was. Our waters, which once seemed so vast and limitless, are not limitless after all.

We stand at a crossroads. We can ignore the evidence of damage and continue extracting resources without regard for their replenishment or the long-term health of the environment, or we can set a goal of sustainable development to pave the way for the success of future generations.

Sustaining The Environmental Infrastructure

In this country, the definition of sustainable development must and will evolve in the marketplace. As economist Michael Silverstein says, "Viewed from the perspective of national and international economics. . . we are on the verge of an opportunity."[9] In order to grasp the opportunities of sustainable development, we must define what we need to sustain us as we develop—what we might call our *environmental infrastructure*. When we look at the environment in that light, it is easy to see that it has value—not just aesthetic value, but hard, cold, cash-value. Like any other infrastructure, it serves us and makes possible our commerce. Moreover, like any other infrastructure, it breaks down and can be broken. Unlike any infrastructure of our making, it repairs itself if the stresses on it are not too severe.

This idea of a valuable environmental infrastructure is somewhat new to us. In an opinion survey published in late 1991, the Roper organization found that only one-fifth of the people surveyed listed protection of natural resources on which our economy relies as a reason to protect the environment.[10]

Yet, any good engineer can tell you what happens to flood control and erosion control without, for example, wetlands. General Williams' Corps of Engineers made a wise financial decision in the 1970s when it decided to preserve wetlands in the Charles River Basin in Massachusetts. By doing so the Corps saved the enormous costs of building dams and levees, and today the wetlands avert an estimated $17 million a year in flood losses.

Safeguarding Our Environmental Capital

Our environmental infrastructure is our capital. It is the factory which feeds and shelters us and often keeps us from harm. How long can we keep spending our capital before production slows and forces us to slow, too? How long can we abuse our environmental infrastructure without affecting the quality of our lives?

In closing, I will share with you a story I found in a little book called *The Quality of Life,* in which author James A. Michener looks at a variety of issues and how best to address them in our daily lives. One of those issues is development, and Michener argues for sustainable development this way,

134

It is quite possible that men require dogs and deer to keep them human. It is possible that we need cleaner air and quieter cities to keep us sane. There is a balance between beauty and business that must not be ignored. The quality of a good life depends in large measure on how a man reacts to his natural environment, and we cannot destroy one without diminishing the other.[11]

Sustainable development sustains us in many ways. I commend the AWRA for addressing this important topic, and I look forward to working with you.

Notes

1. William D. Ruckelshaus, "The Business End of Sustainable Growth," speech to the Globescope Pacific Assembly, Los Angeles, 1 November 1989.
2. Environment Opinion Study, Inc., "EOS2," Washington, D.C., June 1991.
3. "The Best Places to Live in America," *Money* magazine, September 1991.
4. "Voters See Big Needs At Home," *Washington Post,* 4 November 1992, A1.
5. President George Bush, "The President's Message on Environmental Quality," *22nd Annual Report,* The Council on Environmental Quality, 1991.
6. Vaclav Havel, "Rio and the New Millennium," *The New York Times,* 3 June 1992, A21.
7. Paul Lewis, Environment Minister of Germany, "U.S. at Earth Summit: Isolated and Challenged," *The New York Times,* 10 June 1992, A8.
8. Michael Specter, *The New York Times,* 3 May 1992, E5.
9. Michael Silverstein, "In Economics, Green Is Gold," *Christian Science Monitor,* 18 February 1992.
10. *Green Gauge 91,* The Roper Organization, November 1991.
11. James A. Michener, *The Quality of Life* (Philadelphia, 1970).

Comments

Gilbert F. White

The statements of experience and outlook from representatives of the Army Corps of Engineers and the Environmental Protection Agency outline the need for basic reassessment of the intellectual framework in which national water policy is formulated. Together, they suggest that the broad and loosely defined term "sustainable development" may point to an expansion of traditional concepts of optimal economic development and environmental protection.

We are all aware that the goal of sustainable development has a wide spectrum of connotations in the current scene. While several of the definitions are tantalizing in their ambiguity, and others are mutually opposing, I suspect that there is something close to consensus on a few elements. The time horizon is the indefinite future, rather than an investment period. The capacity of the environment is seen as providing opportunity for cultural as well as economic satisfaction, without any impairment of natural systems.

To the extent these concepts are accepted, they call for serious change in ways of using economic, engineering, and ecological analysis. This is anticipated in both presentations. The design concepts developed by the Corps of Engineers are challenging and highly ambitious.

One caution about the recognition of changing public values may be in order. While public opinion polls may reflect the views of people at a given time, they are affected by the information available, and the recent experience of the respondents, and are not necessarily a guide to future behavior. What people say often contrasts with what they do. This is illustrated by the current confusion about national wetlands policy. Concerned groups differ acutely over the aims and performance of the federal government's "no net loss" policy.

Two observations about policy development grow out of the presentations, and may be illustrated by recent experience at the global and local levels.

The media discussion of the United Nations Conference on Environment and Development at Rio places very heavy emphasis on the U.S. position with

136

respect to the proposed framework conventions on atmosphere and on biodiversity. The controversy over setting emission limits on greenhouse gases, and over strategies to reduce further loss of species, obscured consideration on the world scene of the forces driving continued deterioration of air, water, soil, and biota. The massive changes under way in population and in consumption patterns are subjecting the world's environment to tremendous stress. Today's world population of 5.3 billion, for example, may be expected to reach 7-8 billion in the twenty-first century, and possibly as much as 13 billion, depending upon policies and programs in place during the next two decades. Limiting carbon dioxide emissions is important, but far more important is action on problems of population and consumer demand.

Consider at the other extreme the case of government review of the proposed Two Forks dam for municipal water storage in the Upper South Platte Basin. The details of the controversy between water supply advocates and environmentalists are well-known. The environmental opposition, with its reasonable espousal of demand alternatives, prevailed in the final EPA decision. Still, no plan for the sustainable development of the South Platte Basin emerged. As all too often happens, when the goal is upholding standards for protection of one resource, people lose sight of what might be a genuinely harmonious, fruitful use of all resources for a healthy society.

Obviously, the challenges posed by the sustainable development concept in water management are enormous and unprecedented. Two of the possible steps to meet them are to focus on simple demonstrations of what is envisaged in practice, and to join in specifying an agenda for needed research.

The agencies and scientific groups involved should lose no time in demonstrating exactly what they mean by a plan for sustainable water development of an area. To only describe appropriate technologies and standards and regulations will not be enough.

Along with this, the water agencies should join with other management and scientific groups in outlining those problems that are especially deserving of research in the near future. The Sigma Xi Society and the International Council of Scientific Unions have already taken steps to prepare such an appraisal, and the Scientific Committee on Problems of the Environment has launched a more deliberate review on a regional basis. There is no doubt that any demonstration of genuinely thoughtful planning will reveal precise research needs, and that those will call out for early attention.

Myron B. Fiering

Sustainability is in, if only we could define and measure it! Almost exactly 30 years ago, when Arthur Maass and the Harvard Water Program published *Design of Water-Resource Systems*,[1] *optimality* was in. We devoted a lot of time to describing and searching the response surface, in quest of the global optimum. Today, time has tempered our ardor, and optimality has become near-optimality; our jargon now includes such temporizing, even humbling, concepts as fuzzy sets, sensitivity to unknown parameters, negotiation along Pareto frontiers, surprise, chaos, robustness, and Bayes regret. All these reflect our inability to predict the future perfectly, or even to assess the exact state of water-resource systems at any moment. They acknowledge our willingness to make good decisions while hoping for good outcomes; they recognize our need to compromise at less than the optimum.

So it is with sustainability, a vague and curious concept which conveys the notion that inherently stochastic water-resource systems, driven by increasing demands derived from a monotonically increasing population, can somehow manage to achieve long-term stability. It is Ponce de Leon's Fountain of Youth, and sounds much like what mathematicians call "steady state." We know that it sounds good, and that everybody appears to favor it, as we all favored optimality in its heyday.

It is not my intent here to attack the concept of sustainability or its proponents. Rather, it is to establish a context for its consideration and to note that other good ideas—ideas that "felt right" in water-resource usage but defied strict evaluation—have languished because of difficulty in assigning specific numerical values to them. Apart from optimality, resilience, robustness, and surprise come to mind. Mathematics and statistics are the disciplines through which sustainability might usefully be defined.

Suppose we say that a system is *sustainable* if it can be guaranteed to continue to function and to maintain its current characteristics for a long time. At least three qualifiers are required in this definition. First, we ask what is meant by a guarantee. Assign an argument α to be the probability that the guarantee will be honored (that the system will *not* change in a substantive way). We admit there is a small chance that some unforseen outcome will degrade the system, which leads to the second qualifier(s). What constitutes a significant change? Can the system be described by some powerful scalar index whose value traces the sustainability of development? If not, is a vector required? Of what dimension (how do we define the system in the first place)? How do we assess the significance of changes in each of its elements? Some argument β which might be a vector, is needed to assess the significance of the change(s).

Finally, not all statistically significant changes are necessarily bad. Population shifts, climate changes, geopolitical events and other activities occurring over the course of time might alter the demands imposed on the system so that development remains sustainable. This supports the need for an argument γ the time interval over which sustainability is defined. Thus we speak of a system being (α, β, γ)-sustainable, all of which resembles the standard language used in describing *ergodicity* of a stochastic process.

I certainly agree with General Williams' emphasis on the problem of population growth, and his articulation of the role of technology in extending the time through which our systems might serve in an apparently sustainable way, before the pressures induced by inevitable population increases render the system inadequate. In other words, technology properly applied can change α (make the system more reliable), change β (make the system more stable), change γ (extend the time to failure), or some combination of these. In the long run, I suspect we will see a continuing increase in average water demand due to inexorable population pressures, a less dramatic increase in average supply made available through application of the technology and training outlined by General Williams, and a necessarily unstable difference between them. Resource systems are not characterized by nice, neat stationary stochastic processes. To ask if the output of such a multidimensional system is stable or "sustained" is to pose a very hard question; it generally cannot be answered satisfactorily by examining the conventional measures of system performance because these are statistically unreliable, whereupon it becomes impossible to know, except in very gross ways, if system development can be called "sustainable."

I appeal to this audience to reject narrow definitions of sustainability, even though we might seem to have an intuitive sense of the meaning of the term. In our multidimensional world, driven by a continuously rising population, some of these descriptors will move one way and some will move another; some will respond quickly and some will respond sluggishly; but only rarely will there be responses sufficiently overt to support general agreement that system performance is no longer being sustained. The process is more nearly insidious, and in the absence of a clear, statistically based definition, such as those proposed[2] for resilience, the notion of sustainability is not sustainable.

Systems flip around. Holling[3] noted this behavior, along with the role of, and interplay among, slow and fast driving variables; others have studied the migration of environmental systems (including water-resource systems) in multidimensional phase-plane space, with appropriate stochastic elements built into the system description. A new domain of equilibrium, or perhaps cyclic variation between equilibria, or even chaotic behavior, all now appear to offer plausible modes of behavior derived from solutions to defensible system dynamics. Thus, I caution against simplistic, steady-state or equilibrium views of sustainability; it is a much more complicated characteristic.

Ms. Wilcher's paper deals particularly with sustainable health, both of ourselves and our ecosystems. Yet, we know that stress on systems for delivering our own health care has already begun to effect the quality of that care and the uniformity of its delivery. We are on the way to having our health care being homogenized and, ultimately, to having its average quality decrease as health care and budget conflict more powerfully. Why, then, should we not accept *some level* of environmental degradation in response to the increased environmental or resource stresses which population growth will impose? In other words, why should our development trajectories necessarily be fully sustainable? Why should we not develop some socially acceptable levels of (α, β, γ)?

Indeed, systems cannot be fully sustainable (corresponding to limiting values of the three arguments) unless technology, given all the opportunities described in these two papers, produces one major surprise after another. Some argue that man's history indicates we can count on this; I see less reason to be optimistic, and fully sustainable development does not appear to me to be attainable.

Notes

1. Arthur Maass, Maynard M. Hufschmidt, Robert Dorfman, Harold A. Thomas, Jr., Stephen A. Marglin, and Gordon Maskew Fair, *Design of Water-Resource Systems: New Techniques for Relating Economic Objectives, Engineering Analysis, and Governmental Planning* (Cambridge, Mass., 1962).
2. Myron B. Fiering, "Alternative Indices of Resilience," *Water Resources Research* 18, no. 1 (February 1982): 33-40.
3. C. S. Holling, "Resilience and Stability of Ecological Systems," *Annual Review of Ecology and Systematics* 4 (April 1971): 1-23.

Floodplain Management

Floodplain Management and Natural Systems

James M. Wright and Don L. Porter

Introduction

Some of our nation's most important assets are contained in its 3.5 million miles of rivers and streams, 84,000 miles of coastline, and adjacent lands. These riverine corridors and coastal zones provide a variety of valuable resources and contain substantial capital investments in structures important to the people who live and work in the area and to transportation and commerce. They contain most of the 100 million acres of remaining wetlands in the contiguous states and a considerable portion of the nation's most significant and diverse natural areas. These areas are sites with outstanding scenic or recreational importance or are unique in natural or scientific value. Nearly 10,000 miles of rivers have received designation under the Wild and Scenic Rivers Act. Coastal barrier islands are receiving increased protection.

Management of the nation's river and stream corridors and coastal zones involves a variety of disciplines, governments, programs, and activities and includes the private sector. The most resources probably are committed to the floodplain portion— the seven to ten percent of our nation's land area subject to the overflow from adjacent riverine watercourses or from coastal storm surge and wave action. Within these floodplains most management measures aim at reducing the economic losses resulting from flood events. Up to 20 percent of land in urban areas is subject to flood water inundation. About one-half of this flood-prone land is developed.

Present efforts at managing the nation's floodplains reflect an evolution in federal flood control policy and in the respective roles of federal, state, and local governments in minimizing flood losses. The past 25 years have witnessed a major expansion in the field of floodplain management—in legislation, technology, activity, and shifts in governmental roles. Many of these changes are in response to mounting flood losses resulting from unwise occupancy and use of our floodplains. More attention also is being given to the natural resource values and functions of floodplains and associated wetland areas.

Two major legislative acts have had a significant impact on current flood-plain management efforts—the National Flood Insurance Act of 1968 (P.L. 90-448) which focuses on flood loss reduction, and the National Environmental Policy Act of 1969 (P.L. 91-190) which provides for the consideration of environmental values in federal and federally supported actions.

Reducing Economic Losses

Under the National Flood Insurance Program (NFIP), relief from the impacts of flood damages became available to individuals in participating communities in the form of federally subsidized flood insurance, contingent on flood loss reduction measures embodied in local floodplain management regulations. Over 18,000 of some 22,000 flood-prone localities currently participate in the program. Individuals in these localities may purchase flood insurance, intended as a substitute for post-flood disaster assistance, and other forms of federal aid for flood recovery.[1]

Most of the nation's urban floodplains, involving some 40,000 stream miles, have been mapped as a result of efforts by several federal agencies and to a small extent by some states. Most rural areas remain unmapped. The one percent annual chance ("100-year") flood generally has been adopted as a minimum national standard for defining flood-prone areas and for planning flood loss reduction measures. These measures typically are grouped into those that reduce the susceptibility to flood damage, those designed to modify flooding, and those that modify the impact of flooding (Figure 1.1).[2]

In response to the NFIP's goal of reducing flood loss, most floodplain management measures carried out at the local level involve only floodplain regulations. They are not designed or intended to achieve other objectives. At a minimum, those regulations must meet criteria developed by the Federal Insurance Administration to implement the land-use component of the flood insurance program.[3] Most participating communities have enacted the federal criteria, although there are a number that have adopted more stringent regulations.

Where detailed flood hazard data are available, the NFIP criteria require adoption of local ordinances designating a floodway along the river or stream to allow for safe passage of floodwaters (Figure 1.2). Future development within the floodway is restricted to uses which will not further obstruct flood flows. Although new development is not prohibited, it is restricted considerably. Floodways also are considered impractical and unsafe for permanent human occupancy and use because of the depths and velocities of floodwaters.[4]

Through the NFIP, some 7,800 communities have designated nearly 6 million acres of river and stream corridors as floodways. These floodways contain many natural resources and a sizeable portion of our riverine wetlands. By restricting development within the floodway, local measures provide a limited

Strategies and Tools for Floodplain Management
Flood Loss Reduction
Modify Susceptibility to Flood Damage and Disruption

Floodplain Regulations
- State regulations for flood hazard areas
- Local regulations for flood hazard areas
  - Zoning
  - Subdivision regulations
  - Building codes
  - Housing codes
  - Sanitary and well codes
  - Other regulatory tools

Development and Redevelopment Policies
- Design and location of services and utilities
- Land rights, acquisition, and open-space use
- Redevelopment
- Permanent evacuation

Disaster preparedness
Disaster assistance
Floodproofing
Flood forecasting and warning systems and emergency plans

Modify Flooding

- Dams and reservoirs
- Dikes, levees, and floodwalls
- Channel alterations
- High-flow diversions
- Land treatment measures
- On-site detention measures

Modify the Impact of Flooding on Individuals and the Community

- Information and education
- Flood insurance
- Tax adjustments
- Flood emergency measures
- Postflood recovery

Figure 1.1. *Strategies and Tools for Floodplain Management*

144

Typical Floodway/Flooded Area Map

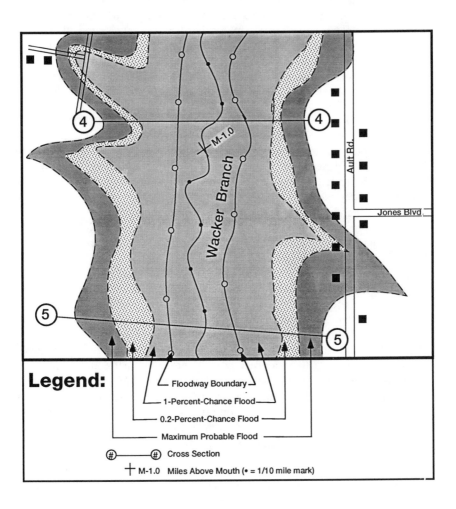

Figure 1.2. *Typical Floodway/Flooded Area Map*

degree of resource protection. More importantly, however, they provide a framework for managing these and other areas for multiple objectives.

In the remainder of the regulated floodplain, established by engineering studies to include those areas that would be inundated by a flood that has a 1 percent annual chance of occurrence, development must be protected by siting and construction practices (Figure 1.3). As a result of flood insurance program requirements, nearly 150,000 square miles, or about 100 million acres of our nation's floodplains, are regulated by local ordinances. The degree of commitment to and effectiveness of these regulations varies considerably from community to community and from state to state. Although there are a few notable exceptions, most communities have not implemented other floodplain management measures listed in Figure 1.1.

The Framework for Managing Natural Systems

Present programs, policies, and interest in the wise management and use of the many natural resources found in our nation's river corridors and coastal zones can be traced in large part to the National Environmental Policy Act (NEPA). In this measure, Congress formally recognized that environmental resources depend upon the functioning of complex natural systems. This act declared environmental quality to be a national goal and established a procedure for assessing the environmental impact of proposed federal projects and programs which could significantly affect the environment.

Federal agencies were required to develop implementing procedures and most assigned staff for this purpose. Thus, the legislative and administrative foundation was formally laid for an evaluation of the environmental resources associated with river corridors and coastal zones.

Interest in better floodplain management, however, preceded NEPA. The National Flood Insurance Act, passed by Congress in 1968, directed the development of proposals for a unified national program for floodplain management. A report prepared by the Federal Interagency Floodplain Management Task Force was issued first in 1976, and subsequently revised and updated in 1979[5] and 1986.[6] It sets two broad objectives: (1) to reduce loss of life and property due to floods and (2) to minimize losses of natural and beneficial resources from changes in land use by promoting the wise use and management of the nation's floodplains.

The report established a conceptual framework to guide the decision-making processes of federal, state, and local officials, as well as private parties. Strategies and tools for flood loss mitigation and for the preservation and restoration of natural floodplain resources were presented in detail. These resources were grouped into three broad categories—water, living, and cultural (Figure 1.4). To manage these resources, the report detailed strategies for restoring lost or degraded resources and for preserving the wide diversity of

Floodplain and Floodway Schematic

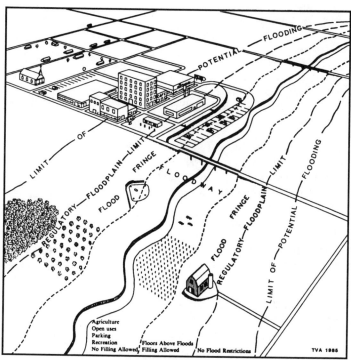

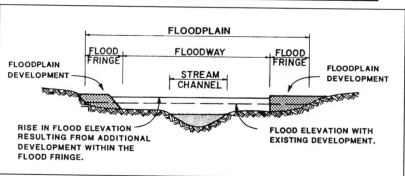

Figure 1.3. *Floodplain and Floodway Schematic*

Floodplain Natural and Cultural Resources
Water Resources

Natural Flood and Erosion Control
- Reduce flood velocities
- Reduce flood peaks
- Reduce wind and wave impacts
- Stabilize soils

Water Quality Maintenence
- Reduce sediment loads
- Filter nutrients and impurities
- Process organic and chemical wastes
- Moderate temperature of water
- Reduce sediment loads

Maintain Groundwater Supply and Balance
- Promote infiltration and aquifer recharge
- Reduce frequency and duration of low flows
    (increase/enhance base flow)

Living Resources

Support Flora
- Maintain high biological productivity of floodplain and wetland vegetation
- Maintain productivity of natural forests
- Maintain natural crops
- Maintain natural genetic diversity

Provide Fish and feeding grounds
- Create and enhance waterfowl habitat
- Protect habitat and rare and endangered species

Cultural Resources

Maintain Harvest of Natural and Agricultural Products
- Create and enhance agricultural lands
- Provide areas for cultivation of fish and shellfish
- Protect silvaculture
- Provide harvest of fur resources

Provide recreation oppurtunities
- Provide areas for active and consumptive uses
- Provide areas for passive activities
- Provide open-space values
- Provide aesthetic values

Provide Scientific Study and Outdoor Education Education Areas
- Provide opportunities for ecological studies
- Protect historical and archeological sites

Figure 1.4. *Floodplain Natural and Cultural Resources*

148

resources existing in relatively undisturbed floodplains (Figure 1.5). Finally, the authors recommended ways to coordinate resource management programs among all levels of government.

The goal of protecting and enhancing environmental quality is emphasized in other important legislation enacted over the past two decades, including the Wild and Scenic Rivers Act of 1968, the Coastal Zone Management Act of 1972, the Endangered Species Act of 1973, the Clean Water Acts of 1972 and 1977, the Coastal Barrier Resources Act of 1982, and the Water Quality Act of 1987.

Of these, the Clean Water Acts undoubtedly are the most important in preserving the natural and beneficial resources within riverine corridors. Section 404 of the Clean Water Act of 1972 supplemented the existing U.S. Army Corps of Engineers permitting program for activities in navigable waters (pursuant to section 10 of the Rivers and Harbors Act of 1899) by requiring permits for the discharge of dredged or fill materials into all waters of the United States. The act also directed the U.S. Environmental Protection Agency (EPA) to develop guidelines to assist in the implementation of section 404 and to prohibit or restrict discharges with unacceptable adverse impacts on fish, shellfish, wildlife, water supply, or recreation. Finally, the Water Quality Act of 1987 made sweeping revisions in EPA's approach to stormwater discharge permitting. It directed the EPA to prepare regulations and implement a permit system for separate stormwater sewer systems. Water quality monitoring and mitigation programs emerged as new responsibilities for river corridor managers.

The Coastal Zone Management Act provided for more attention to coastal resources, and the Coastal Barrier Resources Act placed a general prohibition on all federal activities that might encourage or support further development of barrier islands. Implementation of these and other laws helped set the stage for the 1977 Executive Orders on Floodplain Management (11988) and Protection of Wetlands (11990). These orders accompanied President Carter's *Message on the Environment to Congress* which outlined the scope of environmental issues and pledged firm support to environmental protection.[7]

The Executive Order on Floodplain Management linked concerns for human safety, health, welfare, and property with concerns for restoring and preserving natural and beneficial floodplain resources. The order's policy directive is to (1) avoid direct or indirect support of floodplain development; (2) avoid actions located in or affecting the floodplain, unless the floodplain location is the only practicable alternative; and (3) in the absence of a practicable alternative, require that the action be designed or modified in order to minimize potential harm to or within the floodplain.

The Executive Order for Protection of Wetlands, issued at the same time, is closely related and similar in structure. This relationship has been highlighted in implementation of both orders. Because most inland wetlands are located within riverine floodplains, the orders often cover the same areas. Experience

Strategies and Tools for Floodplain Management
Resource Protection

Restore and Preserve the Natural and
Culltural Resources of Floodplains

Floodplain, Wetland, Coastal Barrier Resources Regulations
- Federal regulations
- State regulations
- Local regulations
  - Zoning
  - Subdivision regulations
  - Building codes
  - Housing codes
  - Sanitary and well codes
  - Other regulations

Development and redevelopment Policies
- Design and location of services and utilities
- Land rights, acquisitiion, and open-space
- Redevelopment
- Permanent evacuation

Information and Education

Tax adjustments

Administrative Measures

Figure 1.5. *Strategies and Tools for Floodplain Management*

in implementation strongly suggests the need for integrated management of wetlands and floodplains within river corridors. *It also shows that floodplain management should be regarded as a process by which decisions are made, rather than simply a set of floodplain regulations, flood insurance, or flood control structures.* This also is true for managing wetlands and other natural resources.

At the state level, numerous regulatory and nonregulatory programs have been developed that apply directly or indirectly to floodplains, wetlands, shoreline, and natural resource protection. Many of these have paralleled federal efforts in resource management and environmental protection.

A New Approach to Floodplain Management

This management framework has led to a greater recognition of the multiple functions of floodplains and provided guidance for maintaining or restoring the resources they contain. With the framework in place, and experience showing the drawbacks of working with limited objectives or floodplain areas, there is a growing interest in looking at the entire river corridor as a functioning system, even encompassing total watershed management. This interest probably results from several factors.

Over the past few decades, better methodologies have been developed to identify and quantify the natural and beneficial resources and values found in river corridors and coastal zones. These resources are described in detail in various reports[8] and are listed in Figure 1.4. They provide many economic, social, and environmental benefits of great value to local communities and their citizens. Their value is evident when the cost of replacing lost or diminished resources is calculated.

In addition, interdisciplinary and intergovernmental cooperation is increasing. Since most riverine wetlands are located within floodplains, wetland managers, floodplain managers, and other natural resources managers are discovering that their program goals overlap and they share many interests and needs. Floodplain managers find that single-objective management approaches do not work as well as they could or should. Most floodplain management objectives and practices use existing watershed and floodplain conditions to determine areas of involvement. They focus on controlling future development rather than on existing problems, look at only a small portion of the floodplain and river corridor and coastal zone (typically, the area that would be inundated by the 1 percent annual chance flood), and have but one purpose—flood loss reduction. To make matters worse, most existing programs deal with floodplain resource management decisions on a case-by-case basis.

As a result, communities and citizens have little interest in floodplain management for the sole purpose of flood loss reduction. Most programs exist because of NFIP requirements. What support exists is often tacit. Not only is the occurrence of the regulatory ("100-year") flood perceived as unlikely; many people believe the government will bail them out if a major flood occurs, restoring everything to preflood conditions or better.

Developing multipurpose management plans and programs to meet a number of community needs helps broaden the political and public support needed for success. This, in turn, enhances the opportunity for funding, especially when the coordination of plans and programs allows for greater efficiencies and the elimination of duplication. Also, individual citizens, organizations, and community groups are now taking a greater interest in the welfare of river corridor and coastal zone areas. They are becoming better organized and increasingly vocal in presenting their views and wishes. Whether government

151

is ready or not, they are demanding an increased level of stewardship of our water resources.

The Record of Accomplishments

Nationwide data to measure the benefits of floodplain management in protecting natural systems are not available. However, some general findings can be offered.

With a wider recognition of the natural and cultural resources found in floodplains, a better understanding of their value, and improved procedures to measure impacts on these resources,[9] floodplain managers are beginning to integrate resource conservation or restoration techniques into more traditional flood loss reduction strategies.

In a 1986 report, the Federal Interagency Floodplain Management Task Force recognized that a unified national program for floodplain management should have two broad national goals: (1) flood loss reduction and (2) preservation and restoration where necessary of the natural and beneficial resources of floodplains.[10] In preparing an assessment of floodplain management in the United States,[11] the task force sought to evaluate the degree of success in achieving these goals.

The work of the task force, made up of ten federal agencies, was aided immeasurably by representation from the U.S. Environmental Protection Agency's Office of Wetlands Protection. Created in response to the continuing loss and degradation of the nation's wetlands, this office helped to integrate the task force's flood loss reduction and resource protection strategies to achieve the two broad goals for floodplain management.[12]

Communities are not required to preserve the natural resources and associated values of floodplains as a condition for participation in the National Flood Insurance Program. However, provisions of the program help to preserve and protect floodplains through restrictions on development within riverine floodways. Therefore, limited preservation and restoration of floodplain natural and cultural resources have been accomplished through flood loss reduction actions. The extent of these accomplishments is unknown.

Over the past five years, the floodplain management community has conducted ten regional or national workshops on the natural resources and functions of floodplains, multiobjective planning, and various regulatory and protection techniques that are commonly employed.[13] The title of the National Association of State Floodplain Managers' annual conference in 1992 was Multi-Objective Approaches to Floodplain Management.[14] Numerous papers reflecting this theme were presented at the conference.

The U.S. Army Corps of Engineers and other federal water resources development agencies are conducting various environmental protection, restoration, and mitigation initiatives to offset the impacts of federally-assisted

152

projects. They also provide support for programs of other resource protection agencies. Recognizing the need to promote the benefits of better management of natural systems at the local level, the Tennessee Valley Authority recently developed a pamphlet entitled *Conserving Your Valuable Floodplain Resources.*[15]

There are many notable examples of communities that are carrying out multiobjective planning and implementation of river corridor management plans for park, parkway, wildlife, conservation, or other environmental or social uses. These include Boulder Colorado; Chattanooga, Tennessee; Minneapolis/St. Paul, Minnesota; Raleigh, North Carolina; Scottsdale, Arizona; and Tulsa, Oklahoma. Some of these efforts have been implemented through flood damage reduction or other floodplain management activities.

New approaches to solving agricultural flood problems are also being developed and implemented. These endeavors recognize the need to maintain stream systems that are functioning or to restore those that are damaged. For example, the Tennessee Valley Authority has provided technical and financial assistance to help develop and implement an environmentally sensitive stream channel restoration program in west Tennessee. Local soil conservation districts covering an eight-county area lead this project. It was designed to improve or restore the within-bank streamflow capacity to reduce the incidence and duration of flooding during the growing season and to provide improved drainage to areas of stressed bottomland hardwood forests. The program has resulted in the restoration of over 100 miles of stream channels without the use of draglines, backhoes, or excavators. Area landowners and conservation and environmental groups are well satisfied with the program's success.

Needs and Oppurtunities for Improving Resource Protection

There are many unmet needs and opportunities for improving resource protection in the field of floodplain management. What has been accomplished thus far has been largely the result of programs, policies, and efforts outside the field. Better integration of flood loss reduction and natural resources protection remains a compelling need. Over the past 30 years, a wide array of new laws and programs have been established to protect natural resources. However, many of the existing programs for flood loss reduction and resource protection apply to differing geographic areas. Most local flood loss reduction programs focus primarily on the "100-year" floodplain, while natural resource protection programs focus on a particular resource which may or may not be located in the floodplain.

Federal agencies can lead the way by identifying opportunities within the context of existing programs to better conserve the natural and cultural resources of the floodplain. They can work to minimize actual and potential conflicts that exist in many agency programs and to bring about changes in the missions of programs and the way they work. The Federal Interagency Floodplain Management Task Force will address this issue as it revises its 1986 report. The National Association of State Floodplain Managers recently formed a task force on multiobjective management.

Significant advances have been made in our understanding of natural resource functions and the importance of maintaining the nation's natural and cultural heritage. However, if floodplain management is to achieve its potential for resource conservation, floodplain management professionals will need to learn more about these functions and possible protection techniques. They also will need to understand better the benefits and to accept the need for their involvement. It is these professionals who develop programs and measures to implement policies and who can advocate changes in present policies and programs to promote resource conservation.

Various information and data sources have been developed which already aid and can continue to aid this understanding. These include sources of data and information on natural and/or cultural resources, including resource quality and quantity; biodiversity; endangered and threatened species; unique resources; and environmental and cultural resource locations, sites, and networks. Of particular note is the national wetlands mapping program of the U.S. Fish and Wildlife Service.

Wetland and other resource information can be juxtaposed on floodplain maps through geographic information systems (GIS) and used in other ways by floodplain managers. For example, the state of Tennessee is currently developing a comprehensive wetlands conservation plan which will be GIS based. Several federal agencies and conservation organizations are assisting in this effort. A companion state-wide rivers assessment program is just getting underway. It also will be GIS-based. In addition, the Tennessee Conservation League has a three-year program underway to develop a state-wide GIS-based system to determine the state's terrestrial biological diversity using neotropical migrant bird species as indicators of overall habitat quality. The rivers assessment program is intended to be the aquatic component of this state-wide biological diversity evaluation. Because these three projects will be established on compatible GIS bases, Tennessee communities with GIS capability will have access to a wealth of natural resource data on which to base floodplain management or other land use decisions.

The Environmental Protection Agency's Office of Wetlands Protection can provide technical assistance to floodplain managers on how to maintain and/or restore the natural resources of floodplains.[15] The National Park Service has assisted communities in planning greenways along river corridors. This has been accomplished primarily through the Service's State and Local Rivers Conservation Assistance Program. Help is available in carrying out statewide river assessments and preparing river corridor plans.[16] This assistance offers floodplain managers many opportunities to carry out resource protection and other multiobjective goals.

Multiobjective management of floodplains, stream corridors, and coastal zones is both a need and a goal. There are increasing opportunities and challenges to put together plans and programs to meet a number of community needs, to increase political and public support for the recommended measures, and to enhance the opportunities for implementation through multiple funding packages. One goal should be to achieve broader resource management and protection.

Floodplains are only one part of the watershed and often cannot be managed effectively unless a total watershed approach is taken. For instance, watershed pollution affects rivers, streams, and their floodplains and associated wetland. Thus, resource management or restoration plans for these waters and lands cannot be implemented effectively without addressing such problems as excessive upland erosion or municipal and industrial pollution. Plans must cross political jurisdictions. Natural resources do not recognize manmade boundaries; neither do floods. By focusing only on the floodplain, many opportunities for examining alternatives to floodplain development are lost, and the particular role of the floodplain within the total watershed is not properly appreciated.

At present, there is not enough nationwide data to document resource losses or to measure accurately the success or failure of various management approaches. This inability to provide for a quantifiable measurement greatly hinders needed policy changes, new approaches to floodplain management decision making, and the allocation of limited resources.

Conclusion

Many of our nation's most biologically productive, environmentally sensitive, and culturally important areas are found in floodplains. All of these natural and cultural resources, however, are not associated exclusively with floodplains. They are a unique and important component of a larger set of resources and values. As a result, with the exception of some riparian and estuarine resource management programs, most programs that serve to protect floodplain resources have not been developed specifically for floodplain application. They apply to resources found outside the floodplain as well. A wide range of such programs, typically containing regulatory measures and requirements, have been enacted at all governmental levels.

Floodplain management has helped to protect beneficial natural and cultural resources found within the nation's river and stream corridors and coastal zones. However, the record of accomplishments to date has been limited. This is because of the narrow focus of agency missions and program requirements, along with a general lack of understanding by professionals, typically engineers and planners, of the natural resource functions and values of floodplains. Moreover, these professionals are often unfamiliar with resource conservation approaches that could be integrated effectively with flood loss reduction strategies.

Because floodplains contain a considerable portion of the nation's most diverse and important natural and cultural resources, floodplain managers will continue to encounter these resources and resource managers on a regular basis. They must be prepared to play an expanding role in helping to protect these resources through coordinated interdisciplinary approaches.

Floodplain management can greatly benefit from a broadened mission. Integrating environmental protection measures with existing flood loss reduction strategies will increase interest and support for floodplain management at all governmental levels and from nongovernmental sources, including concerned citizens and special interest groups.

Notes

1. U.S. Federal Emergency Management Agency (FEMA), *Questions and Answers About the National Flood Insurance Program* (Washington, D.C., February 1990).
2. FEMA, Interagency Task Force on Floodplain Management, *A Unified National Program for Floodplain Management* (Washington, D.C., 1986).
3. National Flood Insurance Program, 44 Code of Federal Reculations (CFR) 60.3
4. American Planning Association, *Regulations for Floodplains*, Planning Advisory Service Report No. 277 (Chicago, February 1972).
5. U.S. Water Resources Council, *A Unified National Program for Floodplain Management* (Washington, D.C., 1976, 1979).
6. FEMA, *A Unified National Program for Floodplain Management,* 1986.
7. Executive Order 1988—Floodplain Management and Executive Order 11990—Protection of Wetlands, Washington, D.C. issued on 24 May 1977 by President Carter.
8. President's Commission on American Outdoors, *American Outdoors, the Legacy, the Challenge* (Washington, D.C., 1987); American Planning Association, *Protecting Nontidal Wetlands,* Planning Advisory Service Report No. 412/413 (Chicago, December 1988); The Urban Land Institute, *Wetlands: Mitigating and Regulating Development Impacts* (Washington, D.C., 1990); Tennessee Valley Authority (TVA), *Conserving Your Valuable Floodplain Resources* (Knoxville, TN, November 1991).
9. The Urban Land Institute, *Wetlands: Mitigating and Regulating Development Impacts.*
10. FEMA, *A Unified National Program for Floodplain Management*
11. Federal Interagency Floodplain Management Task Force, *Floodplain Management in the United States: An Assessment Report* (Washington, D.C., 1992)
12. American Planning Association, *Wetlands Protection: A Local Government Handbook* (Washington, D.C, and Chicago, September 1991).

13. Association of State Floodplain Managers, *Multi-Objective River Corridor Planning,* Proceedings of Colorado Springs and Knoxville Workshops, 1989 (Madison, WI, May 1991).
14. Association of State Floodplain Managers, *Multi-Objective Approaches to Floodplain Management*, 16th Annual Conference, Grand Rapids, MI, 18-22 May 1992.
15. United States Environmental Protection Agency, Office of Wetlands Protection, *America's Wetlands: Our Vital Link Between Land and Water* (Washington, D.C., February 1988).
16. U.S. Department of the Interior, National Park Service, *A Casebook in Managing Rivers for Multiple Uses* (Washington, D.C., October 1991).

Flood Control, Urban Stream Corridors, and Clean Water Strategies

L. Scott Tucker

Introduction

Flood control in an urban environment offers an opportunity to develop valuable multipurpose resources. What is necessary is a vision of utilizing major drainageways as open, green, urban corridors, along with the ability to pursue that vision over a long period of time. The value of urban stream corridors beyond flood control ranges from passive open space, to active parks, to hiker/biker transportation corridors, to wildlife areas, to groundwater recharge basins.

Local governments throughout the nation, in many cases in partnerships with the federal government, have been addressing urban flooding problems for many years. There are no federal mandates requiring local governments to address urban flooding, but they have done so because there is local political support and the problems are of high priority.

Authorities in the Denver, Colorado, metropolitan area created a regional flood control agency, the Urban Drainage and Flood Control District (UDFCD) in 1969 in response to flooding and the multijurisdictional nature of the problem. The UDFCD and its constituent communities have been addressing flooding problems since 1969 on a partnership basis utilizing an array of structural and nonstructural approaches. Funding has been on a pay-as-you-go basis, and priorities and implementation have been kept at the local level.

Fiscal constraints at all levels of government are becoming a painful reminder that government cannot solve all problems. In 1972, with the passage of the Federal Water Pollution Control Act Amendments (the Clean Water Act of 1972 or CWA), the nation embarked on an aggressive program to improve the quality of the nation's waters. Since that time significant progress has been made, but the costs of environmental protection are growing and we need to reevaluate the nation's approaches to environmental problems,

158

including our ability to finance such investment. All problems cannot be solved. Consequently, we need a mechanism to prioritize problems and allocate limited resources to high priority areas. Recent studies by the Environmental Protection Agency (EPA) indicate that annual expenditures for environmental protection will increase from $40 billion in the 1987 base year to $61 billion in the year 2000.[1] Moreover, local governments are bearing a larger and larger portion of the public costs. They spent about $26 billion or 76 percent of the public share of environmental costs in 1981, but EPA expects the local share to be $48 billion a year or 87 percent of public costs by the year 2000.[2]

The competition for public dollars will intensify in the future. There will be pressure to make better use of public resources. This will make multiple use of urban stream corridors an even more attractive and important concept. However, some tradeoffs with environmental protection goals may be necessary, and different approaches to achieving an improved environment may have to be considered. This paper examines urban stream corridor approaches in the Denver, Colorado, metropolitan area; apparent conflicts between the urban corridor concept and the objectives of the CWA; problems with the basic approach to regulation of urban separate storm sewer systems; and considerations of other approaches to water quality protection.

Urban Stream Corridors in the Denver Area

As mentioned, it is essential that managers of an urban stream corridor program have a vision and the ability to pursue that vision over time. In the Denver area the vision of the UDFCD was, and still is, to use major drainageways as open, green, urban corridors. The vision has been pursued by UDFCD and local governments in the Denver area in different ways, including the construction of flood control projects, regulation of new developments along floodways, maintenance of major drainageways, coordination and cooperation with recreational interests and greenway foundations, and construction of trails along major drainageways for maintenance access. For the UDFCD, a corridor of some kind is an end product of all projects except for storm sewer improvements. New land development projects that affect a floodplain are required to meet basic floodplain management criteria including maintenance access, and developers are encouraged to leave as much "green" as possible.

It was not always that way. Denver was founded at the confluence of the South Platte River and Cherry Creek following the discovery of gold in 1858. It was the river, the creek, the trees, and the wildlife that attracted settlers to that specific location. Denver has a semiarid climate and receives about 15 inches of moisture a year. The streams are fairly small with steep gradients and fairly narrow floodplains. Originating in the mountains or high country to the west of Denver, the streams usually have natural base flows; the drainages headwatering in the plains to the east and south of Denver are naturally dry much of the time. Urbanization has changed that, however, and most major drainageways now have a continuous base flow which can largely be attributed to irrigation return waters.

Indians warned the newcomers of flood danger by indicating how high in the trees the flood waters would rise. Yet, it was hard to believe how such small streams in such an arid climate could ever flood to such an extent. Development continued to take place in the floodplain areas, and it was only a matter of time before flooding became a problem. A flood on Cherry Creek that occurred in the early 1860s is shown in Figure 2.1. Eventually the streams and drainageways were channelized and dams were built upstream of the city to control such flooding.

Figure 2.1. *Cherry Creek Flood, 1860.*

The "big" flood in the Denver area occurred on the South Platte River in June 1965. Twenty-one people died, the flood damaged or destroyed some 2,500 homes and 750 businesses, and damage estimates ranged from $103 million to $325 million.[3] The 1965 flood made people realize that flooding could not be adequately addressed on a city by city, county by county basis. The result was the creation of the UDFCD in 1969. The UDFCD encompassed the entire City and County of Denver, portions of five suburban counties surrounding Denver, and thirty suburban cities and towns. The population of the 1,600 square mile area is about 1.8 million.

The regional district gave reality to the vision of open, green, urban stream corridors. It provided the mechanism to focus on the vision, to better define it, to pursue it over a long period of time, and to provide a degree of consistency throughout the metropolitan area. From the beginning, UDFCD personnel believed that urban streams and drainageways had more value than just as a floodway. Granted, the District's interests were drainage and flood control. But what if the drainageways were left open, what if they were green, what if there was a trail for public access, what if they were left undisturbed, what if they became hiker/biker/transportation corridors, what if they hosted wildlife, what if there was boating? All of these uses are compatible with flood control. The idea was to preserve open stream corridors and to develop uses for them over time.

The UDFCD has emphasized the need for maintenance access and all UDFCD-sponsored projects, as well as projects reviewed by the District, are required to have maintenance access. Maintenance access can double as public access, and the District has developed many popular urban trails along the drainageways. Once citizens begin to use these corridors, they usually support trail maintenance and improvements.

The UDFCD attempts to coordinate the development of corridors and to minimize spotty and incompatible approaches. The District developed regional design criteria that are used by all communities in the area. Local governments have adopted and conscientiously enforce floodplain regulations. It is UDFCD policy that local governments own and be responsible for major drainageway facilities and corridors, but the UDFCD provides to local governments the regular maintenance needed for facilities and corridors. Any facilities constructed by others after 1983 must be designed and built to meet UDFCD requirements in order to be eligible for UDFCD maintenance assistance. The UDFCD reviews and comments on proposed developments in floodplain areas at the request of local governments, and the maintenance eligibility policy is the carrot to induce developers to meet basic criteria when they engage in new projects.

The UDFCD has developed a floodplain/floodway preservation policy and has established a $500,000 special fund to purchase floodplain properties. Purchase of floodplain properties is only done when other methods of preventing inappropriate development of floodplains and floodways—such as floodplain regulations, subdivision regulations, and public land dedication requirements—have been exhausted.

In 1987 the Colorado General Assembly provided the UDFCD with funding authorization for the South Platte River (SPR), the major river in the Denver area. The SPR runs throughout the length of the UDFCD from south to north for a total of about 40 miles. A special levy for the SPR generates about $1 million per year, which has been used to clean, maintain, stabilize, revegetate, and acquire rights-of-way on the SPR. The $1 million a year enables us to preserve, improve and maintain this valuable corridor over a long period of time.

Other programs in the Denver area have been effective in developing urban stream corridors, and the UDFCD has encouraged their efforts and participated in many of their projects. Of particular note is the Greenway Foundation which spearheaded an effort that turned the SPR from a dirty nothing of a river into an important regional asset.[4] The Arapahoe Greenway and Adams County Greenway foundations have also made significant contributions to stream corridor development in the Denver metro area.

Figure 2.2 shows the publicly owned or controlled drainageway corridors as of 1992. Examples of various types of urban stream corridors are shown in figures 2.3 through 2.7. The stream corridor facilities are owned by many different public entities including cities, counties, and park and recreation districts. These stream corridors, like highways, link the various communities in a unique way, and have become important components of the Denver area urban infrastructure system.

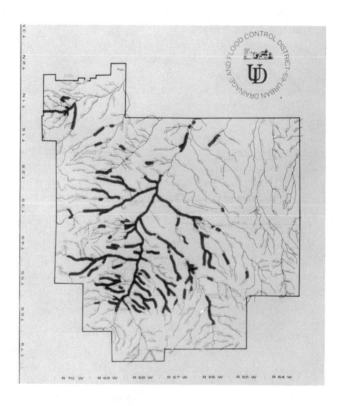

Figure 2.2. *Publicly Owned or Controlled Drainageways in Denver Metro Area.*

Figure 2.3. *Natural Floodplain Corridor Along Bear Creek in Lakewood, Colorado.*

Figure 2.4. *Cherry Creek Corridor in Denver Near Cherry Creek Shopping Center.*

Figure 2.5. *Little Dry Creek in Downtown Englewood, Colorado.*

Figure 2.6. *Portion of 30 Mile Continuous Trail Corridor along South Platte River through Denver Metro Area.*

Figure 2.7. Rafting and Kayaking through Denver Metro Area on South Platte River.

Urban Stream Corridors and the Clean Water Act

Urban stream corridors have inherent value as urban resources. They take on many different forms including hard edges, boat chutes, natural areas, fountains, concrete channels, soft bottoms, rock sides, parallel trails, grade control structures, etc. A common denominator is their value to the people of the urban area. The urban corridor vision must be realistic and must accommodate and indeed encourage different approaches.

It is also important to understand that urbanization has significant impacts on what were once natural streams. Urban streams undergo fundamental changes during the urbanization process that must be recognized and accepted. The impact is obvious when development results in channeling of one kind or another. However, even if a stream or floodplain is not modified directly, the construction of large areas of impervious surfaces cause hydrologic changes, including more frequent runoff events, higher peak flows, and increased volume of runoff which in turn cause erosion problems. Also trash and debris have a way of finding their way to the stream corridors. Regular maintenance, including trash and debris pick-up, mowing in some cases, and erosion control work, is necessary to keep corridors functioning, clean, and attractive.

Because UDFCD assisted three cities in the Denver area in applying for NPDES (National Pollutant Discharge Elimination System) permits for their municipal storm sewer systems, the UDFCD has been introduced to the CWA. From the UDFCD's perspective there seems to be a conflict between the basic premise of the CWA and the concept of an urban stream corridor. The CWA constituted a dramatic national commitment to clean up our rivers, lakes, streams, and wetlands. Strong language was needed as well as lofty goals because there was a long way to go. Because of the CWA, the U.S. has made significant improvements to water quality. However, as obvious problems are addressed, the emphasis is shifting to other pollutant sources where benefits will not be so apparent and easily identified.

The first sentence of the Act states that "The objective of this Act is to restore and maintain the chemical, physical, and biological integrity of the Nation's waters."[5] Taken literally, the word "restore" is troubling. "Good" water quality is critical to developing usable, attractive, and safe urban stream corridors. Yet, it is unrealistic to think in terms of "restoring" the chemical, physical, and biological integrity of developed urban corridors, such as those shown in Figures 2.3-2.7, to conditions prior to the appearance of the first white settlers, which appears to be the literal national objective. The clock cannot be turned back.

Realistically, it is even difficult to apply specific criteria to such goals as biological integrity. For example, the State of Colorado is considering the adoption of biological criteria as water quality standards. The Water Quality Control Division staff has concluded that biological criteria should not be adopted as water quality standards at this time.[6] Among the reasons, the staff cites a lack of data for streams in Colorado that can be used for specifying appropriate "reference reaches" or assessing the comparative biological integrity of affected streams.[7] They also note that it is extremely difficult to find unimpaired reference waters for the water bodies and habitat types which are commonly affected by point source discharges in Colorado.[8] It is time to reassess the goals of the CWA and bring them closer to reality.

Good water quality must remain a high priority, and good water quality is an important and necessary component of a viable urban stream corridor such as those illustrated. However, urban stream corridors have a unique value in an urban context and provide important character to the urban environment. They need to be preserved and enhanced for what they are. It is not practical to think in terms of restoring their physical, chemical, and biological integrity to some predevelopment condition. They are forever changed.

Is it Time for a CWA Midcourse Correction?

The heart of the U.S. effort to clean its waters is the NPDES, which is a regulatory process. Congress establishes goals, objectives, and requirements, and, pursuant to NPDES, the EPA promulgates detailed regulations setting forth specific requirements. While Congress has established mandates limiting pollution, little attention has been given to the question of how to pay for the facilities and programs required to meet the mandates. The result has been a relatively small share of federal dollars committed to environmental clean-up, with the burden increasingly falling on the backs of local governments. The same is true of other federally mandated environmental programs, such as drinking water standards, clean air requirements, sewage treatment plant effluent limitations, sludge standards, combined sewer overflow requirements, and most recently municipal storm sewer discharge regulations.

Each program is addressed without reference to the other mandates, and the cost to local governments of meeting the mandates is not assessed. For example, pursuant to the 1972 CWA and the amendments in the 1987 Clean Water Act all municipalities and the urban portion of counties with a population in excess of 100,000 must apply for NPDES permits for their municipal storm sewer systems by November 1992 or May 1993.[9] The applications will set forth management plans and monitoring programs that will become the compliance basis of a 5-year NPDES permit for the local governments. Congress justified the permit program based on results from the Nationwide Urban Runoff Program (NURP), which indicated the presence of various pollutants in urban stormwater runoff, and on other more general types of assessments showing that urban stormwater runoff significantly impaired beneficial use. However, there were no studies of the costs and benefits of various responses to the problem. Only now are estimates being developed on the cost to local government of implementing an urban stormwater control program. A recent study indicates that the capital cost for nationwide implementation of stormwater management programs could range from $36.2 million to over $420 billion depending on the level of management practices required. Operations and maintenance (O&M) costs would range from nearly $5 billion to over $545 billion for the five levels examined.[10]

On the other side of the equation, the benefits in terms of water quality improvements are unknown on a nationwide scale. There does not seem to be much argument that urban stormwater contains pollutants or that in some locations urban stormwater impairs beneficial use. The issue is whether or not it is cost effective to launch a nationwide program of stormwater controls, rather than evaluating problems at the local level and allocating limited resources to the highest priority problems. For example, the urban stormwater quality problem in Phoenix is distinctly different than it is in a state such as Florida where many inland lakes are surrounded by urban areas. What is missing is a way to prioritize problems on a watershed basis, establish goals and objectives that consider cost effectiveness, identify the various pollutant sources and their impact, and evaluate various approaches that consider available resources and cost effectiveness.

All this is difficult to achieve. One problem is the diffused nature of the institutional arrangements for providing urban water related services. In any one metropolitan area there are numerous water purveyors, sewerage authorities, large cities, small cities, counties, special purpose districts, and in some cases even more than one state involved in water related activities. To this, add a mix of agricultural runoff, silviculture, mining impacts, and industrial sources, and the complexity increases. Unless a mechanism is found to allocate responsibility and costs fairly, it will remain difficult if not impossible to approach water quality enhancement on a more rational basis.

Contrasted to the United States' classic federal command and control approach is the direction taken by Great Britain. All water, sewerage, and pollution regulatory functions in Great Britain are carried out by ten recently privatized water companies.[11] The ten private water companies replaced ten public water authorities in 1989, and the ten public water authorities replaced several thousand different local authorities or other public bodies that were responsible for water, sewer, and pollution regulatory functions prior to 1974. Environmental objectives are developed taking into account the needs of the ecosystem and interests of the water service companies, the regulated community, and regulatory agencies. Their approach is based on the development of strategic plans for pollution control on a watershed scale that provides the most benefit or least damage to the environment at an affordable cost. A notable difference between the U.S. and British approaches is that the U.S. has established somewhat arbitrary and absolute objectives that must be met regardless of cost while British objectives include consideration of cost.

It is hard to imagine how the U.S. could consolidate all its water-related functions into a few water authorities or private companies. There is simply too much emphasis on local control and too many water companies, sewerage authorities, drainage and flood control districts, cities and counties in the U.S. to think that national or regional consolidation is possible—at least within the next 20 to 30 years. The U.S. may have to live with the premise that muddling through is a viable alternative.

The Municipal Separate Storm Sewer Permit System—A Case in Point

The approach being taken to control the impacts of pollution from municipal storm sewer systems is an example of the disjointed and sometimes seemingly illogical approach the U.S. takes toward achieving clean water. Congress clarified its mandate regarding the control of pollution from municipal separate storm sewer systems in the 1987 Clean Water Act, and the EPA published stormwater regulations in November 1990 that set forth the permit requirements to be followed by cities and counties applying for NPDES permits.

Below we will discuss the problems with EPA's approach and recommend some mid-course corrections.

Regulatory Approach

The NPDES program is a classic federal command and control approach. It is by nature adversarial and does not lend itself to cooperative efforts between the local level of government and the state and federal levels. Local communities are defined as polluters because of their storm sewer systems and must obtain permits for the discharge of stormwater or face fines and penalties. Costs of meeting permit conditions are not an issue with the regulators, and the bottom line is that local governments must comply with the promulgated regulations. Costs may become a political consideration, however, if implementation of the mandates forces noticeably higher local taxes, reductions in other services, or both.

It would seem more logical if stormwater pollution is indeed a serious national problem for federal, state, and local governments to address the issue on a cooperative basis. There is certainly no financial support from federal programs for municipal stormwater as there once was for wastewater treatment. Local governments are on their own in terms of meeting the federal mandate.

Municipal Stormwater as a Point Source

Municipal separate storm sewer systems are being regulated as point sources of pollution through the NPDES program. The purpose of the NPDES permit program is to prohibit the discharge of any pollutant from a point source by any person without a permit.[12] Typical point sources include discharges from publicly owned treatment works (POTWS) and industrial treatment facilities. These are generally closed systems with fairly predictable discharges from a single pipe; they can be measured and sampled at regular intervals, and there are relatively few of them.

Municipal stormwater by contrast is a rainfall driven system which varies considerably from region to region, city to city, area to area within a city, storm to storm, season to season, etc. It is an open system with no controls over the inputs, yet a city or county is held responsible for what comes out the ends of the pipes. Potential sources of pollution are diverse, difficult to identify, and variable; the discharges occur at many, many locations. Municipal stormwater runoff is in reality not a point source, yet the regulatory program in which it has been placed is a point source program.

Confusion on Standards to Be Met

In recognition of the difference between classic point sources and municipal separate storm sewer systems, Congress defined a different standard in the

1987 Clean Water Act for municipal stormwater than for other point sources. The standard for stormwater is to reduce the discharge of pollutants to the maximum extent practicable (MEP). Congress did not refer to water quality standards as it had when considering stormwater discharges associated with industrial activities.[13]

However, the issue has been raised that stormwater discharges from municipal storm sewers should eventually be required, like any other point source, to meet numerical effluent limitations based on water quality standards. This raises some fundamental issues and problems. Numerical effluent limits are based on identifying the various pollutants in a water body and then determining the maximum limits to be imposed on each pollutant source in order for receiving waters to meet established water quality standards. Currently there are no standards for wet weather discharges, and allowable pollutant loads are typically determined based on water quality standards established during low flow conditions. What would be an appropriate numerical effluent limit for stormwater? Would all outlets have to be monitored? How would a violation be determined and what would be the consequences of a violation? In the arid southwest there is typically no flow in receiving waters except during storms. What would be the standard in these cases?

In an "attainment study," Sacramento recently determined it would have to collect and treat its stormwater for certain heavy metals in order to meet proposed State of California water quality standards.[14] City officials estimated the cost of a collection and treatment system would be approximately $2 billion dollars or $35 to $45 per household per month for 30 years. The population of the Sacramento area is about 900,000 people. Even with this level of effort Sacramento could not guarantee compliance with proposed standards. In short, within the limits of present technology there does not appear to be a way to meet end-of-pipe numbers effectively or economically. A system is being created where all cities and counties could eventually be in a state of noncompliance.

Currently, local communities are mandated to develop and implement programs that will reduce discharges of pollutants in stormwater to the maximum extent practicable. However, will it eventually become a requirement to meet numerical effluent limitations at the end of the pipe regardless of cost? After all, the goal should be to improve the quality of the nation's waters. But should water quality standards for municipal stormwater systems be translated to numerical effluent limitations at the end of the pipe where exceedences will trigger noncompliance and corresponding penalties? Or should local governments be required to develop management programs to eliminate pollutants to the maximum extent practicable, to provide monitoring to develop a long term measure of progress, and to measure performance by other standards such as implementation of a cooperative management plan by the local governments?

What Are The Benefits and Costs?

The cost of stormwater treatment is unknown at this time but will certainly be tremendous. The Sacramento study concluded that it would cost about $2,200 per person in that area. On a national scale, the cost of the stormwater quality program that is now being implemented, which is not end-of-pipe oriented, is likely to exceed the POTW program. All of these costs of the stormwater quality program are to be borne by local governments. The POTW construction program, on the other hand, was supported by large amounts of federal funding.

At the beginning of the 1990s local and state governments across the nation are facing fiscal problems: bankruptcy in Bridgeport, Connecticut; severe financial difficulties in Philadelphia and New York; and fiscal crises in California, Massachusetts, Rhode Island, and Connecticut. In Colorado a constitutional tax limitation measure passed the electorate in 1992 that limits the tax rate, annual tax revenue increase, and annual spending increases. Several local tax measures were defeated by the voters in the Denver region in the fall of 1990 including a one percent sales tax in Lakewood, a mill levy increase for the Jefferson County School District, and a $\frac{1}{2}$ percent sales tax increase for the City of Littleton. In the November 1990 elections in California, referendum issues including Big Green and other initiatives requiring an outlay of public monies failed to win approval. Local governments are simply not in a good position to continue to take on new programs mandated by the federal government.

Another point is that POTWS were and are better situated to charge for their services. While some communities have been successful with stormwater utilities, such utilities are not a panacea. A stormwater fee is basically another tax and there must be voter approval and/or political acceptability. To compound the problem, there is no readily discernible or definable benefit to a stormwater quality management program. While we may assume there will be an improvement in water quality, we do not know the extent. There is general public support for environmental programs, but there is also a limit on how much the public can be taxed before resisting. In Colorado, a constitutional tax limitation measure is a likely possibility and it would severely limit local government's ability to provide basic services let alone programs such as municipal stormwater treatment and/or management plans.

A Recommendation

When the Federal Water Pollution Act is reauthorized by Congress, amendments should be considered regarding the municipal stormwater program. Because of the confusion it would create, however, any changes should not disrupt the permitting process that is now underway.

Congress should clarify that the MEP standard is the standard of performance for municipal stormwater discharges and not numerical end-of-pipe effluent limits in terms of compliance. The law is now written as if municipal stormwater discharges are point sources of pollution. Legislative requirements should reflect the unique nature of municipal stormwater discharges. They are not point sources in a classic sense.

Congress should clarify that stormwater quality management is to be accomplished through comprehensive programs that emphasize preventing pollution as opposed to treating it, that stress that stormwater quality objectives must be technically and financially feasible, and that establishes realistic timelines for achieving performance. In addition, Congress should provide technical and financial assistance to help local governments define problems and solutions and pay for implementation costs. Also, Congress should create a process that fosters a cooperative approach to the problem rather than the adversarial relationships characteristic of programs dependent on government enforced regulations.

Notes

1. U.S. Environmental Protection Agency, *A Preliminary Analysis of the Public Costs of Environmental Protection: 1981-2000*, (Washington, D.C., May 1990), ii.
2. Ibid.
3. Jay Grelen and Marilyn Robinson, "The Great Flood of '65," *The Denver Post*, 10 June 1990.
4. For complete background on revitalization of the South Platte River in Denver, see Joe Shoemaker, *Returning the Platte to the People* (Denver, 1981).
5. Federal Water Pollution Control Act Amendments (Clean Water Act of 1972), P. L. 92-500, Declaration of Goals and Policy, Section 101(a).
6. Notice of Public Rulemaking Hearing Before the Colorado Water Quality Control Commission, For Consideration of Revisions to the Basic Standard and Methodologies for Surface Water, Exhibit 1, Denver, 20 April 1992, 1.
7. Ibid.
8. Ibid.
9. Environmental Protection Agency, "National Pollutant Discharge Elimination System Permit Application Regulations for Storm Water Discharge; Final Rule," *Federal Register*, 55, 222 (16 November 1990), 47990-48091.
10. American Public Works Association of Southern California, *A Study of Nationwide Costs to Implement Stormwater Best Management Practices*, prepared by James M. Montgomery, Consulting Engineers, March 1991. (Administrative Draft Report).
11. J. M. Tyson, "Institutional Issues in Urban Pollution Management in England and Wales," Paper presented at Engineering Foundation Conference on Urban Runoff and Receiving Systems: An Interdisciplinary Analysis of Impact, Monitoring, and Management, Mt. Crested Butte, CO, (4-9 August 1991).
12. John P. C. Fogarty, *Clean Water Deskbook* (Washington, D.C., 1988), 5.

13. The Water Quality Act of 1987 modified Section 402(p)(3) of the 1972 Clean Water Act by requiring municipal discharge permitters to reduce the discharge of pollutants to the maximum extent practicable.
14. Larry Walker Associates, "Urban Stormwater Controls Necessary to Achieve Water Quality—Based Effluent Limitations Required by the Proposed Inland Surface Waters Plan", Prepared for the City and County of Sacramento, California, December 1990, 23, 33.

Comments

Russell Earnest

The manner in which we view the world is rapidly changing. There is growing recognition that many environmental problems are global in nature and will require international efforts to begin to develop solutions. Similarly there is increasing awareness in the United States that protection and management of natural resources must involve landscape or ecosystem level approaches instead of working with individual species or individual projects on a case by case basis.

The goal of this Forum is "to provide guidance and perspectives to aid water resources managers into the next century." The preliminary program shows that many of the participants here today work with water resources from the standpoint of water supply, stormwater management, flood control, wastewater treatment, navigation, and other human uses of water. I am pleased that a session on managing natural systems was included in the Forum.* From the perspective of the Fish and Wildlife Service, it is extremely important for water resources managers to consider the biological and ecological functions of aquatic and wetlands systems in addition to human uses.

Participants in the session on managing natural systems were asked to address the broad topic of restoration and management of aquatic areas and their natural systems. Management, restoration, and protection of aquatic and wetland systems is quite different from management and protection of terrestrial systems. First, surface waters such as lakes, rivers, streams, and estuaries are generally public resources that have many competing uses. Second, water has generally been regarded as a free, unlimited resource available to all users, except in the midwest and west where water resources are more limited. Third, aquatic systems are much more vulnerable to contamination due to their position in the landscape and surface and groundwater movement.

Present trends show an increasing demand being placed on water resources. Municipal water supply, hydropower projects, navigation, sewage treatment,

---

* The paper by James M. Wright and Don L. Porter was originally presented in a session on "Managing Natural Systems."

port development, agricultural irrigation, flood control, and water-based recreation all affect this nation's water resources. Many of our water resources are concentrated in coastal areas and current estimates predict that 50 to 70 percent of the population will live within 100 miles of the coast by the middle of the next century. Additionally, recreational use of aquatic systems is increasing as more people enjoy boating, fishing, and swimming in the nation's lakes, rivers, streams, and coastal waters. At the same time, we are seeing increasing levels of contaminants in aquatic systems. Contaminant problems range from pollution of surface waters by fertilizers, pesticides, motor oil, toxic landfill leachates, acid mine drainage, and feedlot wastes to pollution of groundwaters by pesticides and herbicides. Not only are waters themselves polluted, but more contaminated sediments are accumulating in aquatic systems. Point source discharges in our surface waters are monitored and must meet discharge standards as required by the Federal Water Pollution Control Act Amendments (Clean Water Act) of 1972, but we are now beginning to recognize that non-point source runoff is causing many water quality problems.

How do water resource managers address management, protection and restoration of aquatic systems with increased human demands being placed on water resources and with increasing contamination problems? Based on material presented in this Forum, I submit five general recommendations to aid water resources managers.

First, management, protection, and restoration of aquatic and wetland systems must be considered from a landscape or watershed perspective. With increasing demands being placed on water resources, better management and protection of these resources will result when decisions are made by looking at the scope of activities and impacts within an entire watershed. Additionally, since contaminants can move quickly through surface or groundwater systems, this further supports the need to develop basinwide or landscape level planning processes.

Within the Fish and Wildlife Service (Service), one example of working at the ecosystem level is the North American Waterfowl Management Plan. The Plan is a strategy for conserving wetland habitats throughout North America (including Mexico and Canada) that are critical to waterfowl and other wetland-dependent species. Strategies for restoration, management and protection of wetlands have been developed for designated geographical areas that are known as joint venture areas. Within these joint venture areas, partnerships have been developed between federal, state and private groups to plan and implement cooperative projects that will benefit wetland habitats.

The second recommendation is that restoration, management and protection of aquatic systems will require coordinated actions between federal, state, and local governments; various organizations; and the general public. Government agencies have different responsibilities under various federal, state, and local statutes and regulations. Additionally, since government budget limitations have affected many programs, these conditions mandate that the most efficient management of aquatic systems will result when actions are coordinated among all interested parties.

One example of such an integrated program is the Service's Bay/Estuary Program which is a national effort involving 23 bay and estuary areas along the coastline. This is a watershed based program where the Service is seeking funding to work cooperatively with federal, state, international, native American, and local agencies; non-governmental organizations; and the private sector to develop and implement ecosystem-based policies and programs that protect and enhance coastal living resources. Emphasis is on data acquisition and advanced planning to avoid problems before they occur, protect key habitats, remediate contamination and pollution, and restore important habitats that have been lost and enhance those that have been degraded.

Third, systematic monitoring must be a component of restoration and management strategies. One program for monitoring aquatic systems resulted from the requirements of the 1972 Clean Water Act. This is the monitoring of point source discharges that measures chemical parameters at the "end of the pipe." However, environmental stresses are generally first detected by biological organisms, and a monitoring system using biological indicators will significantly increase our ability to identify areas of contamination. Some states have implemented the use of biological monitoring criteria and EPA is requiring all states to develop such criteria by the end of 1993.

Monitoring systems should be established that will enable managers to detect problems before they become widespread, and to allow a general assessment of the overall health of specific drainage basins or watersheds. To achieve this goal, monitoring systems should be long-term, site specific, and cover entire watersheds. Such monitoring systems should address biological components, chemical parameters, and hydrologic characteristics in addition to tracking changes in the quantity and quality of different types of aquatic systems. Some examples of existing federal agency monitoring programs that can assist in filling this need include the Fish and Wildlife Service's Biomonitoring of Environmental Status and Trends (BEST) and the National Wetlands Inventory. Other monitoring systems include the U.S. Geological Survey's National Water Quality Assessment Program (NAWQA), EPA's Environmental Monitoring and Assessment Program (EMAP), and the National Oceanic and Atmospheric Administration's status and trends surveys.

Fourth, restoration should be included in planning for management of aquatic systems. The National Research Council recently published a report[1] recommending that a national strategy be developed for a large-scale aquatic ecosystem restoration program. Recommended goals include an overall gain of 10 million wetland acres by the year 2010, restoration of 400,000 miles of steams and rivers within the next 20 years and restoration of 1 million acres of lakes by the year 2000. The report advocated such large-scale aquatic ecosystem restoration projects because of past losses of valuable environmental functions provided by these ecosystems. Additionally, President Bush's Wetland Plan provided for the establishment of an interagency committee on Federal Wetlands Restoration and Creation. In 1992, the committee proposed a strategy for coordinating federal wetland restoration and creation projects that includes criteria for prioritizing projects and recommendations for future funding.

Wetlands restoration is a key component of the Service's Partners for Wildlife Program, which provides protection and restoration assistance to private landowners for wetlands, riparian corridors, and associated uplands. The Service restored over 41,153 acres of wetlands in fiscal year 1991. Over 9,000 individual landowners are now working with the Service to restore wetlands and associated uplands on their private property through voluntary cooperative agreements signed since 1987. The Service's goal is to reestablish native plant species and vegetative communities in order to benefit the broadest array of wildlife possible. Priority is placed on areas where habitat restoration can benefit threatened, endangered, and other declining species.

Restoration is ecological in nature; it restores multiple functions. Effective aquatic system restoration programs establish priorities to target declining systems and those in greatest need of restoration. Restoration also includes the development of criteria for success and of monitoring procedures that allow for corrections when problems are identified.

Lastly, successes and failures must be commuicated to other water resources managers throughout the country. Technology such as geographic information systems (GIS) and the latest research results should be made readily available to water resources managers. More training on biological and ecological functions of aquatic systems should be offered and workshops, such as this AWRA Forum, should be encouraged to promote exchange of information. Management of aquatic systems is complex and water resources face increasing demands from many users. Sharing ideas, technology, and information will result in better management of our aquatic resources.

In closing, I would like to reiterate the importance of working at the ecosystem level and developing partnerships. If we are to successfully manage, protect, and restore our aquatic systems, while providing an adequate supply of clean water for human uses and for fish and wildlife resources, our efforts must be cooperative and be conducted at the ecosystem or landscape level.

Note

1. U.S. National Research Council, Committee on Restoration of Aquatic Ecosystems-Science, Technology, and Public Policy, *Restoration of Aquatic Ecosystems: Science, Technology, and Public Policy* (Washington, D.C., 1992).

David C. Major

The Huainanzi, a Daoist classic of the second century BC, tells us that under certain circumstances it is proper, in the summer season, to publish, to proclaim, and to make clear.[1] I am grateful to my colleagues for having followed this injunction so well, and I append my modest additional contributions in these comments.

Scott Tucker reflects the concerns of many thoughtful water planners when he raises questions about the appropriateness of standards. He notes that regulations, primarily those promulgated by the federal government, profoundly affect the design and operation of water resource systems for both quality and quantity. His remarks open up fundamental issues in water resources planning. The questions suggested for the session on Integrated Urban Water Management, "What is the best way of obtaining the necessary information for setting water quality priorities?" and "What kind of deliberative process will produce effective standards and clear priorities for metropolitan water management?" are only two of the questions that arise, albeit two of the most important.* The effects of the regulations or standards in question are not trivial, nor are they simple or short, as is indicated by, for example, the May 1990 Fact Sheet, "Drinking Water Regulations under the Safe Water Drinking Act,"[2] which has 43 pages of regulations guaranteed to give pause to even the most compliant and well-funded water utility manager.

It is easy enough to fault the current system, although many devoted professionals have tried to make it work. As one of many possible examples: for volatile organic chemicals (VOCs) in the Fact Sheet,[3] if a utility system served 10,000 people, it was to have begun initial monitoring by 1 January 1989; if a utility served 10,001 people, it was to have begun monitoring a year earlier, on 1 January 1988. It does not take a whole lot of exposure to engineering, systems, or economics to know that the functional shape implied by this is rather unlikely, and to infer that not enough effort went into optimizing the imposition of costs as a function of the number of persons served by a utility. This is not a criticism of the people who did the work; rather it reminds all of us, whether we work in public agencies, in university labs, or in consulting firms, of how very hard it is to figure out anything, let alone the optimal levels of dozens of contaminants in public water supply systems, or whether it is right, as in the example in Tucker's paper, to require that streams should revert to natural status. As one example from my own experience, a river basin modelling effort that would now be thought fairly straightforward, a multiobjective and multipurpose analysis of a relatively small river in Argentina, cost more than $.5 million and two years of effort 20 years ago, and would cost much more and take not much less time now.[4]

---

* The paper by L. Scott Tucker was originally presented in a session on "Challenges in Integrated Water Management."

Comments

I do not think there are easy ways out of this. It is not enough to call for price incentives rather than regulations; price incentives and regulations have the same ultimate goals, and even in a situation well-suited for price incentives instead of regulations, the government must still study the problem, set up the incentive system, set boundary conditions, and monitor the results. (A useful treatment of price incentives vs. regulation is in Baumol and Oates[5]; see also Cropper and Oates.[6]) Another factor is that we will inevitably become still more sensitive than we have already become to multiple objectives,[7] and confronting these makes clear that the analytic problems are complex. An additional consideration is that, amazing as the machines already on our desks now seem to us, we are still in an era of continued rapid advances in computational techniques. This suggests that imposing requirements now that are relatively poorly analyzed may be a mistake; the benefits of delay resulting from better analysis with better techniques may substantially exceed the costs of delay (see Ausubel[8] for the delay argument).

What should be done? It is unfashionable in Washington today, and might even be regarded by some as being in poor taste, to give what is in my view the correct answer. We need substantially more resources than have been devoted to training, research, analysis, and applications in water resources for many a year. The stakes are very high, as indicated by the papers under review. We do not want to repeat the social experiment that we performed with the National System of Interstate and Defense Highways, which was apparently based ultimately on a map drawn for General Pershing in the 1920s. This was a very large experiment conducted on a very small planning base. We are not in so bad a state with respect to water quality regulations, but in my view we have nothing remotely comparable to what is needed. I am not talking just about money; in my recent experience as a senior planner for the New York City water supply system, I was struck by the shortage of qualified planners, and by how the dedicated people in the agency labored mightily and produced very well, but could not conceivably do all that was required given the challenges. There are not enough well-trained people to go around. We need many more—those who have social science, natural science or engineering training together with a sense of the public policy process and public involvement.

More resources cannot be made available? We professionals have to make the case for them to be made available; it is our responsibility. We are told that the federal government cannot do any more, that there is no money, that we will have to use the research that we have now and make do. This is simply wrongheaded. The papers that we have heard today, by making clear the extent to which regulation drives huge expenditures and forces decisions that will affect us for decades, buttress the case for far greater expenditures— which will still be a very small proportion of what is at risk—for training, research, analysis, and applications. We must do better.

Notes

1. For a translation of and commentary on the cosmological chapters of the *Huainanzi*, see John S. Major, *Heaven and Earth in Early Han Thought: Chapters Three, Four and Five of the Huainanzi*, (Albany, NY, [in press]). The reference given is from Chapter 3, Section 36.
2. U.S. Environmental Protection Agency, Criteria and Standards Division, Office of Drinking Water, "Fact Sheet: Drinking Water Regulations under the Safe Drinking Water Act," May 1990.
3. Ibid, 11.
4. David C. Major and Roberto L. Lenton, *Applied Water Resource Systems Planning*, (Englewood Cliffs, NJ, 1979).
5. William J. Baumol and Wallace E. Oates, *Economics, Environmental Policy, and the Quality of Life*, (Englewood Cliffs, NJ, 1979).
6. Maureen L. Cropper and Wallace E. Oates, "Environmental Economics: A Survey," *Journal of Economic Literature* 30, no. 2 (June 1992): 675-740.
7. For multiobjectives, see Arthur Maass et al., *Design of Water-Resource Systems*, (Cambridge, MA, 1962); Stephen A. Marglin, *Public Investment Criteria*, (Cambridge, MA, 1967), and David C. Major, *Multiobjective Water Resource Planning*, (Washington, DC, 1977). Some of the background is given in Martin Reuss, "Water Resources People and Issues: Interview with Professor Arthur Maass," U.S. Army Corps of Engineers, Office of History, Fort Belvoir, VA, 1989.
8. Jesse H. Ausubel, "A Second Look at the Impacts of Climate Change," *American Scientist* 79 (May-June 1991): 210-21.

Risks and Uncertainties

The Economics of Risk in Water Resource Planning

Kenneth D. Frederick

Changing Sources of Risk

Large seasonal and annual variations in precipitation and runoff pose major challenges for planners and risk for water users. In the absence of flow regulation and storage, the ratio of the maximum to minimum streamflow within a year may exceed 500 to 1. Furthermore, climatic variability results in large interannual streamflow fluctuations. The ratio of very high annual flows (those exceeded in five percent of the years) to very low annual flows (those exceeded in 95 percent of the years) is 2.9 for the conterminous 48 states. Annual flow variability in most of the water-scarce western river basins is significantly higher than the national average.[1]

Floods and shortages are common outcomes of hydrologic variability, and dams and reservoirs are the primary means of reducing the risk of these events. At the start of this century, the welfare and even the survival of countless people living in arid, semiarid, and flood-prone areas were vulnerable to hydrologic extremes. Over the next seven decades or so, progressively larger investments in dams, reservoirs, canals, and pumps altered the nation's plumbing and, thereby, its vulnerability to fluctuations in natural water supplies. More than 60,000 dams and reservoirs with nearly 850 million acre-feet of storage were completed between 1900 and 1982.[2] The use of groundwater, which is less susceptible to the vagaries of the climate, increased from about 7 billion gallons per day (bgd) in 1900 to 83 bgd in 1980.[3]

Water control and supply projects were the accepted solution to water problems during the first two-thirds of this century. An indication of the initial success of this strategy is that well before the middle of the century the availability of high-quality water at the turn of a tap was taken for granted by virtually everyone in the United States. In recent decades, however, several factors have made the task of providing high-quality water on demand increasingly difficult. First, the structural approach, which has provided water managers with unprecedented control over the timing and location of water supplies, has encountered sharply diminishing returns in its ability to prevent and resolve water problems. Second, demands for both instream and withdrawal water uses have increased rapidly. Third, concerns as to the quality of supplies have grown. These changes are discussed below.

The costs of developing new supplies have increased markedly in recent decades, and further cost increases are inevitable because (a) the best reservoir sites already have been developed, (b) the quantity of water that can be supplied with a high degree of probability rises only at a diminishing rate as storage capacity on a stream increases, and (c) the opportunity costs of storing and diverting water rise as the number of free-flowing streams declines and the demand for instream flows rises. Water-project construction trends reflect these changes. The average number of dams completed annually in the United States declined from 1,411 in the 1945-1969 period to 1,069 in the 1970-1982 period, and the average storage capacity of these dams fell from 13,000 acre-feet in the earlier period to 9,000 acre-feet in the more recent period.[4] A basic principle of reservoir planning is that the risk of deficiency increases if the storage period (available storage divided by average daily withdrawals) is not increased as withdrawals rise. The storage period, which had increased for at least six previous decades, declined from 216 days in 1970 to 201 days in 1980.[5]

Growing demands on the resource have made water more valuable and the competition for supplies more intense. Offstream water use rose from 40 bgd in 1900 to 440 bgd in 1980.[6] Increasing values for instream flows and the dependence of some users on nonrenewable groundwater supplies may make it difficult to increase and, in some areas, to even maintain the level of withdrawals reached in 1980. Moreover, the past policy of placing the risks associated with hydrologic variability overwhelmingly on instream flows is giving way to the growing concerns over the impacts of low flows on the environment.

In addition to the increasing risk of shortages, there is growing concern over water quality. Water is rarely pure. Impurities are added as water precipitates through the atmosphere and as it comes in contact with soils, rocks, and, most importantly, with society's products and wastes. The quality of the resource can be an important source of risk for water users. Some industrial uses have stringent water-quality requirements while others may be able to get by with brackish water. Drinking water quality is the most important and difficult to guarantee. Contaminated water was a major cause of morbidity and mortality in the United States during the nineteenth century, and it continues to be a principal health problem in the developing world. Improved understanding of the linkage between water quality and human health together with the development of technologies for treating supplies enabled the United States to provide most of its citizens with reliable drinking water by about

1920. In recent years, however, the growing quantity and toxicity of wastes reaching or threatening the nation's water supplies have revived fears about drinking-water quality and produced new concerns about the long-term health of aquatic ecosystems. Salinity is virtually a universal problem for irrigators, and it can impose large costs on urban and industrial users.

Rivers, lakes, and estuaries have been common disposal sites for municipal and industrial wastes. Concentrations of conventional pollutants such as fecal coliform and organics that create biochemical oxygen demands had reached levels that threatened human health, impaired aquatic life, and eroded the recreational values of many of the nation's surface waters when the Clean Water Act was enacted in 1972. In the following two decades, in excess of $100 billion have been spent to reduce and treat these point-source discharges. Although these investments produced significant improvements in water quality, more than 5 percent of the assessed lakes and reservoirs did not meet the fishable and swimmable goal of the Clean Water Act in 1986-1987. And the quality of 30 percent of the assessed river miles and 26 percent of the assessed area of lakes and reservoirs did not support their designated uses.[7] Industrial and municipal wastes continue to add BOD, bacteria, nutrients, toxics, and other pollutants to these waters, and large additional investments are planned to further reduce these discharges. Yet, investments to curb pollutants from municipal and industrial sources are encountering diminishing returns in their ability to restore the remaining waters to a fully-usable status. Non-point sources such as runoff from farms, urban areas, and construction sites and seepage from landfills and septic systems are now the principal sources of both conventional and toxic water pollutants.[8]

Groundwater contamination and depletion are growing concerns. Groundwater is the source of more than one-fifth of the nation's freshwater withdrawals and about one-half of its drinking water. Only a small fraction of the nation's aquifers are known to be contaminated such that they fail to meet drinking-water standards. Still, the potential threats to groundwater quality are ubiquitous. Chemicals applied to agricultural and other lands, millions of septic and underground storage tanks, on-site and municipal landfills, abandoned waste sites, surface impoundments, and oil and gas brine pits are all possible sources of water pollutants. Coastal aquifers are also susceptible to saltwater intrusion.[9] Because ground and surface waters are part of a single hydrologic system, contaminated surface water can pollute groundwater and vice-versa.

Confidence about the availability of high-quality water has eroded in many areas. For example, New York City is confronting its fourth drought in a decade, and the quality of the once pristine reservoirs that supply this city is threatened by development activities that have led to high fecal coliform and summer algae levels. Prolonged drought in California has forced large reductions in water use and growing concerns about the availability of supplies for future population and economic growth.

Furthermore, in spite of the increased capacity to control water flows and the growing concerns over shortages, flood damages have been rising in recent decades. Higher flood damages are attributable to intensive development and rising property values within floodplains as well as to upstream developments that increase runoff rates and flood peak frequencies. In the absence of effective counter measures, flood losses are likely to continue increasing because urban expansion within the floodplains is growing at 2 percent per year.[10]

The limited opportunities for adding to supplies, the increasing scarcity of the resource, the rising flood losses, and the varied threats to water quality have created new challenges for planners and added uncertainty for water users. Planners and policymakers face an increasingly complex task of risk management in which hydrologic variability is just one of several major sources of uncertainty. Protecting and restoring water quality and allocating scarce supplies effectively among competing uses have joined, if not displaced, the construction of new water-supply facilities as the principal water-policy concerns.

The Role of Economics in Managing Risk

Many individuals are quick to attribute the costs of droughts to misguided legislation or poor planning. In an attempt to avoid such criticism, politicians often pass laws that seem to suggest that they can legislate a riskless world and planners attempt to design facilities capable of performing under the most extreme conditions. Yet, as Wildavsky has succinctly stated: "Risks as well as resources must be allocated. Risk cannot be reduced for everyone. The sheer supply of resources that have to be devoted to minimizing risk means that surpluses are less likely to be available for unforeseen shocks. What is spent to lessen risk cannot be used to increase productivity."[11]

Economics, which involves the allocation of scarce resources among competing ends, offers insights for water resource planners in managing risk. Benefit-cost analysis provides a framework for evaluating water development investments, alternative drought-prevention and flood-control strategies, and regulatory measures. Least-cost or cost-effectiveness analysis can be used to assess alternative means of achieving desired water quantity and quality objectives. Economic analysis can also be used to assess alternative institutional arrangements for allocating risk among alternative segments of society and different generations and for encouraging practices that conserve and protect vulnerable resources. The application of economic tools, however, provides few easy answers and is not without controversy.

Benefit-Cost Analysis

The principle that the benefits of a water project should exceed the costs is widely accepted. The Flood Control Act of 1936 states that flood control

185

projects should be undertaken only "if the benefits to whomsoever they may accrue are in excess of the estimated costs. . . ."[12] The Reclamation Project Act of 1939 established a similar benefit-cost criterion for Bureau of Reclamation projects. This principle, however, provides only limited guidance to planners in a world where water and investment capital are scarce. Furthermore, the application of this principle is apt to be controversial when there is great uncertainty as to the magnitude and allocation of the benefits and costs associated with alternative policy strategies.

The criterion that project benefits exceed costs implies that a project will not impoverish a society; it does not imply that society's resources are used efficiently. Economic efficiency implies maximizing the net present value of all the nation's scarce resources over time, taking into account all alternative uses of the resources. While this ideal implies a level of information, certainty, and sophistication that is unattainable in practice, economic analysis can assist in evaluating alternative project designs and in sequencing water development investments to reduce society's overall risk and to distribute the remaining risk among individuals and over time.

Evaluating the relative merits of alternative water plans involves making judgments about the likelihood of various physical, economic, demographic, and social outcomes. Synthetic streamflow-generating models are used to incorporate hydrologic variability and to estimate the probability of extreme events. All such models assume that the values of the flow parameters are time invariant. This assumption becomes increasingly suspect as land use changes, water resources are developed, and anthropogenic climate change is a possibility.[13] Moreover, hydrology is just one element of uncertainty surrounding water-project design, and the probability of alternative hydrologic regimes may be one of the easier variables to estimate with a tolerable degree of accuracy.[14] Indeed, hydrology ranked last in an analysis by James, Bower, and Matalas of the relative importance of four variables involved in the water resources planning decision. The most important, in descending order, of the variables analyzed were the projections of economic development, the water-quality objective, and the physical model used to reflect how various factors affect dissolved oxygen levels in the estuary.[15] The historical record is apt to be of less use in illuminating the future behavior of the economic, demographic, and social factors that are important to the outcome of a project. Even if all these variables were known with certainty, there might be major uncertainties as to the impacts of a project on water quality and the health of the aquatic ecosystem.

Krutilla summarized the role of economics as follows: "Economic analysis of benefits and costs of long-lived investments involve as much art as science. There is need to project the relevant course of events within the area of project influence over a very long period of time, and getting to understand human responses to changes in the social and physical environment does not come easily."[16]

Several approaches might be used to reduce the risk associated with these uncertainties. Traditionally, planners have adopted conservative engineering criteria in designing the scale of a water supply or flood control system. Most water systems were designed to be "robust" (able to respond to the range of uncertainties associated with future events) and "resilient" (able to operate under a range of conditions and to return rapidly to designed performance levels in case of failure.[17] Planners generally sought to construct facilities large enough to protect against a 100-year flood and to provide withdrawal users full supplies during all but the most severe droughts. Yet for reasons detailed above, the high costs of and limited opportunities for constructing new water projects and the increasing importance of instream flows make this fail-safe approach to project design expensive, economically inefficient, and inconsistent with the full range of demands on the resource. The traditional approach tends to shift the costs associated with extreme hydrologic events without necessarily reducing the overall costs to society. For instance, constructing and operating a water-supply system to protect withdrawal users from hydrologic risk transfers the costs associated with drought to the instream users.

An efficient strategy would attempt to minimize the sum of the costs of expanding the water-supply or flood control systems and the expected losses that would result from a drought or flood. Comprehensive water planning would consider nonstructural measures for reducing the costs of extreme hydrologic events. Evaluating the expected losses from droughts and floods under alternative investments or the expected net benefits of a water project is done by assigning probabilities to various outcomes associated with the project. As suggested above, the uncertainties surrounding these probabilities are large. Still, even if planners had confidence in the probability distributions, the design that produces the highest expected value is not always to be preferred. For instance, people buy insurance even though the insurance premiums are invariably greater than the expected value of the losses insured against.[18]

Sensitivity and Risk-Cost Analysis

Sensitivity analysis provides a means of estimating the implications of alternative outcomes. The *Principles and Guidelines* for federal water planning and project evaluation calls for the consideration of "a limited number of alternative forecasts that would, if realized, appreciably affect plan design. . . ." Planners are expected to consider the advantages and costs of reducing risk and uncertainty through methods such as (1) collecting more detailed data to reduce measurement error, (2) using more refined analytic techniques, (3) increasing safety factors in design, (4) selecting measures with better known performance characteristics, (5) reducing the irreversible or irretrievable commitments of resources, and (6) performing a sensitivity analysis of the estimated benefits and costs of alternative plans.[19]

Risk-cost analysis, which examines the cost of being wrong to varying degrees, is a variation on sensitivity analysis. Alternative plans can be evaluated by assigning probability distributions to independent variables and identifying social risk preferences. With this information, planners can design systems that will impose limited and acceptable costs on society when they fail. That is, they are "safe-fail" as opposed to "fail-safe," which has become a costly and often unrealistic objective of water planning.[20]

Valuing Public Goods

The problems of applying economics to water resource planning and regulation are not limited to the uncertainties surrounding the outcome. Other areas of controversy include the valuation of nonmarket goods, the benefits of pollution controls, and the choice of a discount rate. Planning decisions and the risk associated with various water uses depend on the values assigned to these factors.

Water projects often affect public goods such as fish and wildlife habitat and scenic amenities provided by streams and lakes. Such goods are not marketable because there is no easy way to exclude those who do not pay for them from enjoying their benefits. For privately traded goods, observed prices and quantities can be used to derive a demand curve and quantify consumers' willingness to pay. The value of public goods must be estimated if they are not to be ignored in the benefit-cost calculus.

The first efforts to value nonmarketed goods attempted to infer the value individuals place on these goods from observable behavior related to the good. The travel-cost method pioneered by Marion Clawson assumes that the distance traveled is closely correlated with the cost of enjoying the recreational experience at a given site.[21] Because households are located varying distances from a recreation site, their costs of using the site differ. Use tends to decrease as the distance from the site increases, suggesting that travel costs can be used to estimate a willingness to pay for the experience. Although the travel-cost method has been used to estimate the recreational demand for numerous sites, there are important limitations to this method. For instance, the assumption that travel costs are an accurate proxy for site entry fees is invalid if visitors stop at multiple sites on a single trip. Visits to national parks located far from major population centers commonly involve multiple stops. Moreover, demand estimates derived from this method are biased when visitation rates are distorted by congestion at the site.

Hedonic pricing is used to estimate the marginal value of various site attributes. Differences in property values among sites can be used to estimate the value of being located near a recreation site. Another application of hedonics draws on the travel-cost method; decisions to visit a particular location, selected from among many sites with varying attributes, are used to reveal a willingness to pay for greater quality. This method can be used to evaluate the benefits of investments in upgrading recreation sites.[22]

The contingent valuation method relies on surveys to value public goods. Individuals are asked to reveal their personal valuations of varying amounts or quality attributes of unpriced goods within contingent markets described in the survey. Contingent markets precisely define the initial level of the good, how it would be altered, how the respondent would pay for the changes, and the institutions for providing the good and the changes. The responses elicited from the survey are contingent upon the specified markets.

A number of potential sources of bias can distort the results of these surveys. Strategic bias arises when a respondent wants to influence the outcome. Information bias arises when respondents are asked to value unfamiliar or poorly defined attributes or goods. Starting point bias results when the predefined range of possible answers does not include the full range of the willingness-to-pay of the respondents. And hypothetical bias results when respondents give ill-considered answers because they are not required to pay the values they attribute to the goods.[23] Supporters of this method believe careful survey design and implementation can keep the biases within an acceptable range. Yet designing and conducting surveys to minimize bias in the estimated values are expensive. On the other hand, when it is done well, contingent valuation offers some important advantages over the travel-cost and hedonic-pricing methods. It is the only method that can estimate the value of goods not yet supplied as well as nonuse (or existence) values. The willingness of some people to pay to preserve natural areas that they never intend to visit may be a significant component of the value of some public goods.

Valuing the Benefits of Pollution Controls

Avoided damages to human health and environmental resources are the principal benefits of pollution controls. The problems of evaluating these benefits are particularly acute where toxics are involved. Many toxics are invisible, odorless, and difficult to detect in the low concentrations that may still be harmful. Moreover, some toxics persist in the environment for long periods. Just identifying what substances are toxic and in what concentrations or combinations may be an impossible task. Knowledge of exposure levels is very incomplete and even very large additional investments in detection would surely leave significant gaps. Even with full knowledge of contaminant levels, the effects of exposure can be only indirectly estimated because large numbers of people cannot be subjected to controlled experiments. While laboratory studies on animals and epidemiological studies help to identify problems, they fall well short of quantifying the effects of human exposure to individual or combinations of substances. Laboratory experiments are expensive and extrapolating from the impacts of large doses of a chemical given to animals over short periods of time to estimate the effects on humans of small doses over extended periods is tenuous at best. Statistical studies of human populations exposed to different levels of a chemical are also likely to be expensive. Moreover, it is probably impossible to control for all variables that might affect mortality and morbidity rates in these studies. The possibility of synergistic and antagonistic effects among chemicals presents an overwhelming number of combinations of potentially detrimental substances. Since latency periods may involve decades, long-term studies may be needed to understand the effects of the substances that are studied. Yet, postponing action until the results of such studies are known risks amplifying the problem and not being able to do much about it for an entire generation.[24]

Once a substance is determined to pose a significant risk to human health or the environment, the task becomes one of valuing the net benefits of limiting exposure to the substance. This task opens up the controversial issues of placing values on extending human lives and reducing the incidence of illness. Economists have no generally-accepted formulas for making these calculations. They recognize, however, that policy decisions do commonly affect the length and health of various segments of society and that tradeoffs involving human lives have to be made because resources are finite.

The Discount Rate

The choice of a discount rate is one of the more important and controversial aspects of water resource planning. The importance of the discount rate for evaluating future streams of benefits and costs is apparent when one considers that the present value of $1,000 fifty years hence is $1,000 without discounting (a 0 percent interest rate), $87.20 at 5 percent, and only $8.52 at 10 percent. Almost any positive discount rate gives the impacts on future generations little to no influence over today's plans. Consequently, some environmentalists argue that discounting of future benefits and costs is inappropriate for considering the impacts of actions that deplete the resource base over time or impose risks on future generations.

The lack of agreement as to the appropriate rate for discounting the benefits and costs of public investments and regulations has resulted in the use of a wide variety of practices, often motivated by a political agenda. In the late 1960s, the practices of U.S. federal agencies varied widely. Some did not discount at all, and the rate varied from 3 to 12 percent among those agencies that did discount. In 1972 the U.S. Office of Management and Budget directed most federal agencies to use a 10 percent real rate of discount, which was believed to approximate the marginal real rate of return on capital in the private sector. Yet, at the insistence of Congress, water projects were exempted from using this rate.[25]

Differences in the opportunity costs and riskiness of the projects and changes in the social rate of time preference suggest that there is no single rate of discount that should be used to compute the present value of benefits and costs of all public investments and policies. Moreover, appropriate adjustments for risk and the opportunity cost of capital often cannot be corrected simply by adjusting the discount rate.[26]

Cost-Effectiveness Analysis

The need for government measures to protect unique natural environments and to limit environmental pollution has become widely accepted in recent decades. On the other hand, there is little agreement as to when and how the government should intervene. The lack of agreement is attributable in part to the problems of valuing the benefits provided by natural environments and reduced exposure to toxics and other contaminants. One consequence of these valuation problems has been the tendency of policymakers to establish broad, unattainable objectives. The goals of restoring all navigable waters to a "fishable and swimmable" condition by July 1983 and eliminating all discharges of pollutants to these waters by 1985 that were incorporated into the Federal Water Pollution Control Act Amendments of 1972 illustrate this point. Even though these and similarly ambitious environmental objectives have been established without analyzing the benefits and costs associated with attaining them, sensible policy should attempt to achieve a given level of environmental quality at the lowest possible cost. Cost-effectiveness analysis provides a systematic method for evaluating policy alternatives with a common objective.

Measurement problems make it difficult to determine if the nation's sizable water-quality investments could pass a benefit-cost test. Still, economics can be useful in determining whether the same water-quality improvements might have been achieved at a lower cost or whether the same level of investment could have purchased even greater improvements in water quality. For instance, the technology-based effluent standards used to curb point-source discharges provided industry with little incentive to develop improved technologies, and federal subsidies distorted investment incentives in wastewater treatment facilities. With the federal government subsidizing 75 percent of the capital costs of these facilities, municipalities had little incentive to contain costs or to develop innovative techniques to reuse effluents.[27] Federal subsidies also discouraged investments in more efficient irrigation technologies that would reduce the salts, agricultural chemicals, and other pollutants from irrigated lands that end up contaminating downstream supplies.[28] Society's costs of achieving a given water-quality level would be reduced by policies that encourage development of new technologies and do not distort incentives to adopt particular pollution-control measures.

Notes

1. U.S. Water Resources Council, *The Nation's Water Resources 1975-2000: Second National Water Assessment*, 4 vols. (Washington, D.C., 1978), I:15.
2. U.S. Army Corps of Engineers, *National Program of Inspection of Non-Federal Dams: Final Report to Congress,* (Washington, D.C., 1982).
3. Kenneth D. Frederick, "Water Resources: Increasing Demand and Scarce Supplies," in *America's Renewable Resources: Historical Trends and Current*

Challenges, eds., Kenneth D. Frederick and Roger A. Sedjo (Washington, D.C,. 1991), 72-73.

4. Ibid., 72.
5. U.S. Geological Survey, *National Water Summary 1983 -Hydrologic Events and Water Supply and Use* (Washington, D.C., 1984), 34.
6. Frederick, "Water Resources," 72.
7. U.S. Environmental Protection Agency, *National Water Quality Inventory: 1988 Report to Congress* (Washington, D.C., 1990), xii-xiii.
8. U.S. Environmental Protection Agency, *National Water Quality Inventory: 1986 Report to Congress* (Washington, D.C., 1987), 3.
9. U.S. Environmental Protection Agency, *1988 Report to Congress,* 126-27.
10. Kyle Schilling, Claudia Copeland, Joseph Dixon, James Smythe, Mary Vincent, and Jan Peterson, *Water Resources: The State of the Infrastructure* (Washington, D.C., 1987), 42.
11. Aaron Wildavsky, "No Risk is the Highest Risk of All," in *Readings in Risk*, eds. Theodore S. Glickman and Michael Gough (Washington, D.C., 1990), 121.
12. Sec. 1, 49 Stat. 1570, 33 U.S.C. 701a, Flood Control Act of 1936.
13. Nicholas C. Matalas and Myron B. Fiering, "Water-Resource Systems Planning," in *Climate, Climate Change, and Water Supply,* National Research Council (Washington, D.C., 1977), 99.
14. Robert Dorfman, "Basic Economic and Technologic Concepts: A General State-ment," in *Design of Water Resource Systems: New Techniques for Relating Eco-nomic Objectives, Engineering Analysis, and Governmental Planning*, eds. Arthur Maass, Maynard M. Hufschmidt, Robert Dorfman, Harold A. Thomas, Jr., Stephen A. Marglin, and Gordon Maskew Fair (Cambridge, MA, 1962), 158.
15. I.C. James II, B.T. Bower, and N.C. Matalas, "Relative Importance of Variables in Water Resources Planning," *Water Resources Research* 5 (December 1969): 1165-73.
16. John V. Krutilla, "The Use of Economics in Project Evaluation," in *Transactions of the 40th North American Wildlife and Natural Resources Conference, 1975* (Washington, D.C., 1975), 375.
17. Matalas and Fiering, "Water-Resource Systems Planning," 101-9.
18. Dorfman, "Basic Economic and Technologic Concepts," 139.
19. U.S. Water Resources Council, *Economic and Environmental Principles and Guidelines for Water and Related Land Resources Implementation Studies* (Wash-ington, D.C., 1983), 5-6.
20. Mark W. Mugler, Eugene Z. Stakhiv, Hanna J. Cortner, and Michael Rubino, "Planning for Climatic Variability and Uncertainty," (Washington, D.C., nd), 1-4.
21. Marion Clawson, "Methods of Measuring the Demand for and Value of Outdoor Recreation," Resources for the Future Reprint No. 10 (Washington, D.C., 1972).
22. Michael D. Bowes and John V. Krutilla, *Multiple-Use Management: The Econom-ics of Public Forestlands* (Washington, D.C., 1989), 177-212.
23. Robert Cameron Mitchell and Richard T. Carson, *Using Surveys to Value Public Goods: The Contingent Valuation Method* (Washington, D.C., 1989), 120-26.
24. Clifford S. Russell, "Lessons from the Drinking Water Conference: One Man's View," in *Safe Drinking Water: Current and Future Problems,* ed. Clifford S. Russell (Washington, D.C., 1978), 593-637.

25. Robert C. Lind, "Introduction," in *Discounting for Time and Risk in Energy Policy,* eds. Robert C. Lind, Kenneth J. Arrow, Gordon R. Corey, Partha Dasgupta, Amartya K. Sen, Thomas Stauffer, Joseph E. Stiglitz, J.A. Stockfisch, and Robert Wilson (Washington, D.C., 1982), 6.
26. Ibid., 1-18.
27. U.S. Congressional Budget Office, *Efficient Investments in Wastewater Treatment Plants* (Washington, D.C., 1985), ix-xv.
28. Kenneth D. Frederick, "Controlling Irrigation Return Flows," Resources for the Future Discussion Paper ENR 92-08 (Washington, D.C., 1992), 4-19.

Are We Doomed to Fail in Drought Management?

Stanley A. Changnon

Introduction

Droughts continue to rate as the most severe weather-induced problem in the United States.[1] Global attention to natural hazards reduction over the current decade includes drought as one of the major hazards.[2] During the 1987-1991 period, a sequence of severe droughts occurred affecting many parts of the United States, bringing home once again a complex myriad of losses and forgotten lessons about drought management.[3] In general, too much response to drought has been performed under a crisis management mode. My thesis is that most U.S. droughts reveal a management cycle associated with drought that begins with 1) using emergency responses after drought has become well developed, 2) making a few permanent adjustments in critical areas during and after droughts, and 3) forgetting to do much else in the succeeding years, or "out of sight, out of mind."

In attempting to address drought as one of the major risks to water resources facing water management policy, one is faced with the challenging question, what new can be said, once again and with feeling, about droughts, their impacts on water resources, and related water management options that has not been said many times during the past 60 years? If the past is a useful predictor of the future, then the major lessons learned about drought responses and management in the past appear to be a good place to start in defining the problems that drought portends for future water management policies *at all levels of government.*

Lessons about Drought: 1932-1992

The 1987-1991 drought which affected most parts of the United States at different times and at different levels, helped illustrate problems and indeed lessons from the past.[4] Depending upon how one categorizes the lessons, I believe there are at least seven identifiable "truths," or lessons, emanating out of study of the major droughts of the 1930s, 1950s, 1960s, 1970s, and 1980s. Almost every decade has experienced serious droughts in some portions of the United States. However, the frequency of drought in any given area is generally greater than decadal.[5]

Lesson Number One

Major drought is a pervasive condition affecting most portions of the physical environment as well as the socioeconomic structure. Hence, the definition of drought is difficult, complex, and multifaceted. The net effect is that drought, as such, is poorly understood, and often a lack of concerted action exists until the drought is well-developed. Droughts are so pervasive that they require action at all governmental levels, from the local to the federal, and this alone often produces inertia in decision making.[6]

Lesson Number Two

Droughts are a major but unpredictable part of the climate of all parts of the United States. Moreover, they occur infrequently and this results in a decay in the attention to drought preparedness and mitigation. This loss of "corporate memory" for dealing with drought is a major management problem. Typically, inexperience with drought problems is found among those who must make drought-related decisions (e.g., who is in charge and what should I do?)

Lesson Number Three

Responses and adjustments to drought problems can be sorted into two classes: 1) short-term fixes and 2) long-term improvements. The short-term adjustments often ignore long-range effects and can be damaging in the post-drought situation.[7] Cloud seeding is certainly not the answer during drought. Long-term adjustments to water shortages, typically accomplished locally, have been made after every drought since those of the 1930s.[8] Reservoirs have been built, spillways altered, water distribution systems installed, contingency plans developed, wind breaks planted, drought-resistant crop varieties developed, irrigation developed, etc.

Lesson Number Four

Although many long-term adjustments have been made as a result of the major droughts of the last 60 years, many factors make today's society generally more vulnerable to drought than ever before. This was evident in the 1988-89 drought.[9] Ever growing population, expanding irrigation,[10] aging and wasteful water delivery systems, and dependence on international trade make us ever more vulnerable to drought, both at home and abroad.[11]

Lesson Number Five

Agriculture, in general, cannot escape from experiencing major drought losses in the future, even with healthier crop strains and increased irrigation. Federal, and to a lesser extent, state relief likely will remain a major means of coping with agricultural drought. Drought and weather insurance has not been found to be adequate.[12]

Lesson Number Six

Opportunities for improvement in water management exist and could make the nation's water resources more impervious to drought. However, many serious water-related problems are localized and at the substate scale and often do not get needed attention.[13] Regional differences, related to the physical settings and law, further complicate obtaining the action and funding needed in a given region.

Lesson Number Seven

Drought is ubiquitous: everything and everybody is affected, and yet no one (or everyone) is in charge. All levels of government—local, state, regional, and federal—must be involved in drought issues, but within this chain of intermingled responsibility, there typically is confusion about drought and its impacts with a resulting lack of action. There has been a rapid increase in state action and 22 states now have drought contingency plans. There are at least 11 major federal agencies that have mandates affected by droughts. Some of them, such as the USDA, have several major branches that must deal with drought (Soil Conservation Service, Agricultural Stabilization and Conservation Service, the Forest Service, and the Federal Crop Insurance Corporation). This large collection of well-established bureaucracies makes it difficult to plan or react coherently to drought.

Future Uncertainties and Risks

The authors of papers in the conference session, "Risk and Uncertainty in Water Resources," were asked to comment on the question, "What risks and uncertainties do we face?" With the danger of ignoring a major facet of risk or uncertainty, I identify several uncertainties that we face in the future as a result of the certainty of drought.

First, we have the gnawing continuing uncertainty of when and where will the next drought occur? Predictive capabilities for drought—including its beginning, intensity, and ending—are meager.[14] Thus, for water managers, the inability to predict drought remains a major uncertainty.[15]

Another uncertainty relates to whether the inefficient use of water for irrigation, and the waste in aged water delivery systems, will be reduced and by how much in the future? A major and shifting risk related to drought is the growth in demand for water and the loss of water through inefficiency, pollution, and waste. Aged and leaking water systems, both urban and rural, enhance this risk. Will improvements in water conservation occur? Can water laws be altered and pricing of water changed to reduce the impact of drought?

A major problem in anticipating, responding, and managing droughts relates to the lack of understanding of the impacts. The relationship between meteorological drought and its effects on the hydrologic system, other environmental systems, and on socio-economic patterns is poorly understood—and ever changing. We lack the quantitative models in many sectors to relate droughts to specific effects. Furthermore, many existing impact models are no longer valid (a shifting target), and lack routine updating requirements.[16]

Another uncertainty with associated risks that the nation faces is the potential for climate change. Future changes could be due to the greenhouse effect, or could be due to natural controls. In either instance, shifting climate conditions could bring more droughts, more intense droughts, and different regional patterns of drought than in the past.[17]

Coping with the Uncertainties: Policy Recommendations

The second question asked from this assessment of droughts was, "How do we cope with uncertainties?" I have attempted to identify a series of actions which would reduce uncertainties through drought preparedness, more effective responses, and long-term adjustments.

Planning at the Federal Level

A major lesson derived from the latest (1987-91) drought was that many federal agencies in charge of drought-sensitive environmental sectors lacked definitive plans for dealing with drought.[18] These agencies and their regional counterparts such as the river basin commissions, either need to update existing and often out-dated plans, or need to develop new plans as has the Corps of Engineers.[19] The Great Lakes Commission has prepared an excellent drought information document.[20]

Reaction at the Federal Level

The number and type of agencies dealing with drought at the federal level makes cross-agency solutions difficult.[21] President Reagan established an ad hoc federal interagency drought committee at the height of the 1988 drought, but the committee was disbanded before the drought terminated. The message is clear: a standing interagency drought committee is needed with considerable authority to plan, monitor, and respond to droughts.

Monitoring, Detection, and Warning

The 1988 drought provided many examples of inadequate monitoring of the incipient drought, poor warnings of the drought severity, and inappropriate responses.[22] This problem was compounded, as with the Yellowstone Park fires, by the lack of physical understanding of how weather aberrations relate to environmental conditions. U.S. agribusinesses were similarly "caught with their pants down," with no contingency plans and unable to react to the drought in a timely fashion.[23] Existing climate monitoring entities, including regional climate centers, state climatologists, and national climate centers, need to establish a "drought monitoring and information network," in concert with other water and agricultural monitoring bodies, to detect, monitor, and warn about drought. This will become ever more important if the U.S. climate shifts to a more drought-prone regime.

Research on Drought Impacts and Indices

Much of the inaction in addressing drought impacts has resulted from the lack of up-to-date, quantified relationships between weather conditions and affected sectors.[24] Considerable research is needed in both federal laboratories and the university community to measure and define these complex relationships.

State Planning

Considerable progress has been made in the last 10 years in developing state drought contingency plans. Twenty-two states have developed plans, and many have standing drought committees. Every effort should be made by the federal and regional agencies to encourage the remaining states to develop drought contingency plans.

Case Studies of Sensitive Areas

The concept of dealing with drought in specific regions, such as outlined by the Corps of Engineers in their *National Study of Water Management During Drought*[25] is essential. Climate, water resources, law, and agriculture, the main components of droughts, all have regional characteristics that are geographically and geophysically integrated. At the regional and local levels there are generally a number of agencies that deal with water management for multiple-purpose reservoirs and river systems. The effects of the 1988 drought on transportation along the Illinois-Mississippi River areas,[26] and on water availability in the Atlanta region, are examples of how different areas of the country have recently become more sensitive to drought. Anatal and Glantz provide other excellent examples of case study investigations of different areas that are now "sensitive to drought."[27] More such analyses are needed to identify other and newly developing sensitive areas. These drought preparedness studies will help identify the options for addressing drought before the danger occurs.

Emphasis on Drought Prediction Research

Physically-based predictions of droughts, based on understanding of hemispheric and global weather patterns, are not yet available, but effort needs to be focused on this issue. Improvements in empirically-based, climate predictions of drought can be made but await attention.[28] Emphasis must be placed on every means to improve climatological and hydrological predictions of drought.[29]

Development of Drought Mitigation Facilities and Crop Strains

It will be obvious, as we get the findings from improved state and federal planning for drought response, that various water management facilities are needed, either to be constructed or improved, in various parts of the United States. Similarly, improvement of crop varieties is needed to make them more drought resistant. Increasing the flexibility in our water and agricultural systems is simply good business, particularly with the growing likelihood that the future 50 to 100 years will provide a climate different than that of the past 50 to 100 years. Decisions as to how to develop these mitigation devices, new crop strains, and new facilities, should logically follow from the recommended development of federal, regional, and state plans for drought management.

Conclusions

Assessment of the 1987-89 drought, which extended across much of the United States, indicated that government agencies were particularly weak in:
• Pre-event planning and mitigation efforts
• Efforts to reduce the vulnerability to drought in several weather-sensitive sectors
• Monitoring drought and methods for information transfer

An overriding theme was confusion, largely caused by two issues: 1) the sudden development of the drought (and its definition), and 2) uncertainty about the drought's severity. This confusion was compounded by widely different views expressed by government agencies, scientists, and media-presented information. Losses from the 1988 drought amounted to $40 billion. Among the numerous responses were lawsuits relating to crop insurance.[30]

The recent major droughts in the United States, and the resultant responses, provide the basis for declaring some "good news" about drought management. In some regions, coordinating management groups were established that functioned effectively. They addressed complex local drought problems involving overlapping jurisdictions at the local, state, and regional levels. Several positive actions have been made since 1989. These include the national study of water management during drought by the Corps of Engineers, the construction of some new water management facilities in Illinois and elsewhere, the production of new information about droughts and their management, and the development of the nation's six regional climate centers. These centers are now able to provide updated, regional-scale information on incipient drought conditions and their intensity and additionally perform some of the research needed on drought indices and impact models.[31]

There is plenty of "bad news" that still exists in drought management. In my judgment, the nation has and will continue to become ever more vulnerable to drought. Increasing population, waste, aged leaking water systems, pollution of water, and shifts in land use are collectively making many existing water systems, management facilities, and drought management plans outdated. Furthermore, the age-old problem inherent in drought management is that those in decision-making management positions constantly shift, continuously removing the "corporate memory" about droughts and their management. Existing drought plans, old alliances, and management procedures are frequently forgotten, or even unknown by today's decision makers.

Finally, there is no interagency committee for addressing drought. Drought is such a pervasive phenomena that it absolutely requires a broad national view and interagency attention as a part of a well-functioning U.S. water management program.

Are we doomed to fail in achieving effective drought management? If the events of the past 60 years are the best predictor of the future, the answer appears to be "yes."

Notes

1. Stanley A. Changnon, "Climatological Aspects of the 1988 Drought in the United States," paper presented at the AGU meeting, San Francisco, 1988.
2. U.S. National Committee for the Decade for Natural Disaster Reduction, *A Safer Future: Reducing the Impacts of Natural Disasters,* National Research Council, National Academy Press, (Washington, D.C., 1991), 67.
3. International Drought Information Center, *Drought Management and Planning,* IDIC Technical Report Series 91-1, (University of Nebraska-Lincoln, 1990), 245.
4. William E. Riebsame, Stanley A. Changnon, and Thomas R. Karl, *Drought and Natural Resources Management in the United States, Impacts and Implications of the 1987-89 Drought,* (Boulder, CO, 1991), 150-70; David H. Moreau, "Water Supplies and Nationwide Drought of 1988," *J. Water Resour. Planning and Management,* 117 (1990): 460-70; California Department of Water Resources, *California's Continuing Drought: 1987-1991, A Summary of Impacts and Conditions,* (Sacramento, 1991), 4-49.
5. U.S. Geological Survey, *National Water Summary, 1988-89,* (Washington, D.C., 1991), 89-98

6. Riebsame, et al., *Drought and Natural Resources Management,* 150-56.
7. U.S. Geological Survey, *National Water Summary,* 147-56.
8. Stanley A. Changnon, "What Can the Atmospheric Sciences Do to Aid in Drought Management?" Invited paper presented at the Workshop on Drought Management, National Science Foundation, Washington, D.C., 1988.
9. Riebsame, et al., *Drought and Natural Resources Management,*158-60; Moreau, "Water Supplies and Nationwide Drought," 465-68.
10. Jean A. Bowman and Mark A. Collins, *Impacts of Irrigation and Drought on Illinois Ground-Water Resources,* Report of Investigation 109, Illinois State Water Survey, (Champaign, 1987), 4-11.
11. E. Anatal, and Michael H. Glantz, *Identifying and Coping with Extreme Meteorological Events,* Hungarian Meteorological Service, ISBN963-7702-253, (Budapest, 1988), 1-371.
12. Stanley A. Changnon and Joyce M. Changnon, "Use of Climatological Data in Weather Insurance," *J. Climate,* 3 (1990): 568-76.
13. Donald A. Wilhite, *Drought Network News,* (University of Nebraska-Lincoln, 1992).
14. U.S. Geological Survey, *National Water Summary,* 117-22.
15. U.S. Army Corps of Engineers, *A Research Assessment: The National Study of Water Management During Drought,* Institute for Water Resources (IWR) Report 91-NDS-3, (Ft. Belvoir, VA, 1991), 1-6.
16. Riebsame, et al., *Drought and Natural Resources Management,* 164-65.
17. Michael H. Glantz, *Societal Responses to Regional Climatic Change,* (Boulder, CO, 1988), 27-31.
18. Riebsame, et al., *Drought and Natural Resources Management,* 165-66.
19. U.S. Army Corps of Engineers, *A Preliminary Assessment of Corps of Engineers' Reservoirs, Their urposes and Susceptibility to Drought During Drought: The National Study of Water Management During Drought,* IWR Report 91-NDS-2, (Ft. Belvoir, VA, 1991), 1-122.
20. Great Lakes Commission, *A Guide Book to Drought Planning, Management, and Water Level Changes in the Great Lakes,* (Ann Arbor, MI, 1990), 1-61.
21. Riebsame, et al., *Drought and Natural Resources Management,* 161-167.
22. Stanley A. Changnon, "Improving Responses to Drought at the State, Regional, and Federal Levels," Strategic Planning Seminar "The Drought of 1988 and Beyond," National Oceanic and Atmospheric Administration, Washington, D.C., 1988.
23. Stanley A. Changnon, Steven T. Sonka, and Steven Hofing, *Assessment of Uses and Values of Climate Predictions on Agribusiness,* Agricultural Education & Consulting (Champaign, 1991), 55.
24. U.S. Army Corps of Engineers, *Report on the First Year of Study: The National Study of Water Management During Drought,* IWR Report 91-NDS-1, (Ft. Belvoir, VA, 1991), 70.
25. U.S. Army Corps of Engineers, *A Research Assessment,* 28-32.
26. Stanley A. Changnon, "The 1988 Drought, Barges, and Diversions," *Bulletin,* Amer. Meteor. Soc., 70 (1989): 1092-1104.
27. E. Anatal and Michael H. Glantz, *Identifying and Coping with Extreme Meteorological Events,* Hungarian Meteorological Service, (Budapest, 1988), 365-70.

28. International Drought Information Center, *Drought Management and Planning,* IDIC Technical Report Series 91-1, (University of Nebraska-Lincoln, 1990), 9-16.
29. Stanley A. Changnon, "The Dilemma of Climate and Hydrologic Forecasting for the Great Lakes." in *Proceedings of Great Lakes Water Level Forecasting and Statistics Symposium,* Great Lakes Commission, (Windsor, Ontario, 1990).
30. Changnon and Changnon, "Use of Climatological Data in Weather Insurance," 568-76.
31. Stanley A. Changnon, Peter J. Lamb, and Kenneth G. Hubbard, "Regional Climate Centers: New Institutions for Climate Services and Climate Impacts Research," *Bulletin,* Amer. Meteor. Soc., 71 (1990): 527-37.

Comment

Christopher D. Ungate

Kenneth Frederick and Stanley Changnon have illustrated the difficulties that uncertainties present to water managers. The public we serve often forgets about the variation of natural events and human actions. Even though annual rainfall in the Tennessee Valley can range from 50 percent to 150 percent of normal, wet years and droughts take many people by surprise. Within any given year, some portion of the Valley experiences a flood or dry period; there is no such thing as a normal year. Yet the memory of those who experience a flood or a drought event seems to last no more than two or three years. It is difficult to obtain public support or develop consensus among elected officials for effective floodplain management or drought preparedness plans after the immediate effects of the last event have passed.

We should not be too hasty to criticize these reactions. We all know, for example, that the risks of dying in an automobile accident are considerably greater than those of an airplane crash, but we take risks behind the wheel that we would never accept from an airline company. Similarly, despite well-publicized exhortations about diet and exercise, we often do what pleases us the most in the short term.

Nevertheless, we still must find an approach to coping with the risks and uncertainties in water resources. Changnon and Frederick have provided us some insights into how to think about risks and uncertainties in water resources. The common context is a decision maker facing a decision problem, whether it be Congress debating whether to approve a water resources project or pollution control law; a public water system manager trying to determine how to allocate resources to address sources of groundwater contamination; or a local, regional or state agency deciding how to supply water during droughts.

Every decision maker seeks a sound basis for the decision he or she faces. Ronald A. Howard, one of the founders of the field of decision analysis, defines this basis as consisting of: (1) clearly defined alternatives; (2) values that are affected by the decision and for which quantifiable performance measures can be specified; (3) all the available, relevant information to evaluate the alternatives, including the uncertainties which could affect the decision; and (4) the application of correct logic to the alternatives, values and uncertainties to highlight the implications of the alternatives.[1] By applying the techniques of decision analysis, such as influence diagrams and decision trees, the decision maker can be guided into understanding the effect of uncertainties on the decision at hand.

A recent project I completed at TVA illustrates this framework, and relates to the topics addressed by Frederick and Changnon. In September 1987, the Board of Directors of the Tennessee Valley Authority (TVA) authorized a study of the priorities for operating the system of 30 major dams on the Tennessee River and its tributaries. In February 1991, the board adopted the recommendations of the study to provide minimum flows and aerate the releases from 16 dams to improve water quality, and to improve summer lake levels on 10 tributary lakes to increase recreational use and associated economic development. In the intervening 41 months, the study team developed a high quality decision basis using the discipline of decision analysis, complemented by the procedures of the National Environmental Policy Act for incorporating public input and environmental concerns into the decision process.[2]

The decision to delay the drawdown of tributary lakes until 1 August provides the most interesting example of how uncertainties were factored into decision making. A system of tributary reservoirs was constructed by TVA in the 1930s and 1940s to regulate flood crests at Chattanooga, Tennessee, and to store late winter and early spring runoff for use later in the year. Before this decision, lake levels typically reached their peak around Memorial Day, after which the water in storage was used primarily to meet summer seasonal peak power demands.

Delaying the drawdown of tributary lakes beyond Memorial Day was found to increase recreation visitation and tourism activity by making the lakes larger and more accessible for a longer time during the summer months. Residential development would be encouraged and economic activity would increase. Scenic views would improve because more of the unvegetated drawdown zones would be covered. The quality of reservoir fisheries would eventually improve because newly spawned fish would have greater food and cover in shoreline areas, promoting their survival. Navigation depths on the lower Ohio and Mississippi rivers would be increased because flows at the mouth of the Tennessee River would be increased as tributary lakes are drained after 1 August. In a dry year, this would yield navigation benefits by reducing the impacts on channel depth during the dry months on those rivers (September and October).

Other factors discouraged delaying drawdown until Labor Day or beyond. These factors included interference with the navigation and flood control operations of the U.S. Army Corps of Engineers during the late fall and early winter months; significant hydropower losses because water that is normally used to meet summer power demands would no longer be available; and environmental concerns due to increased coal-fired power plant emissions from replacement power generation.

Before the board decided to adopt the proposed change in reservoir operating policy, it requested a clear presentation of the effects of the change on the operation of the TVA power system. By delaying drawdown of the tributary reservoirs until 1 August, hydropower generation would be shifted from mid-March through July to August through December. This shift could have implications for thermal unit maintenance scheduling, generate-buy decisions (whether to generate power from TVA plants or buy from another utility), and the next capacity expansion decision, among others.

The effect of shifted hydropower generation could be calculated in terms of the energy and capacity costs for the TVA power system. Four uncertainties were found to have the biggest effects on cost: hydrology (spring and summer rainfall), the expected growth in power demand, the timing of the peak summer season power demand, and whether large thermal units were returned to service from spring maintenance outage before the beginning of the summer peak power season. Hydrology and load growth affected both energy and capacity costs; the timing of the system peak and maintenance scheduling affected energy costs only. Probability distributions were developed for each uncertainty based on historical data and staff judgment. The effects of each uncertainty on the cost of the alternative was examined for high, low and average values of the variable.

Hydrology dwarfed the effects of other uncertainties on energy costs. During a wet spring and summer, energy costs could be ten times higher than average ($20 million versus $2 million) with recreational lake levels because the capacity of reservoirs to store added runoff is reduced, leading to spilling of water without generating power. However, total hydropower generation is above average in these years, mitigating the impact of the lost energy. In a dry year, there would be a benefit of $9 million rather the average cost of $2 million because water is saved to generate power during the month of August, when the probability of the peak summer season load is highest. Delaying drawdown until 1 August would increase the flexibility of hydropower to respond to peak power demands in years when this flexibility is impaired by low rainfall.

The cost of replacement capacity was eliminated by developing methods for improving tributary lake levels that permitted extra hydropower generation during periods when high cost power sources might be used to meet power demands, or supply to power customers may have to be interrupted. The effects of uncertain hydrology and load growth were not significant once this method was implemented.

This example shows how uncertainties can be considered when making decisions about water resources. It seems similar to the sensitivity and risk-cost analysis which Frederick describes and is adaptable to the techniques for valuing public goods he describes. In the early stages of the TVA study, we analyzed the value of recreation visits, improved scenery, increased land values, and other public goods, and compared them to power costs. We did not develop these analyses beyond a preliminary level because we wanted to focus the public review of the evaluation of alternatives on the issues involved in selecting one over another, rather than on how TVA staff valued public goods.

The framework that decision analysis provides for analyzing uncertainties would be very useful for examining the lessons about droughts that Changnon presents. The analysis of summer lake levels on TVA tributary lakes included a consideration of how droughts would affect recreational summer pool levels. We found that recreation target elevations in tributary lakes could be met or exceeded in 90 percent of the years. In the remaining 10 percent, there simply was not enough water to fill the lakes. The implementation procedure was carefully designed to account for how summer peak power demands would be met during droughts. Realistic summer lake level targets would be set, and extra water would be used to generate hydropower when incremental power costs reached high values. The frequency of both occurrences (hours of high incremental power cost and drought conditions) was so small that the capacity cost was insignificant.

The authors are to be commended for providing a thought-provoking discussion of the risks and uncertainties in water resources and how we might cope with them.

Notes

1. Ronald A. Howard, "Decision Analysis: Practice and Promise," *Management Science* 34, no. 6 (June 1988): 679-95.
2. Tennessee Valley Authority, *Tennessee River and Reservoir System Operation and Planning Review*, Final Environmental Impact Statement (Knoxville, TN, 1990), TVA/RDG/91-1.

America's Water
Infrastructure Needs

Short-sighted Policy Impacts on the Long-term Viability of Public Water Systems

Frederick A. Marrocco, Thomas M. Franklin, and William J. Sedlak

Introduction

In Pennsylvania, as in many states, public water systems were established at a time of relatively little regulatory control by federal, state, or local governments. They were intended to support urban and industrial growth in the nation's early years; in more recent years, they have supported suburban sprawl.

At a time of relatively small population and an abundance of uncontaminated water, the operative policy for years was to provide all of the water demanded by users at the cheapest possible price. Little was invested in the operation, maintenance, and replacement of the system. In fact, many of these systems became "cash cows" to fund other needs in the community.

This cheap water policy continues in practice today in a large number of public water systems. Until very recently, one prominent Pennsylvania city, which serves corrosive, unfiltered surface water to over 50,000 people, was transferring $2.5 million of water system revenue annually to subsidize general government operations. The Pennsylvania Department of Environmental Resources (DER) was forced to take the city to court to get it to spend an estimated $25,000 to install corrosion control treatment.

The Legacy

In this country, there are tens of thousands of community systems that serve between 25 and 500 people. It is probable that there are untold thousands more serving populations below 25. In Pennsylvania, there are 723 community systems for between 25 and 100 people each, with another 763 serving between 100 and 500 people. Collectively, these 1486 systems serve only about 233,000 people, or 2.2 percent of the 10.6 million people protected under the State's Safe Drinking Water Program (see Figures 3.1 & 3.2). Conversely, these small systems represent sixty percent of the 2,456 community systems regulated by Pennsylvania and are overwhelmingly comprised of mobile home parks and associations

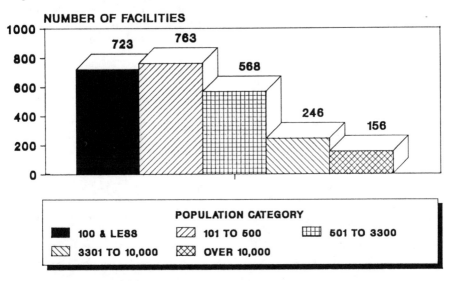

Figure 3.1. *Pennsylvania Active Community Water Systems—Number of Systems by Population Category*

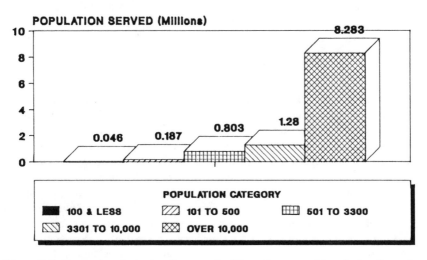

Figure 3.2. *Pennsylvania Active Community Water Systems—Population Served by Population Category*

The map in Figure 3.3 illustrates that these systems are not confined to the stereotypical Appalachian community in western Pennsylvania, but exist in high concentrations as well in the more economically vibrant eastern part of the state. These systems will be hard pressed to generate the revenues to address existing deficiencies, let alone make the investments in capital necessary to comply with the 1986 amendments to the Safe Drinking Water Act (SDWA).

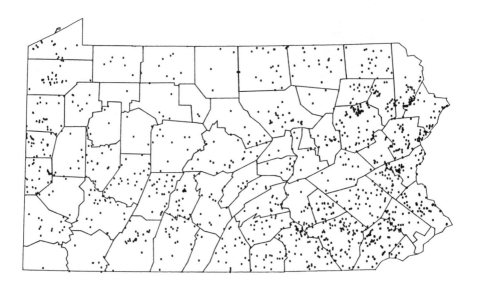

Figure 3.3. *Community Water Systems in Pennsylvania—Serving 500 or Fewer People*

The small size of these systems is not only a barrier to generating the revenues to properly operate, maintain and replace the facilities, but it is also a barrier to securing the necessary management and technical expertise to perform these functions competently. Based on DER's experience with enforcing the SDWA, from 75 to 90 percent of all monitoring and reporting violations occur at small systems. Small systems also account for about 90 percent of all violations of the bacteriological contamination standard. Clearly, the state's program work load is driven by the very large number of small systems regulated under the program. It is reasonable to project that non-compliance at these hundreds of small systems will become considerably worse as the many new and complex regulatory requirements mandated by Congress in the '86 amendments take effect.

Impact on Operations (TAPSS and FPPE)

The cheap water policy associated with large systems and the revenue-generating limitations of small systems have contributed to poor operations of public water systems. Policymakers working with big systems infrequently understand the complexity of the regulatory requirements and technology, nor do they do fully appreciate the important public health protection function provided by the facilities. As a result, they tend to undervalue the service provided by the system's personnel, offer relatively low compensation packages, and may find it difficult to hire and retain individuals with the level of technical knowledge and expertise required to operate the facilities properly. Two initiatives recently undertaken by DER's Safe Drinking Water Program staff point up the magnitude of the operational deficiencies in the public water systems of Pennsylvania. The Technical Assistance Program for Small Systems (TAPSS) and the Filter Plant Performance Evaluation Program (FPPE) identified serious operational deficiencies in a broad cross-section of public water systems.

TAPSS was established to help small system operators improve their knowledge and skills in three specific areas of operation: filtration, disinfection, and corrosion control treatment. Operators from 360 small systems received training under this program. There were three common operational deficiencies that instructors observed during the training: lack of an on-site operator during hours of operation, insufficient monitoring for water quality and process control, and the lack of a preventive maintenance program.[1] Very few of the operators participating in TAPSS had even a basic understanding of water treatment plant chemistry or sufficient knowledge to make necessary process adjustments for water quality changes. Although well-intentioned, most of the operators participating in this program had insufficient knowledge, skills, and treatment facilities to carry out the important public health protection responsibility with which they are charged.

The DER's FPPE Program grew out of the Giardia monitoring program which was initiated in 1985 as a result of a number of waterborne giardiasis (usually associated with diarrhea in human beings) outbreaks at community water supplies. At the time, there were about 175 filtration treatment plants in operation in the state, and about 277 systems using unfiltered surface water sources for public consumption. Following the outbreaks, a policy decision was made to require all surface water sources to be filtered and disinfected. Since this policy action would more than double the number of filtration treatment plants in the state, it was recognized that a special effort must be put forth to assure that operator skills were adequate for these more complex and demanding responsibilities. As a first effort, Department staff determined if operating personnel at existing filter plants were performing their responsibilities satisfactorily. The findings forthcoming from this first phase of the FPPE Program were revealing.

211

A filter plant's ability to reliably remove giardia-sized particles from the finished water was the primary measure of performance for the FPPE Program. Of the plants evaluated in 1988, the first year of the program, about 60 percent of the facilities were judged to be providing unsatisfactory performance and exposing the public's health to an outbreak of giardiasis. Through expanded technical assistance initiatives at these facilities, and enforcement actions in some instances, the unsatisfactory evaluations have been reduced to only about 50 percent of the plants evaluated in 1991. Improvements in filter plant performance have been real and measurable, but very slow to make the turn.

The explanation for this high level of unsatisfactory performance at filter plants derives from the same deficiencies discussed above under TAPSS. Operational problems, equipment and design deficiencies, inadequate operator training, and lack of administrative support combined to adversely affect a plant's effluent water quality. One of the major problems observed during plant evaluations was the lack of treatment process monitoring and control. In many cases, operators did not understand basic concepts of chemical pretreatment and filter operation. Design deficiencies existing at a number of plants constructed in the early 1900s, as well as the numerous responsibilities loaded on many plant operators, contributed to the pervasive unsatisfactory performance at these facilities.[2]

Waterborne Disease Outbreaks and Their Costs

Public water system owners who fail to invest adequately in their systems also expose themselves to potentially significant liability damages and expose the community to large economic losses. In the aftermath of one of Pennsylvania's giardiasis outbreaks, Resources for the Future conducted a study[3] of the economic impacts experienced by the affected community. Estimates of total losses reported in the study ranged up to $55.5 million. Local commerce suffered considerable economic losses as well, the largest of which was attributed to actions taken by individuals to avoid drinking contaminated water.

The local economic impacts were reported[4] to have resulted in two precedent-setting rate decisions by the Pennsylvania Public Utility Commission (PUC). In the first case, the Commission ordered a 25 percent rate reduction during the six-month period that the public was under a boil water advisory. In the second case, the PUC denied a requested rate increase of over $100 million to the same public water system for failure to provide an acceptable quality of water service. Class action suits totalling close to $1 billion were also filed against the Company by the affected public.

Deferred Needs (PENNVEST)

To provide the necessary financial assistance for public water and sewer system improvements, the Pennsylvania Infrastructure Investment Authority (PIIA) Act, commonly known as PENNVEST, was enacted in March of 1988. PENNVEST was capitalized by over $1 billion in state and federal funds to provide low interest loans and limited grant assistance for publicly and privately owned drinking water and sewerage facilities. PENNVEST is a revolving loan program. Estimates indicate that it allows the financing of over $2.5 billion of new construction over a 25-year period. Eligible projects are evaluated based primarily on public health, safety and environmental impacts.

PENNVEST has been a very important source of funding for many systems in Pennsylvania. Since 1988, 271 applications were approved for PENNVEST funding of approximately $404 million. Of this amount, about $75 million was approved for 161 projects for small systems. PENNVEST funding figures also illustrate the economy of scale enjoyed by larger systems. Based on service area population of systems approved for funding, the total PENNVEST assistance provided for each customer amounts to about $77 while the amount approved per customer served by small systems, a subset of total assistance, is about $429.

In the early stages of the PENNVEST Program operators of some small water systems were concerned that the funds were insufficient to pay a consultant to determine the most cost effective alternative for resolving their problems and then to design the project and submit a construction application to PENNVEST. In 1989 two types of "advance funding" applications were made available to applicants. One application was for financial assistance to perform feasibility studies and the other was for project design. Since 1989, twelve advance funding applications have been approved for small communities, providing over $ 1.3 million in financial assistance for those purposes.

One distressing statistic of the PENNVEST program is that through fiscal year 1991 fewer than 40 projects have been proposed to address unfiltered surface water sources. It appears that even after the serious outbreaks of giardiasis and the adoption of Pennsylvania's filtration rule in March 1989, operators continue to defer improvements on systems. At the PENNVEST board meeting in April 1992, 31 applicants requested funding in excess of $145 million to address requirements of the filtration rule. PENNVEST water system funding normally amounts to about $100 million annually and would have soon been significantly reduced if Pennsylvania voters had not recently authorized $350 million in additional state indebtedness to subsidize program funding. Nevertheless, to comply with the filtration rule deadlines, it is likely that many of these systems may still have to look elsewhere for funding assistance.

To maximize the benefits of the PENNVEST Program and ensure the long-term viability of systems receiving assistance, the PIIA Act also required that a comprehensive plan for piped drinking water facilities and wastewater disposal be developed by 31 December 1990. Two of the required elements in this plan were an inventory of existing facilities and an inventory of drinking water construction needs. Department staff gathered information on existing facilities and construction needs while performing sanitary surveys on the state's 2,456 community water systems. Water suppliers or Department staff identified potential projects and their estimated costs but they did not evaluate the cost effectiveness of various project alternatives. Department cost estimates were based primarily on information from the U.S. Environmental Protection Agency (EPA) and the Means Construction Cost Guide. Actual construction costs for some projects over the past year have exceeded the Department's estimate by 30 percent or more. Since construction cost is about 70 percent of the total project cost, another 30 percent needs to be added to estimate the cost of the entire project. Adding another 30 percent to reflect the actual construction cost experience to date yields a total project cost for all systems of about $1.6 billion. The estimated construction cost for community water systems serving 500 or fewer people is about $85 million and for systems serving 501 to 3300 people, around $205 million. Adjusting for total project cost and actual construction cost experience yields new estimates of about $136 million and $328 million, respectively.

Many of the identified water system improvements are the result of the 1986 amendments to the federal SDWA. About $868 million or 87 percent of the total construction needs are associated with treatment, distribution system improvements, and finished water storage. Most of this cost relates directly to the treatment requirements established under the filtration rule. Old distribution systems that allow for the loss of more than 20 percent of treated water must be replaced to allow for a reduction in size of costly water filtration systems. Uncovered finished water storage facilities must be covered or replaced, and systems with insufficient finished water storage or storage at inappropriate locations to support their new filtration system are constructing additional storage facilities.

The increased user costs to support system improvements will be the greatest for customers of small systems. The increased cost per household will be large in many cases because user rates were too low to allow for proper system operation and maintenance; thus deferred needs are the greatest. Figure 3.4 shows current average user rates and estimated rates after improvements have been made for various size systems.

Given the complexity and variability of current user rate structures, the data presented in Figure 3.4 should be considered in a relative sense rather than an absolute one. In other words, it is unlikely that twelve percent of system average annual user charges currently exceed $600 per year. However, it is very likely that there will be at least a ten percent increase in the actual number of systems with such high rates.

214

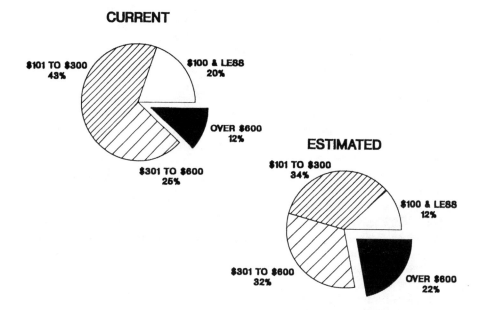

Figure 3.4. *Annual Pennsylvania Active Water Bill—Percent of Systems*

EPA assumes acceptable user rates, based on a customer's ability and willingness to pay, are about 1 to 1.5 percent of the median household income. In Pennsylvania, based on a state-wide median household income of about $29,000, annual users rates greater than $435 may not be acceptable. For many small systems, physical or administrative consolidation may be the only answer to long-term system viability.

Conclusion

Can the many years of neglect in the public drinking water field be corrected? If the '86 Amendments are rigorously enforced at the larger systems with a good rate base potential, there certainly will be substantially increased investment in facilities and personnel at these systems. The need to gain access to public markets and government funding programs should strengthen the internal management at these systems. The increased pressure on available water resources is also likely to change pricing policy to reflect the true cost of service and promote water conservation.

The solution at the hundreds of small systems which do not have a viable rate base will be much more elusive. For this large body of systems, the regulatory agencies do not have the resources to enforce the regulations, and the systems cannot generate sufficient revenues to comply. A different approach will be needed. To this end, the Department, with funding assistance from EPA, undertook a study to find effective solutions to overcome the viability problem extant at the many small systems.

The Viability Study Report[5] determined that the basic problem was the inability of managers to cope with new economic realities. Water was always abundant, inexpensive to treat and deliver at small scale, and almost completely taken for granted by consumers. The performance demands placed upon small water systems were historically so low that many were created with no reserve or depreciation fund mechanism to provide for eventual capital replacement.

The 1986 SDWA amendments significantly expand the performance requirements for small systems. Many now require much more operation and maintenance than were ever envisioned at the time they were created. Compliance will necessarily entail replacement of many existing, deteriorated plants; additional capital investment to install treatment technology; additional monitoring to document the absence of exotic contaminants; and further elevation of the operational standards of performance. Unfortunately, an increasing number of the small systems are proving incapable of meeting these new demands for improved public health protection.

The Viability Study Report recommends that programs be instituted to put these systems on a sound business basis through the development of facilities, management, and financial plans. The facilities plan will define the physical scope of necessary services and identify the most cost-effective method for providing them. The management plan will specify the commitments needed for the effective operation and maintenance of the system. The financial plan will explain how to generate the revenues necessary to cover the full costs of capitalization requirements under the facilities plan and operation and maintenence costs under the management plan. Those systems unable to demonstrate a sound business footing for the facility and establish long-term viability would be forced into restructuring under the Study's recommended strategy. Restructuring options could include interconnection, acquisition, or consolidation under a regional authority.

Tens of thousands of public water systems have been established in this country in a regulatory environment that placed few demands on the owners to invest in their facilities. As a result decisions were delayed, funds were used elsewhere, and many investment decisions were deferred. The result—as exposed in implementing the 1986 amendments to the Safe Drinking Water Act—is a crisis of enormous magnitude. It has been observed[6] that resolution of the small system problem will involve much broader questions of infrastructure policy, economic development and rural poverty. New institutional arrangements will be required to respond efficiently to the deferred investment liability facing thousands of the nation's public water systems. Success in this area will require leadership and commitment from federal, state and local governments to establish the necessary new legislative authorities, provide access to funding, require vastly improved planning, and return the water supply industry to a sound business footing.

Notes

1. Walter L. Harner and Jay C. Africa, "Pennsylvania's Technical Assistance Program for Small Water Systems," Pennsylvania Department of Environmental Resources, Division of Water Supplies, Harrisburg, PA.
2. "Pennsylvania Safe Drinking Water Program: Filter Plant Performance Evaluations—A Summary of Procedures and Results, January 1988 through December 1990," Pennsylvania Department of Environmental Resources, Division of Water Supplies, Harrisburg, PA.
3. W. Harrington, A. J. Krupnick and W. O. Spofford, "The Benefits of Preventing an Outbreak of Giardiasis Due to Drinking Water Contamination," U.S. Environmental Protection Agency Grant No. CR 810 466 010 (September 1985).
4. Frederick A. Marrocco, "Does EPA's Surface Water Treatment Rule Include Filtration?," *Annual Conference Proceedings of the American Water Works Association* (Kansas City, MO, 1987), 931-37.
5. Wade Miller Associates, Inc., "State Initiatives to Address Non-Viable Small Water Systems In Pennsylvania," Pennsylvania Department of Environmental Resources Contract BCEC RFP 10-89, ME #90014 (August 1991).
6. John E. Cromwell, III, Walter L. Harner, Jay C. Africa and J. Stephen Schmidt, "Small Water Systems at a Crossroads," submitted for publication in the May 1992 issue of the *Journal AWWA*.

Alliances: The New Foundation for America's Ports and Waterways

Arlene L. Dietz

The web of alliances which enable the smooth functioning of the U.S. water transportation system is a remarkable net of private and public commitments. Each partner shares in the development, maintenance and operation of this system, whether it is the federal government contributing the common channels, the state, port authority, regional or local government providing shoreside infrastructure, or the private terminal operator and vessel owner moving the goods. The traditional alliance of federal, state and local governments and their roles are shifting, while private-public and private-private sector alliances are being woven together to create a new foundation.

U.S. Port and Waterway System

The commercial water transport system of the U.S., comprised of 25,000 miles of waterways and over 200 deep draft ports, moves 16 percent of inter-city freight, 99 percent of overseas foreign trade by volume, and, by value, 60 percent of overseas exports and 75 percent of overseas imports. The nation's competitiveness in the world is directly influenced by this one transport mode. Indispensable for the nation's economic well-being, national defense, and environmental health, waterway transport offers the most economical, safest, cleanest and energy efficient transportation per ton-mile for both overseas and domestic traffic. Figure 1 depicts the waterways and principal U.S. ports.

Waterway Use

Use of water transport grew quite slowly but steadily during the 1980s, exceeding 2.1 billion tons in 1990, an increase of over 100 million tons from 1980. This traffic growth was led by foreign commerce, which grew from 921 to 1029 million tons, an 11.7 percent increase from 1980 to 1990. Imports

PRINCIPAL PORTS OF THE UNITED STATES
(10 Million Tons or Greater)

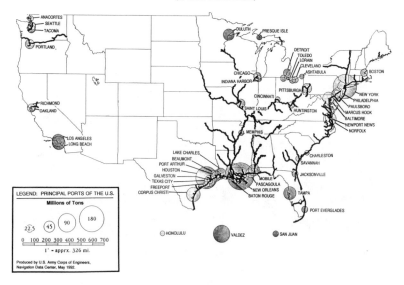

Figure 4.1. *Principle Ports of the United States*
(10 Million Tons or Greater)

dominated, surging ahead by 16.7 percent, from 517 to 603 million tons. Figures 4.2 and 4.3 display the breakdown of U.S. waterborne commerce between 1981 and 1990.[1]

In 1991, the United States was the world's top merchandise importer and exporter with 13.9 percent and 12 percent of the world trade, respectively.[2] Since nearly all overseas traffic moves by water, the value of the U.S. seaports to the U.S. and global economy cannot be overstated.

Energy products continue to dominate waterborne commerce, comprising over half of all foreign and domestic tonnage. The leading commodity category by far is petroleum, capturing in 1989 over 40 percent of foreign and domestic waterborne tonnage. Domestic petroleum moves predominately by pipeline and water. In 1989, on a tonnage basis, 23 percent moved by water and 52 percent moved by pipeline.[3] Since petroleum imports are nearly all waterborne, U.S. energy policy must involve the U.S. seaports and all its connecting waterways. Internal waterborne coal movements primarily serve the electric utility industry which will use over 40 percent more coal by the year 2010. These internal coal movements are expected to triple to over 300 million tons by 2010.[4] Second to petroleum in volume of both foreign and domestic waterborne commerce, coal is primarily an export, unlike petroleum. The shipment of coal overseas will more than double to 236 million tons by 2010, with most of the coal going to Europe.[5]

219

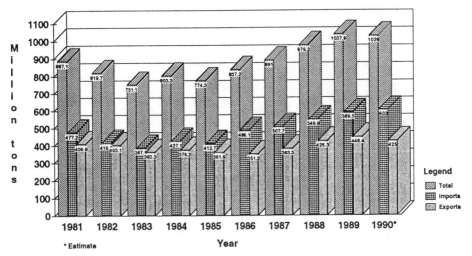

Figure 4.2. *Foreign Waterborne Commerce 1981-1990*

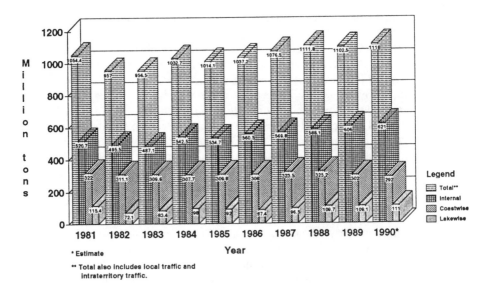

Figure 4.3. *Domestic Waterborne Commerce of the U.S. by Type of Traffic 1981-1990*

The U.S. grain and oilseed overseas exports moving through U.S. ports bring in $25-$27 billion to the U.S. economy. Sixty-five percent of these exports are moved to export terminals via the inland waterway system. Agriculture and allied industries contribute 20 percent to the U.S. GNP (Gross National Product).[6] Thus, just as U.S. energy policy is linked to the ports and waterways, so too is U.S. agricultural policy.

Waterborne transport, besides being highly energy efficient, is also very competitive. As an industry, it is always pressing through technological and managerial efficiencies for continuous improvements. Vessel size, capacity, and speed have all increased over the last 20 years. However, during the 1980s, with modern fuel management technologies, operating speeds actually have declined. In the late 1960s and early 1970s, containerships handled 500 containers and required 25-27 feet of water. Today, the sixth generation of ship carries 4000 TEUs (Twenty-foot Equivalent Units) and draws 40 feet. Economies of scale have similarly affected dry bulk carriers; for example, today's 150,000 dwt (deadweight) coal vessels draw 55 feet. The changing ship size drives the need for deeper and wider channels, berthing areas, longer and stronger wharves, more back-up acreage next to wharves, and new cargo handling equipment. More pressure is placed on ports to increase their handling efficiency. Fewer and fewer ports are capable of handling the world fleet of today. Instead, we see the rise of mega-ports with niche ports interspersed.[7]

Responding to economies of scale, the number of vessel operators on the U.S. inland waterways has declined 30 percent over the past decade, and the number of barge lines continues to shrink. However, the 1990s should bring a surge in investment since nearly 40 percent of the self-propelled U.S. vessel fleet and one-fourth of the barges are over 20 years of age.[8] From $140 million to $260 million must be invested annually in the hopper barge fleet over the next twenty years, while the new tank barge fleet probably will require $2 billion cumulatively over the same time.[9] In the meantime, working cooperatively with shippers, the barge and towing industry is improving barge utilization. Vertical integration in the rapidly consolidating industry helps control more aspects of service and allows for greater efficiency.[10] In the last 10 years alone, waterway carriers' management practices resulted in a 25 percent increase in fuel efficiency from 400 to 500 ton-miles per gallon. This compares with railroad's 36 percent improvement over the same period.[11] Increased fuel efficiency is important since the barge and towing industry pays for half of the construction and rehabilitation costs of federal improvements through user fees on the fuel.

Investment in Water Transportation Infrastructure

General tax support to waterways and ports continues to decline following the long term trend of diminishing federal investment. According to Nancy Dorn, Assistant Secretary of the Army for Civil Works, total civil works expenditures have spiraled downward for the last 20 years for a 25 percent reduction in constant dollars.[12] Waterway and harbor investment reductions have led this decline. Harbor projects in constant 1988 dollars displayed a 23 percent decrease in annual expenditures in 1990 compared to 1980. Similarly, annual federal investment in the inland waterway system fell 41 percent in the past decade. Only inland waterway operations and maintenance (O&M) grew by a modest 12 percent; harbor maintenance fell 25 percent.

Inland

Investment needs are rapidly increasing on the federal system as the inland locks and dams age. Today 122 (42 percent) of all lock chambers are over 50 years old. In fact, the Inland Waterway Users Board announced in its December 1991 annual report that 50 lock and dam sites plus another dozen channels will require major improvements over the next 20 years.[13] However, given the current trust fund arrangement of 50 percent cost sharing, only three or four locks can be replaced per decade, leaving a growing need. Table 4.1 shows the trust fund receipts, expenditures and balance from 1987 to 1991.

Table 4.1. Inland Waterway Trust Fund Status for Fiscal Years 1987-1991 (Millions of Dollars)

Fiscal Year	Tax Receipts	Expenditures	Fund Balance
1987	48.3	24.5	300.6
1988	48.1	62.1	310.8
1989	47.0	62.8	321.1
1990	62.8	117.3	292.8
1991·	60.5	148.6	225.9

U.S. Army Corps of Engineers

Federal inland waterway facilities pose a serious future constraint to the continuing efficiency of this mode of transportation. For example, along the Upper Mississippi and Illinois rivers there are a total of 35 locks at least 50 years old with half approaching capacity by the year 2000.[14] Without necessary repairs and replacements of these locks, American grain exports could be seriously hampered with potentially major economic and foreign policy consequences.

Corps of Engineers O&M funding for inland waterways is the only area that increased in real expenditures over the past decade. This O&M increase is directly related to the growing number of aging locks. Aging means increasing closures of waterways for repairs with commensurate increases in costs to users. Investment in the waterways goes a long way. Since waterways have characteristics of a declining cost industry, once a channel is dredged or a lock modified, the added cost of one additional vessel or ton-mile is small.[15] Improvement to the waterway infrastructure, allowing for predictable depths and safe conditions, enhances the productivity of users and, therefore, the U.S. economy.

The consequence of disinvesting in the waterways is a shift from waterways to alternative modes. This shift is counter to the nation's economic, environmental, and energy policies. According to a recent study of selected barge movements in Minnesota, shifts from water could increase fuel consumption as much as 250 to 825 percent, exhaust emissions by 400 percent, accidents by 150 percent, and also add to waste disposal and traffic congestion.[16]

Ports

Coal exports in 1991 increased at Hampton Roads, Baltimore, the Lower Mississippi River, and Mobile. All these ports had been recently deepened. These dredging projects involved local-federal partnerships with local sponsors paying up to 60 percent of the first costs (until 1986, the costs had been fully federally funded). They enabled large world-class ships to use these ports economically. Norfolk alone handled over 50 percent of U.S. coal exports in 1991. The federal government invested over $1 billion in deep draft projects from 1980 to 1990. However, 25 years ago annual federal investment in constant dollars was triple that of 1990. Since passage of the 1986 Water Resources Development Act, ports are obligated to contribute from 20 to 60 percent of the costs of a federal project, depending on the depth.

The trend toward port self-sufficiency is evident in the shift in the funding of port maintenance and operations. From the 1970s through the 1980s, port revenue as a funding source at public ports increased from 27 to 48 percent,[17] but governments at all levels reduced their financial support to ports. Regardless, ports must continually modernize to be competitive and attract carriers. In a similar way, private industry within a port must also continue to invest in handling facilities. Considering the 200 major ports, the 5,500 cargo terminals and 2,900 marine service facilities, the magnitude of investment required to utilize federal channels and facilities is formidable.

After *Fragile Foundations*—Unrealized Investment

In 1988, *Fragile Foundations*, a federal report, claimed if the U.S. failed to reverse the decline in investment, the U.S. would fall further behind in world economic competitiveness. This reversal has not happened in water transportation. Also, the report noted that spending for O&M is the key to overall longevity and efficiency of public works capital assets. Four years later both federal and state investments continue to decline, with O&M increasing only slightly. In constant dollars, federal deep draft and shallow draft navigation investments have fallen 23 percent and 41 percent, respectively, from 1980 to 1990.

The report concluded that the federal government "should continue its primary role in . . . inland waterways, highways of national significance, [and] intermodal freight transportation." *Fragile Foundations'* strategy to carry out these roles was to double overall capital spending, clarify roles of various governments, accelerate trust fund dollars, increase beneficiaries' share, offer incentives for maintenance, and increase added research and development support. Accomplishments since its publication are major increases in user fees—harbor maintenance tax tripled and the inland waterway fees increased 50 percent.

The U.S., according to *Fragile Foundations*, is obliged to support national defense, economic vitality, and community well-being with safe and productive public works.

> Thus by reorienting public spending to upgrade and expand the public capital stock, the productivity of the nation's workforce, our competitive position internationally could be improved. . .If there is no excess capacity to accommodate growth in public works facilities capacity must increase at the same rate as use if service quality is to be maintained. . . .To improve service quality, capacity must increase faster than use.[18]

Unfortunately, federal, state and local waterway investments continue to decline. This, coupled with a mounting backlog in private sector requirements, suggests major challenges to U.S. productivity, economic security, and global competitiveness.

Alliances: Key to America's Future

The solution to the waterway infrastructure investment dilemma is new arrangements among all players—governments, ports, labor, shippers and carriers. Infrastructure and assets need to be shared, common information systems developed, and federal-private research and development increased. These actions can be realized through a mix of alliances—intermodal, shipper-port, shipper-carrier, as well as intergovernmental. Although these alliances will not compensate for the absence of major infrastructure investment, they will enhance productivity and offer new efficiencies until the nation can shift its priorities to increase investment in the water transportation infrastructure.

Federal

Giving the nation a predictable federal investment program is part of the current strategy that is played out in the biennial water resources authorization process reestablished in 1986. Assistant Secretary Dorn, recently testified that the Corps of Engineers' aging projects have a replacement value well over $125 billion.[19] Knowing that 122 lock chambers exceed their economic life in 1992 speaks volumes, especially when coupled with the ability to invest in new facilities at a rate of only three to four locks per decade.

Local cooperation agreements between port authorities and the Corps of Engineers now total $7 billion. Another $1.5 billion of inland waterway trust fund monies, derived from the barge and towing industry users, have been authorized for the inland system.[20] The shippers involved in deep sea commerce pay for all the maintenance of U.S. ports and waterways. Nevertheless, whereas inland waterway carriers and shippers have a user board to hear their concerns, deep draft shippers cannot turn to any similar organization.[21]

The Corps of Engineers, a federal leader in cooperative arrangements, not only works with state and local sponsors on project planning and design, but also shares regulatory responsibilities with these agencies. As the nation's regulator of wetlands, the Corps shares policy-making with several federal agencies and cooperates with state and local agencies. In accordance with the Intermodal Surface Transportation Efficiency Act of 1991 (ISTEA), the Corps, Environmental Protection Agency, and the Department of Transportation signed a joint memorandum on 1 May 1992 to expedite environmental and other reviews that must take place before transportation improvements can begin. Strategic alliances among governmental bodies, such as this agreement, have become the watchword for environmental and economic advancements in the 1990s.

According to ISTEA, Section 2, "It is the policy of the U.S. to develop a National Intermodal Transportation System that is economically efficient and environmentally sound, provides the foundation for the Nation to compete in the global economy, and will move people and goods in an energy efficient manner." The Act continues, "Systems shall provide improved access to ports and airports, the Nation's link to world commerce." In Section 133, the Surface Transportation Program, the act authorizes states to apportion funds for construction or reconstruction necessary to accommodate other transport modes. The states may act directly to reduce congestion and thereby contribute to attainment of national ambient air quality standards. Since water transport is the least polluting and most energy efficient mode of transport, any means to shift to water in urban areas will contribute to air quality and energy self-sufficiency. The act includes energy use as an objective of state planning. It also addresses rural access projects with an end goal of promoting economic development in rural areas.[22] The provisions of ISTEA hold out new opportunities in intermodal and interagency cooperation, offering positive signs for the future health of the U.S. transportation system.

Carriers and Terminals

Driven by carrier initiatives, U.S. companies continue to forge new management alliances. Malcom McLean, the father of containerization, has allied his Trailer-Bridge organization with Tidewater, Inc., to shuttle barges between the mainland and Puerto Rico, operating as a truck line.[23] Recently a LASH barge operator from New Orleans joined with a stevedore company out of Mobile, Alabama, to provide an all-weather rapid cargo transfer facility at Memphis, Tennessee for LASH barges. The result is the only mid-continent covered facility in the U.S. to serve water, rail and truck.[24]

At ocean ports, terminal operators are reducing costs by sharing equipment, consolidating, and expanding services. Like shipping lines, terminals are forming partnerships to reduce capital equipment costs. Terminals which are not subsidiaries of shipping lines may find survival difficult. As with the successful transportation companies and ports, those providing terminal services will have to expand the nature of these services in the future.[25]

Modal efficiencies are used wherever possible. The transportation of western coal exemplifies the importance of this approach, utilizing complex transportation partnerships. Driven by the Clean Air Act and the requirement to control sulfur dioxide emissions, a 120-car train winds 1,200 miles from Wyoming, to Paducah, Kentucky where it switches to another line for a 20-mile leg to a Kentucky terminal where its load is dumped into eight barges. Towed upriver for 220 miles, the coal is unloaded at an Alabama facility for blending with higher sulfur, higher BTU Illinois coal. The Illinois coal had a similar rail-barge haul. The blended coal, 90 percent Illinois and 10 percent western, is moved to its final destination by rail.[26]

Shippers and Carriers

Historically, rail carriers provided service between the rail terminals they operated. Steamship companies connected the ports. Ports provided shore infrastructure. Truckers and draymen did the intervening service, and customs brokers or forwarders managed the paperwork transactions. The paperwork was always the most complicated part of a transaction. Today, a railroad may provide door to door service in addition to the line haul. Roles change from customer to customer. In many respects, companies are creating new products, as did Federal Express with its overnight delivery service, thus stimulating and creating demand.[27]

Craig Philip, Vice President, Ingram Barge, noted, ". . . because few carriers will be in a position to provide all of the services required by even a single one of their large customers, developing alliances and partnership is a key to the future." Philip sees continued alliances between transportation suppliers and buyers. Barge lines, railroads, and truck lines will tie themselves more closely into large integrated service organizations. Some of the key owners of barge companies today include grain, oil and petroleum companies, coal producers, and even railroads.[28]

Logistics services offered today provide the ultimate in alliances. U.S. freight forwarders and customs brokers are world-wide operations providing what the industry calls seamless operations services from purchase order all the way through to delivery. This requires the most modern communications coupled with the right partners. Freight forwarders and customs brokers do not have assets such as vessels, trucks, planes, and trains, but have partners world-wide that do. These companies not only handle all logistics, but customs clearances as well. They clear cargo before it leaves for its destination. An integrated management information system is what makes it all work.[29]

Five vessel operating companies seek to address cost and asset utilization issues in the difficult Atlantic trade. Shipping lines in the route already had formed the trade line agreement for discussion. Collectively, they will withhold a proportion of space carrying European imports to the U.S. in order to reduce capacity. Also, the five are considering sharing or leasing space on each other's ships.[30] The net results are reduced operating costs, fewer capital requirements, and greater individual and collective productivity.

Space-sharing on ships or at port facilities by shipping lines reduces the market for port facilities. This encourages load centers and larger terminals, resulting in fewer ports of call. It is these load centers and selected niche ports which must make major investments in infrastructure improvements.[31]

Ports and States

Provisions of ISTEA, which explicitly include port access, have spurred port-state partnerships. This is needed considering the downward trend in state support for public ports. Of the new partnerships, the most important is the closer involvement of ports with metropolitan and statewide transportation committees. In New York, the Port of New York-New Jersey (NYNJ) actively participates in state planning commissions. The Port of NYNJ proposes expansion of railroad tunnels to accommodate double-stack railcars and building access roads from interstates to seaports. Similarly, Virginia ports have been discussing port access and congestion with state planning organizations. Philadelphia is looking into improved terminal access.[32] The Bi-State Delaware River Port Authority compact change was ratified by New Jersey and Pennsylvania in 1991 to include economic planning and development. When approved by Congress, this will permit direct investment in marine facilities.[33] Rhode Island is joining with the Providence and Worcester Railroad in its plans to construct a new $30 million highway to the railroad's new 40-foot deep berth, a $26 million investment.[34]

Directly affected by the load center phenomenon are the domestic highway, railway and waterway systems connecting to the ports. Cooperative national, state, local, and private efforts are required to realize domestic transportation connectors. Dedicated highway and rail corridors, such as the Alameda Transportation Corridor, must be created if cargo is to move freely in and out of these ports. As Sid Robinson, Director of Planning and Research, Port of Los Angeles, claims, "The construction, maintenance and development of port access to highway and rail corridors with sufficient capacity to move the nation's commerce is arguably the most important strategic issue facing the port industry today."[35]

Alliances with competing entities at the waterfront are becoming an imperative. By the turn of the century, three-quarters of the population will be within a couple hours of a waterfront. These people are demanding access for recreation, aesthetics, environmental preservation, and residential developments. Similarly, air quality, water quality, and soil contamination directly influence a port's ability to operate and construct.[36]

Partnerships in Southern California's Intermodal Container Transfer Facility (ICTF) involve vertical cooperation between a single rail carrier and five ports. Cooperation is possible vertically or horizontally among players in the organizational chain. Antitrust restrictions differ on either side of the port. The waterside is testing horizontal integration. The Ports of Los Angeles and Long Beach cooperate and compete. They cooperate on attracting cargo and fight to see who gets it.

U.S. seaports, because of their essential roles in international trade, are attracting foreign partners into port development projects. Japanese participants, including major trading houses and power suppliers, are currently working with western mining companies on a $120 million joint venture to upgrade coal and dry bulk facilities at the Port of Los Angeles. The plan also calls for improving rails from western states.[37]

Conclusion

Water transportation policy is shaped by multiple national objectives, among them economic development, environmental quality, energy efficiency, and national security. Economic growth is the overarching reason cited for transportation investment.[38] To obtain effective water transportation investment in today's global economy requires investors to perform masterful balancing acts that require new alliances and innovative solutions. These solutions require not only increases in investments which have been carefully prioritized, but bold disinvestment strategies and marked increases in rehabilitation and maintenance expenditures. Since the forecast for added funding is bleak, increasing productivity within this aging system must call on new arrangements among all players—governments, ports, terminals, shippers, and carriers—to enhance efficiency through cooperation. Collective creativity of all participants on both land and water sides of the equation must continue.

Notes

1. U.S. Army Corps of Engineers (USACE) Navigation Data Center, *Waterborne Commerce of the United States*, Part 5, 1980-1989 and *Estimated Waterborne Commerce Statistics for Calendar Year 1990*, (Ft. Belvoir, VA, 20 December 1991).
2. "U.S. Top Merchandise Exporter," *The Journal of Commerce* 391, no. 27687 (18 March 1992) 1A and 3A.
3. Eno Foundation, *Transportation in America*, 9th ed., 1991.
4. Connie Holmes, Presentation to National Coal Association, Sarasota, FL, 29-31 January 1992.
5. Major General Arthur Williams, Presentation to National Coal Association, Sarasota, FL, 29-31 January 1992.
6. Steve Lucas, Testimony to U.S. Senate Water Resources Subcommittee, Environment & Public Works Committee, 9 March 1992.
7. Sid Robinson, "Strategic Issues for Ports," *Transportation Research Circular* 392 (March 1992).
8. USACE, Waterborne Commerce Statistics Data Center, *Waterborne Transportation Lines of the U.S.* (New Orleans, 1989).
9. John Lane and Kevin Horn, "A Forecast of Mississippi River System Hopper and Tank Barge Construction, 1990-2014." Transportation Research Board (TRB) presentation, (Washington, D.C., 13 January 1992).
10. Craig E. Philip, "Inland Barge Operators: Migrating From an Era of Surplus to Shortage," Transportation Research Board (TRB) presentation, (Washington, D.C., 13 January 1992).
11. Frank Wilner, "Railroad Productivity," *Transportation Practitioners Journal* (Winter 1991): 28-29.
12. Nancy Dorn, Assistant Secretary of the Army (Civil Works), Testimony to Senate Water Resources Subcommittee, Environmental and Public Works, 11 March 1992.
13. United States Army Corps of Engineers, *Inland Waterway Users Board, 5th Annual Report,* (Washington, D.C., 1991).
14. Steve Lucas, Testimony to U.S. Senate Water Resources Subcommittee, Environment and Public Works Committee, 9 March 1992.
15. Edith Page "Charging Users of Inland Waterways—Draft," Office of Technology Assessment, (Washington, D.C., 2 December 1991).
16. William Newstrand, "Environmental Impacts of a Modal Shift," Paper No. 9201171, Transportation Research Board, (Washington, D.C., 1992).
17. U.S. Department of Transportation, Maritime Administration, *U.S. Port Development Expenditure Report,* (Washington, D.C., February 1991).
18. National Council on Public Works Improvement, *Fragile Foundations: A Report on Americas Public Works: Final Report to the President and Congress,* (Washington, DC, 1988).
19. Nancy Dorn, Assistant Secretary of the Army (Civil Works), Testimony before Senate Water Resources Subcommittee, Environmental and Public Works Committee, 11 March 1992.

20. Ibid.
21. Steve Lucas, Testimony to U.S. Senate Water Resources Subcommittee, Environment and Public Works Committee, 9 March 1992.
22. *Intermodal Surface Transportation Efficiency Act of 1991*, P. L. 102-240, 18 December 1991.
23. "Return of the Trucker," *American Shipper* (March 1992): 16.
24. "LASH Terminal Planned at Memphis," *The Waterway Journal* 106 (24 February 1992): 5.
25. K. A. Wheeler, "Intermodal Transportation Shaping Economic Growth and Natural Policies for the '90's," *Waterways and Transportation Review* 1, no. 1 (Fall 1991): 92-93.
26. Ibid.
27. Craig E. Philip, "Rail Linkages to Ship, Barge and Truck," *Transportation Research Circular: Maritime Transportation Strategic Planning* 392 (March, 1992): 27-29.
28. Ibid.
29. John Saylor, "Logistics Service: Provider's Perspective," *Transportation Research Circular: Maritime Transportation Strategic Planning* 392 (March, 1992): 24-25.
30. "North Atlantic Ship Lines Consider Partnerships," *Journal of Commerce* 391 (30 March 1992): 1A.
31. Sid Robinson, "Strategic Issues for Ports," *Transportation Research Circular* 392 (6 April 1992): 21.
32. "Ports Accelerate Their Participation in Transport Plans," *Journal of Commerce* 392 (6 April 1992).
33. "Bill Would Expand NJ-PA Port Agency's Power, Flexibility," *Journal of Commerce* 392 (6 April 1992).
34. "Dredging Completed for Twin Ports Project," *Journal of Commerce* 391 (March 1992): 3B.
35. Robinson, "Strategic Issues for Ports," 21.
36. Ibid.
37. "U.S.-Japan Plan to Upgrade LA Port for Coal Exports Almost Complete," *Journal of Commerce* 391 (11 June 1992): 6B.
38. *Data for Decisions, Requirements for National Transportation Policy Making*, Special Report 234, Transportation Research Board, (Washington, D.C., 1992).

Managing Community Wastewater in the 1990s: What is Needed to Attain National Water Quality Goals and Why

Kenneth I. Rubin

In 1987, The National Council on Public Works Improvement (NCPWI) found that the nation's wastewater treatment program had accomplished some, but not all, of its goals.[1] In particular, some $50 billion in federal investment (since 1970) in community wastewater treatment plants had arrested degradation of many waterways, but had not improved water quality universally. Gains in the purity of treated wastewater were offset, in many instances, by the effects of population growth and economic expansion. Perhaps more importantly, however, improvements in ambient water quality that many had expected as a result of 20 years of investment in wastewater treatment had not occurred, largely because of the effects of unaddressed runoff from urban and rural lands and continued environmental releases of toxic contaminants.

This article addresses the relative importance of community wastewater treatment in attaining national ambient water quality goals. It begins with the conclusions of the National Council on Public Works Improvement on the physical and financial health of wastewater treatment systems and their contribution to clean water goals. From this perspective, remaining problems and their solutions appear to be financial in nature. The article then argues that the merits of upgrading community wastewater treatment must be viewed within a broader, watershed context. From this perspective, solutions to water quality problems lie not in whether or how to finance and build more or better wastewater treatment systems, but in how to manage natural resource systems for environmental and economic health. Under these circumstances, issues of finance are important, to be sure, but so too are issues of locally responsive management institutions, strategies to change polluting behavior in all sectors of society, and individual and collective responsibility for action.

231

NCPWI's 1987 Evaluation of the National Wastewater Treatment Program

In a thorough evaluation of the nation's wastewater treatment program, the National Council on Public Works Improvement concluded that wastewater treatment services improved significantly between 1972 and 1987, but that many issues remained unresolved, including:

- Costs of providing wastewater treatment facilities needed to comply with the federal Clean Water Act were substantial, despite 20 years of joint federal/state/local investment.
- In many communities, cost recovery conventions failed to ensure sustainable, business-like performance of wastewater treatment systems.
- Wastewater management regulations were inflexible and failed to allow for efficient, economic-incentive and market-based alternatives to technology-based, uniform effluent quality standards.
- Areawide planning for water resources management and economic growth was nearly non-existent.
- The nation's industrial wastewater pretreatment program —one of the key programs to reduce releases of toxic contaminants into the environment— was judged uneven at best.
- The pace of technological innovation in the wastewater treatment field was inadequate, especially considering the $6 billion to $8 billion a year domestic market for such technologies.

Water Quality Conditions and the Role of POTWs

So far in the twentieth century, much attention has focused on the potential to clean up America's water bodies by installing municipal wastewater treatment systems. By 1986, in fact, the U.S. could point to over 15,000 municipal treatment plants worth over $140 billion, serving 186 million people.[2] Yet, several significant questions remain unanswered.

The first key question is whether and to what extent this level of investment has resulted in improved water quality. Most observers would agree that a simple answer is not possible, in large part, because we have not measured results routinely or directly. Based on the most comprehensive and internally consistent reports on ambient water quality, however, one characterization is that wastewater controls over the last few decades prevented further degradation in ambient water quality conditions despite a 25 percent growth in population and a 50 percent growth in Gross National Product (GNP) between 1970 and 1990. So while ambient conditions may not be better universally, they surely would be worse had we not invested in wastewater treatment.

The second key question is, what role will continued investment in wastewater treatment plants play in improving ambient conditions in the future;

indeed, how can we meet the objectives of the Clean Water Act—at the lowest cost to society? To what extent should the nation choose to strengthen controls at municipal or industrial point sources, begin the process of controlling agricultural or urban runoff, or invest scarce resources in some combination? The answer undoubtedly is specific to local watershed conditions and the relative importance of different sources of water quality impairment.

The Water Quality Debate in the Early 1990s

In light of these and related questions, NCPWI's conclusions began to reshape a national debate on the future of U.S. water quality programs. The debate began to coalesce around the issues of financing water quality infrastructure, managing total water resources systems for environmental results, and recognizing the interrelationships between natural and economic systems.

Financing Water Quality Infrastructure

The NCPWI study intimated, and recent data confirm, that under current policies, the U.S. will probably always face a price tag for water quality infrastructure that exceeds reasonably available resources. Figure 5.1 presents a historical perspective on joint EPA/state biennial estimates of needs for publicly owned treatment facilities (costs of providing minimally acceptable treatment levels as directed by the 1972 Clean Water Act) and aggregate, cumulative public expenditures to meet these needs. Over the last ten years, needs have fluctuated more in response to changes in definition of what is needed than to progress toward paying for the backlog. In fact, needs in 1990 were roughly what they were in 1982—some $110 billion—despite a net investment of nearly $60 billion over the nine-year period.

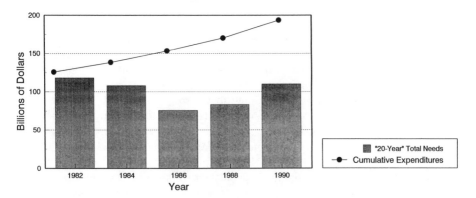

Figure 5.1. *Cumulative Expenditures v. Aggregate Needs— Wastewater Treatment Infrastructure*

233

Given these trends, one might logically conclude that the backlog in waste-water treatment needs is structural, that the annual accrual of costs to replace outdated or undersized facilities in some locations will just match expenditures for construction of new capacity elsewhere in the United States. On balance, our current $6 billion to $8 billion a year program may never reduce "needs" as currently calculated.

Wastewater treatment needs could, in fact, grow substantially over the next few years as certain new "needs" begin to enter the "needs" calculus. In particular, EPA's needs study includes only about $16 billion for remediation of combined sewer overflow problems—the discharge of raw sewage when combined storm and sanitary sewers overload treatment facilities during rain events.[3] Based on recent analysis, this estimate is low by perhaps $100 billion or more. In addition, EPA's needs estimate also overlooks tens of billions of dollars that must be spent to control untreated runoff of urban stormwater.

With cost estimates this large, and needs so greatly outstripping current payments, one conclusion is plain: a national debate on spending more will be useless if our overall goal is obtaining the greatest water quality improvement per dollar invested. Whatever marginal gains in public expenditures that could possibly be expected to emerge from such a debate, especially given today's fiscal realities, will be dominated by newly discovered demands and changes in how statutes define what is and is not a need. Needs, as we now know them, may never be met in a timely fashion.

This is not to say that we should stop thinking of new ways to meet our financing challenges. Quite the opposite; this debate is critical, but it must be elevated beyond a simplistic argument over spending more to build capital-intensive facilities.

Managing Total Water Resources Systems for Environmental Results

This debate continued in 1988 under the auspices of Water Quality 2000—an 86-member consortium of public, private, academic, and nonprofit organizations concerned with water quality. Water Quality 2000 published an interim report in 1991, *Challenges for the Future,*[4] which elevated the national water quality debate by acknowledging that current water quality programs fail to address some of the fundamental societal norms that are largely responsible for impairing water quality. As a result, EPA and state data clearly demonstrated that the overriding objective of the Clean Water Act—to restore and maintain the chemical, physical, and biological integrity of the nation's waters—had not been met for a large percentage of our surface waters.

The way we farm, live, transport people and goods, produce, and consume, are the real, largely unaddressed, root causes of degradation. Historically, individuals and society as a whole have made choices that reflected values specific to these aspects of life that seemingly were unrelated to water quality. Yet, we now acknowledge that societal norms are inextricably linked to water quality, and indeed, to all natural ecosystems.

In the fall of 1992, WQ2000 released a report recommending fundamental changes in the way we manage water resources in the U.S. These ideas are not new. In fact, they are based on nearly 50 years of policy thinking and experiments in the field.[5]

The single most important recommendation to emerge from Water Quality 2000's four-year process is a call to adopt a new national policy of total resource protection based on the concepts of pollution prevention, individual and collective responsibility for water resources, and watershed planning and management. In short, it advocates an integrated, national water policy that supports society living in harmony with healthy natural systems.

Recognizing the Linkage Between Natural and Economic Systems

With over 20 years of a concerted national program to address water quality impairment behind us, it is time to recognize certain principles that can help guide the next 20 years of progress.

Where We Stand on the "Unit Removal Curve." The first principal stems from an acknowledgement of our current position on the "unit removal curve." Considering a very simplistic model of water pollution in which all water is a single body and all pollutants from all sources are lumped together, Figure 5.2 presents an idealized "unit removal curve." The curve plots the marginal cost of removing successive units of pollution against the cumulative percent removed. With no pollution controls in place, the cost of removing the first unit is low. But as increasingly more effective treatment is put in place, removal costs increase substantially, until at some point the cost to remove the next unit is prohibitive.

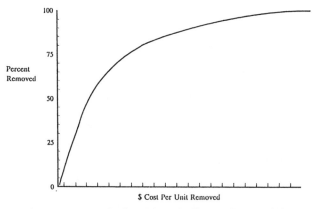

Figure 5.2. *An Idealized Unit Pollutant Removal Curve*

While the real unit removal curve varies from one source to the next, in the aggregate it is probably fair to assume, at least for point sources of conventional pollutants, that the U.S. is almost uniformly above 75 percent removal. The cost of further removal, therefore, is approaching levels beyond the reach of many communities. By the year 2000, for example, one recent EPA analysis found that simply maintaining today's level of environmental quality will consume nearly 6 percent of household income, compared to 2.8 percent in 1987 for the average household in the nation's smallest communities.[6]

Measured in the aggregate, environmental expenditures consumed about one percent of the GNP in 1972 (see Figure 5.3).[7] By 1990, environmental spending accounted for 2.1 percent of GNP and by the year 2000, environmental programs are expected to equal 2.8 percent of GNP. The cost of moving up the unit removal curve appears significant even when measured against the value of all goods and services produced in the United States.

Dealing with a Great Number of Sources Linked to Land Use. Second, we must acknowledge that the last 20 years has focused largely on industrial and municipal point sources. In this area, the command-and-control approach was well-suited to reach and force changes in a relatively small group of economic interests. Today, remaining water quality problems stem more from dispersed activities in or on the land—agriculture, land development, mining, forestry, suburban life, and the like. Using command-and-control approaches to change the polluting behavior of this much larger population is inconceivable. A smarter strategy is needed, one that creates incentives for a variety of economic interests and numerous actors dispersed across the land to act in their own self-interest. The key is to align the interests of these actors with environmental values.

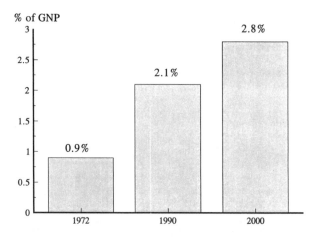

Figure 5.3. *Environmental Expenditures as a Percentage of GNP, 1972-2000*

Changing the Debate from Pollution Control Costs to Investments in a Clean Environment. Typically, investments in municipal wastewater treatment are structured to minimize the cost of meeting national standards for municipal wastewater effluent. Yet there is growing evidence that examining the benefits side of the transaction may be equally or more important.

Economic benefits of clean water investments deserve more attention. In a recent study, for example, public investment in wastewater treatment capacity was shown to improve the productivity of the private economy in the short term.[8] In the longer term, a more productive private economy stimulated additional private investment in plant and equipment, which in turn, led to additional gains in output. In this example, an original federal investment in treatment capacity was more than paid back in increased tax revenues within a 15 year period (see Figure 5.4).

Environmental benefits of alternative investments in clean water also deserve additional attention, even if analysts never fully agree on their monetary value. Water Quality 2000's interim report noted that one key prerequisite to understanding the benefits of clean water programs is improving the monitoring of waterbodies and the measurement of progress:

> Neither the quality of the nation's waters nor the health of ecosystems is measured regularly. Current ambient monitoring of the chemistry and biology of aquatic resources is far too limited to be of use in assessing the performance of water programs.[9]

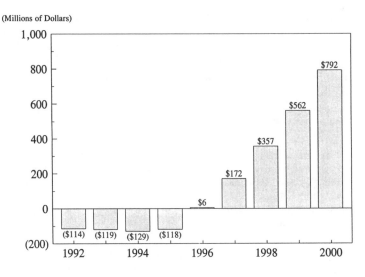

Figure 5.4. *Net Federal Tax Revenues from $23.2 billion in Environmental Investments Investments Financed with Tax Exempt Bonds 1992-2000*

What is Needed for the Future

The 1987 NCPWI report on wastewater treatment provided a very useful road map to solutions that remain appropriate today. Water Quality 2000 largely endorsed, and updated, this map essentially by arguing for a broader context under which we might view alternative pathways to cleaner waters. Based on these efforts, let me summarize four modest policy directions:
• Watershed planning and management.
• Pollution prevention.
• Economic and market-based alternatives to uniform technology-based regulations.
• Motivational financing strategies.

Watershed Planning and Management

On one level, investments in wastewater treatment systems are required by law. Yet they may not be the most efficient or effective way to attain ambient water quality objectives. Congress recognized this in the original framing of the 1972 Federal Water Pollution Control Act Amendments (now commonly called the Clean Water Act). In Section 208, they called for area-wide water quality management planning, which would direct future water quality activities of federal, state, and local governments. Unfortunately, the 208 program fell prey to a much more powerful program of 75 percent federal grants to build wastewater treatment plants.

Now federal grants for wastewater treatment are no longer available. Gone too are their perverse incentives for over-investment. The current system of federal/state loans to build treatment facilities offers the prospect of more rational investment decision making. Moreover, we now face the renewed opportunity to evaluate the effectiveness of municipal wastewater treatment in relation to other pathways to improved water quality.

What's needed is a framework to conduct such evaluations. Water Quality 2000 put it succinctly:[10]

> Most natural events and economic activities affect the quality of water resources principally within watershed boundaries. As a result, watersheds constitute the most sensible hydrologic unit within which actions should be taken to restore and protect water quality. In fact, watersheds also may define the appropriate spatial boundaries for total environmental and economic planning.

The next reauthorization of the Clean Water Act is a logical vehicle to institute a new national program of watershed-based planning and management. Such a program could take many shapes, as could the institutions that organized themselves in response to the program. It would be difficult to argue here that one structure is necessarily better suited to today's conditions than another. One central component of any structure, however, is that watershed plans should create the legal, institutional, and economic framework that directs all other water quality activities within its boundaries.

Pollution Prevention

In recent years, both the public and private sectors have paid considerable attention to industrial waste reduction. After all, who would dispute that an ounce of prevention is worth a pound of cure? It is surprising then, that much less attention has been paid to the application of pollution prevention strategies in other sectors (households, agriculture, transportation, land development) responsible for water quality impairment.

Practices that can reduce contamination from agricultural activities, for example, are well known to environmental professionals. What is missing is the information, incentives, and/or regulatory programs that can help agribusiness understand and adopt such practices. Just as states are beginning to require industries to develop and implement pollution prevention plans, states could expand their Section 319 (1972 Clean Water Act) non-point source management programs to require farm-level pollution prevention or total resource management plans for certain size operations in particularly contaminated watersheds. Plans could specify how and when technologically and economically feasible actions would be taken to reduce loadings of sediment, pesticides, and nutrients.

Similarly, pollution prevention from land and resource development activities could be incorporated in ongoing Section 319 plans. Transportation planning is already beginning to incorporate concerns for environmental pollution prevention by virtue of Clean Air Act requirements.

Many types of pollution prevention activities are possible within households. However, some households are unaware of their options, and incentives to adopt them are incomplete. Energy and water conservation are key components. Others include product labelling, more convenient solid waste recycling programs, and substitution of less harmful substitutes for pesticides, fertilizers, high-phosphate detergents, household cleansers, and solvents.

Economic and Market-Based Approaches

In early 1991, EPA's Office of Water convened a series of two symposia on economic-incentives and market-based approaches to attain water quality goals. These events brought together academic and applied economists and water quality program administrators to debate the merits of such approaches. Their recommendations to the agency formed the basis for an EPA proposal to incorporate certain economic incentive programs in the 1991/1992 amendments to the Clean Water Act. Whether these proposals become statute is still unclear, partly because Congress will not address Clean Water Act amendments in 1992, and possibly not even in 1993. Many states also are considering programs that incorporate economic incentives.

Under consideration or inplace, either within the federal establishment or within state water quality programs are:

• Tradeable discharge permits, either among all sources, or between point and non-point sources to attain ambient water quality standards at least cost to all dischargers.
• Mitigation banking to preserve the total acreage, functions, or values of wetlands.
• Tradeable development rights to preserve wetlands while compensating owners of undevelopable wetlands.
• Assurance/performance bonding to promote restoration of degraded or altered land masses attributable to mining, forestry, or suburban development.
• Deposit/refund systems to assure environmentally compatible handling of materials that could contaminate waterways when improperly disposed.
• Tradeable pretreatment credits to reduce the discharge of toxic contaminants to publicly owned wastewater treatment systems.
• Effluent or activity fees that attempt to "internalize" the cost of water quality degradation in private production decisions.

Whether and how these options are adopted tend to depend on specific economic, institutional, and other characteristics of individual watersheds. Some incentive programs could substitute for additional investments in wastewater treatment plants. Others may be necessary in addition to improved wastewater treatment. For example, only a handful of trading programs are operating today, even though recent studies suggest that watershed conditions in about 1,000 areas are conducive to such programs (see Figure 5.5).[11] As the economy continues to expand and the population grows, conditions in many more watersheds are expected to support trading programs.

Motivational Financing Strategies

While good water quality science is critical to making sound management decisions, financing water quality improvements may be more responsive to water quality public relations. No longer is it possible, for example, to finance a wastewater treatment facility just because some politician claims it is needed. Federal funds are no longer free. In the future communities will largely pay for only the amount of water quality they judge worth the cost. Under these circumstances, the tools needed to finance remaining water quality improvements will include public education, public relations, benefits evaluation, and responsive public processes. According to one analysis, the following conditions were essential to gaining consensus on a financing strategy for the clean-up of Puget Sound:[12]

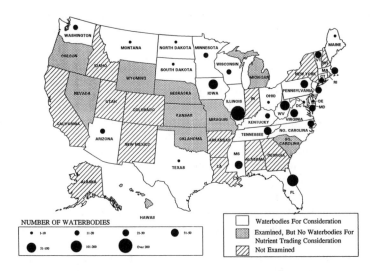

Figure 5.5. *Distribution of Waterbodies for which Point/Non-point Source Nutrient Trading Appears Applicable Now*

- A committee approach structured to blend technical skills, political positions, and the ability to commit their interests to a consensus product.
- A communications strategy that stressed frequent meetings among stakeholders, constant contact with administrative agencies, and sharing of ideas with the legislature.
- A well-orchestrated public involvement process that focused on the effects of endorsing alternative financing strategies on households, businesses, and other economic interests.
- Complete and thorough analysis of the economic effects, equity considerations, and environmental improvements associated with each financing alternative.
- A complete financing plan that was widely endorsed and presented to key decision makers well within time frames needed to assure political support.

In this example, the issue of financing approach was debated using a committee comprised of the major stakeholders, administrative agencies, and legislative staff. Of course, not all processes can or need be this complex. Yet, some consideration of a process or vehicle to raise, debate, and resolve issues probably is a necessary condition of finance. The process must devise some way to educate those asked to pay for water quality improvements on the benefits they will receive. The public and specific interests must further be convinced that their share is equitable compared to the share that similar individuals or groups are asked to pay, either now or over the useful life of the investment.

In short, financing strategies need to be more than feasible; they need to be motivational. They must prove the benefits are worth the costs and that costs are allocated fairly across like groups of users or beneficiaries in space and in time.

Conclusion

How will wastewater treatment plants compete for scarce water quality dollars in the future? While there is probably no simple answer, it is clear that wastewater treatment plants will be a part of future water quality strategies wherever they are needed to manage natural resource systems for environmental and economic health.

Such a determination will be efficient and effective only if it is made on a watershed basis. Moreover, such a determination may be possible only after exploring the full range of alternative pathways to cleaner water, including pollution prevention in all sectors of society and for all environmental media—air, water, and land. One key option for the future is economic incentives to align better the interests of widely dispersed constituents with common environmental values, such as concern for the integrity of a wetland.

Finally, proposals to finance municipal wastewater systems will be subject to a fuller range of investment criteria than they have been in the past. Prerequisites to approval will include a demonstration of environmental results and equitable allocation of costs to motivate all stakeholders. The fundamental question for the future is not what is needed to improve the nation's municipal wastewater treatment systems, but what is needed to improve the quality of the nation's waters.

Notes

1. National Council on Public Works Improvement, *The Nation's Public Works: Report on Wastewater Management* (Washington, D.C., 1987).
2. Apogee Research, Inc., *A Consolidated Performance Report on the Nation's Public Works*, prepared for the National Council on Public Works Improvement (Bethesda, MD, 1987).
3. U.S. Environmental Protection Agency, *1990 Needs Survey Report to Congress*, Office of Water (Washington, D.C., 1991).
4. Water Quality 2000, *Challenges for the Future: An Interim Report* (Alexandria, VA, 1991).
5. Apogee Research, Inc, *Watershed Planning and Management*, prepared for the Steering Committee of Water Quality 2000 (Bethesda, MD, 1991).
6. U.S. Environmental Protection Agency, *A Preliminary Analysis of the Public Costs of Environmental Protection: 1981-2000*, Resources Management Division, Office of Administration and Resources Management (Washington, D.C., 1990).
7. U.S. Environmental Protection Agency, *The Cost of Clean Air and Clean Water*, Office of Policy, Planning, and Evaluation, (December, 1990).

8. To be sure, more research is needed to demonstrate causality underlying these statistical macroeconomic correlations. For additional details, see Environmental Financial Advisory Board to EPA, *Incentives for Environmental Investment: Changing Behavior and Building Capital,* an Advisory to the Administrator of the U.S. Environmental Protection Agency, Washington, D.C. (9 August 1991).
9. Water Quality 2000, *Challenges for the Future,* xiii.
10. Water Quality 2000, *Phase III Report (tentative title)* forthcoming, Fall 1992.
11. Apogee Research, Inc. *Incentive Analysis for Clean Water Act Reauthorization: Point Source/Non-Point Source Trading for Nutrient Discharge Reductions,* prepared for the Environmental Protection Agency, Office of Water and Office of Policy, Planning, and Evaluation (Bethesda, MD, 1992).
12. Apogee Research, Inc., *The Puget Sound Experience: Financial Planning for Implementation of Comprehensive Conservation and Management Plans Developed under the National Estuary Program,* prepared for the U.S. Environmental Protection Agency, Office of Wetlands and Watersheds (Bethesda, MD, 1991).

Reducing the Risks: The Need for Comprehensive Flood Damage Reduction Policies

Neil R. Fulton

Introduction

Any discussion of flood damage reduction could be very expansive. It could easily include urban and agricultural flood control and drainage, streambank and shoreline protection, and dam safety. If it were extended to multipurpose projects, the effects of municipal and industrial water supply, hydropower, recreation, and navigation would have to be addressed. The impacts of these activities involve socioeconomic as well as environmental or natural resource issues. This essay is limited to a discussion of flood control and stormwater. I will review the state of the flood damage reduction system, comment on the relationship between investment in public works and productivity, and suggest ways to reduce the risk of damage from floods.

The State of the System

A review of flood damage statistics is disturbing. Flooding continues to be a very serious problem in the United States, resulting in major loss of life and significant property damage. The National Science Foundation estimated in 1980 that seven percent of the land in the United States was in a floodplain[1] and that urban expansion into the floodplain was increasing by about 1.5 to 2.5 percent annually.[2] Adjusted for inflation and based on 1985 dollars, the figures in the following chart show flood damage for the period from 1920 to 1990. A five-year running average[3] is used to indicate trends more clearly.

An analysis of flood damage figures from 1916 through 1990 shows a trend of increasing flood damage in constant dollars.[4] This is true even when the same unit of population is used over time. Flood damage is increasing at about $200 per one thousand people, or about 1.5 percent, every year. This indicates that the state of the system is not improving and, at best, is holding steady. If

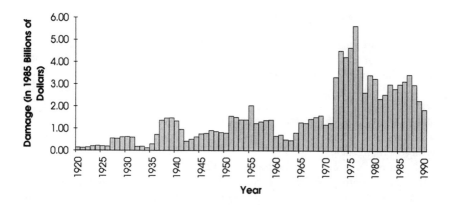

Figure 6.1. *Flood Damage (5-Year Running Average)*

this rate continues, average annual flood damage will increase by one-half billion dollars between 1990 and 2000.

There are many agencies and interests involved in flood damage reduction. The system is complex and sometimes unnecessarily complicated. This is partly because of the way the system evolved. On the public side, international, federal, state, and a multitude of local agencies are involved in flood damage reduction activities. On the private side, the insurance industry, developers, and builders, among others, are active participants.

Five Principle Federal Agencies

Looking just at the federal system reveals the complexity of flood control decisionmaking. Approximately 26 federal agencies are involved in flood damage reduction to some degree. These represent only executive branch agencies and do not include the significant number of committees of Congress. In some cases the complex and difficult challenges of working with the federal system are overly simplified or ignored.

Of the 26 federal agencies with roles in flood damage reduction, four are most active in the construction, operation and maintenance of flood control facilities, and one is very active in reducing flood risk and providing emergency assistance. The construction agencies are, in order of size according to recent water resources expenditures, the Army Corps of Engineers, the Bureau of Reclamation, the Soil Conservation Service, and the Tennessee Valley Authority. The Corps of Engineers has been in the business the longest and has a budget larger than all of the other water-resource budgets combined. Through its National Flood Insurance Program and its Disaster Assistance Program, the Federal Emergency Management Agency oversees reducing risk through improved land use practices and providing emergency assistance.

State and Local Agencies

Many states are very involved in flood damage reduction activities, as are many units of local government. The involvement of states varies considerably across the country. Some states play a role analogous to the federal government. They provide planning and construction assistance and, in cooperation with federal and local agencies, financing as well. In other cases, the role of states is fairly limited. In these cases, local municipal or special-purpose governments perform most flood control activities either alone or in cooperation with federal agencies.

Local governments are the focus of one important part of the flood damage reduction program. The National Flood Insurance Program is principally implemented through units of local government that have zoning code and building code powers. It is a carrot-and-stick approach. The carrot is the provision of subsidized flood insurance for existing buildings and supposedly actuarial-based flood insurance for other buildings. The stick requires the unit of local government to pass and enforce zoning and building code requirements consistent with the regulations of the program before local residents can participate in the flood insurance program. Flood insurance is required for a federally-insured loan or grant. This has been a very effective program in reducing the risk of damages by flooding.

Investment and Maintenance

The federal investment in the water resource system has generally declined since the mid-1960s. At the same time, spending at the state and local level has remained about constant. As a result, if the federal, state, and local investment in water resources is considered as a percentage of the Gross National Product, there has been a rather significant reduction in investment in the water resources of the nation and in flood control activities.

While total federal appropriations are declining in real terms, a larger percentage of the federal budget is being appropriated for operation, maintenance, and rehabilitation of the water resource system. Much of this increase is in support of the operation and maintenance of the national water transportation system.

The report *Fragile Foundations: A Report on America's Public Works*[5] identifies a continuing and serious problem of inadequate and deferred maintenance; maintenance is often postponed in the interest of other more visible expenditures. Potholes in highways are visible and produce a public reaction followed by political action. The same is not true of many of our basic infrastructure systems that are not normally visible. These include water mains, sewers, dams, levees, channels, streams, and stream-banks. Deferred maintenance ends up costing more than timely and periodic maintenance. The aging of major portions of the existing main-line flood control systems, some built in the 1930s, may pose serious problems in the future.

Innovation

In order to reduce the risk from flooding, we continually need to look at more effective and efficient ways of managing the waters of the nation. Fortunately, some excellent steps are being made in this area.

Community Rating System. One of the innovative activities of the National Flood Insurance Program is the Community Rating System. The Community Rating System encourages local communities to be more aggressive in managing their prevention and cure-related activities. A community is provided a rating based on a number of factors that relate to the level of flood damage reduction activity within the community. The higher the rating a community receives, the greater the reduction its residents receive in their flood insurance premiums. This provides an economic incentive for more effective local agency response to the risk of flooding, as well as a direct and measurable link to reduction of premiums for the local electorate.

Of approximately 10,000 communities that participate in the National Flood Insurance Program, about 625 have applied to participate in the Community Rating System. These communities are evaluated using 18 creditable activities that include Public Information, Mapping and Regulatory functions, Flood Damage Reduction, and Flood Preparedness. The maximum reduction in insurance premium is 45 percent, although currently the typical reduction is 10 percent. One community achieved a reduction of 25 percent. This translates into an annual premium savings for a typical residential structure of $75.

This system is in its initial stages of implementation, but I have great hopes for its future. I think it demonstrates a very creative way to encourage effective organizational response to reduce the risks from flood damage at the local level through an economic linkage that relates to the risk of flooding.

Stormwater Management. Another area where state and local governments are becoming increasingly involved is in stormwater management. The stormwater programs are becoming more effective. One reason is that managers are recognizing that water does not respect municipal or local boundaries. Many programs are now becoming more regional in scope.

The basic concept behind stormwater management is that urban development increases the volume of water that needs to be conveyed by the natural drainage system and decreases the time it takes the water to get to the system. This provides a double-barreled increase in peak flows with resultant downstream impacts. In effective stormwater management programs, the impacts of development are identified, and through local regulations or incentives, developers are encouraged and required to use techniques to reduce or minimize the downstream impacts of development.

Some creative financing techniques are also being considered in this area where local or regional agencies are authorized to impose impact fees on existing or proposed development based upon the contribution to increased runoff. The fees provide for the construction or maintenance of facilities to minimize the impact of development.

While this is a beginning, at least one recent study has shown that the impact of development increases as one moves downstream and therefore the amount of storage needed to minimize or eliminate the impact on peak stream flow increases.[6] In most cases, sufficient storage is not provided to minimize the far-downstream impacts of upstream development, which means that there will be a continued increase in the risks of flooding in the downstream areas.

Integration of Quantity and Quality

In the last decade, non-point source pollution received considerable attention. Standards are being developed for the control of discharges from non-point sources and from urban drainage (storm sewers). Stormwater management involves more than controlling the increase in flow and volume resulting from urbanization and other uses. Higher loads of phosphates, heavy metals, and other contaminants, can significantly affect water quality and the uses of streams and water courses. At the same time, development practices are destroying one of nature's primary treatment facilities—wetlands. This is an area of opportunity for the integration of quantity and quality. Construction of facilities to allow preliminary treatment (i.e., settling and biological treatment) of discharges can also provide water quantity benefits by reducing peak flows in streams and waterways. The use of aquatic plants and of lakes of varying depths to provide a variety of habitats to detain and treat stormwater requires continuing investigation. Interestingly, a patent was recently granted for the design of a man-made lake that uses pondweed and coontail to absorb pollutants.[7] Unfortunately, the integration of water quality and quantity is still paid little attention, and in many states as well as in local governments the integration or linking of quantity and quality is talked about but not acted on.

Public Works and Productivity

Few deny the importance of sound local and national infrastructure to economic and social well-being or the need and appropriateness of government involvement in building, maintaining, and rehabilitating the infrastructure. Indeed Adam Smith, the originator of the "invisible hand" of a free economic policy, wrote in *The Wealth of Nations*, first published in 1776, that:

The third and last duty of the sovereign or commonwealth is that of maintaining, those public institutions and those public works, which, though they may be in the highest degree advantageous to a great society, are, however, of such a nature, that the profit could never repay the expence [sic] to any individual, or small number of individuals, and which it therefore cannot be expected that any individual or small number of individuals should erect or maintain. The performance of this duty requires too, very different degrees of expence [sic] in the different periods of society.[8]

Smith defined the first duty of the sovereign as defense; the second, administering justice; and the third, in addition to public works, establishing institutions for facilitating commerce, education, and instruction. Evidently an early advocate of "user charges," Smith considered the use of tolls and port duties to be an appropriate form of revenue collection to offset costs whenever the beneficiary can be defined.

While there may be general societal and political consensus on government involvement in building, maintaining and rehabilitating the nation's infrastructure, there is not a similar consensus on what level of government should take the lead or what level of investment is needed. This situation has become more difficult in recent decades as government funding of and commitment to "entitlement" programs have increased. The competition for a portion of the pie (i.e., the public purse) has increased and the nation's infrastructure has suffered. This most probably has been one of the contributors (though how important a contributor is hard to define) to reduced growth in the nation's productivity.

Relation of Investment to Productivity

Dr. David Aschauer, an economist formerly with the Federal Reserve Bank of Chicago, argues that there is a significant and definable link between reduced public investment in public infrastructure and private sector productivity. He argues that, if the average level of infrastructure investment relative to the Gross National Product had been maintained between 1950 and 1970, the average rate of return on private capital would have been 21.5 percent higher and the average annual rate of private sector productivity growth would have been 50 percent higher.[9] These figures are strongly disputed by Charles Schultze of the Brookings Institution who questions both the methodology and the results.[10] If Dr. Aschauer's figures are correct or even half correct we should add reduced investment in infrastructure to the list of significant factors that have reduced productivity growth in the United States.

In addition to the purely economic benefits, there are the equally, if not more important, benefits to public health and safety that result from efforts to reduce the significant social and economic costs of continuing flood damage.

Flood damage reduction reduces the risks to individuals and society of flood-related deaths, the disruption of the operation of water supply and water treatment facilities, job interruption or loss, and the psychological stress on families and individuals. As contradictory as it may sound, flood damage reduction is more than reducing flood damage. It is an investment in our future and in the economic and social security of the residents of the United States.

Reducing the Risk—A Comprehensive Flood Damage Reduction Policy

The elements of an effective and comprehensive program to reduce the societal and economic impacts of flood damage are well-known. Most, if not all, of the components have been or are being implemented somewhere in the United States. A comprehensive program requires a high level of cooperation and the investment of intellectual and financial capital.

There needs to be a basic change in our mindset regarding the management of surface waters. If we truly want comprehensive management of surface waters, which is crucial to reducing the risk of flooding, we need to recognize the need to manage the water from where it hits the ground. A comprehensive program will contribute toward the prevention of new or increased damage, cure or reduce structural damage that does occur, and provide damage compensation through insurance funds and disaster aid. Prevention of flood damage needs as much emphasis as curing flood damage. A comprehensive approach to flood damage reduction needs to include all levels of government acting as true partners and building on the best available technology in the public and private sectors.

Communication, Coordination, and Cooperation

Improved communication, coordination, and cooperation is needed to develop a true partnership between federal, state and local agencies and between government and the private sector. From the beginning, those closest to the problem should be involved as equal partners. In place of conflict and confrontation, cooperation must be the goal. This means cooperative decisionmaking rather than having one agency or level of government force its decisions on other agencies or levels of government. The idea of cooperation and of coordinated decisionmaking is not new. The National Water Commission stressed this in its 1973 report, *Water Policies for the Future.*[11] A few years later, the *Interim Report On Water Policy*, issued during President Carter's administration, advocated a stronger role for the states in the federal water project decisionmaking process. A decade later, the first recommendation of *The Nation's Public Works: Report on Water Resources*, prepared for the National Council on Public Works Improvement, was ". . . to establish an intergovernmental coordinating forum, initiated at the federal level, for information and technology transfer."[12] The U.S. Advisory Commission on Intergovernmental Relations approved a resolution in December 1991 calling for a national water governance commission.

All of these argue for improved communication, cooperation and coordination. There is not any one agency or level of government or even government itself that has all the answers. Working smarter involves working together, recognizing that there are differing strengths and weaknesses in our system, and building on the strengths even if they are in a different agency or different level of government. It also includes recognizing the importance of listening to and hearing those that are closest to the problem—those at the grass roots level.

A committee for water resources coordination is needed. It may not need to be formal and perhaps its initial life should be fairly short so that senior policy makers at all levels will stay involved. The committee's purposes should include (1) the promotion of efficiency, effectiveness, coordination, and cooperation in intergovernmental relations and (2) the development of an open process for federal-state-local government and private sector coordination of water policy. Its objectives should include:

• Providing an institutional framework for the formulation of goals and objectives related to water.
• Reviewing interagency and intergovernmental policies and programs to promote consistency, fairness, and efficiency.
• Providing a forum for constructive dialogue and potential resolution of water issues of national import.

The demands placed on water resources are great and varied. Overlapping and confusing jurisdictions and levels of government permeate the water resources field. Developing better intergovernmental coordination and cooperation is just one step toward improving our delivery of services. Certainly, our resources are limited, and every effort needs to be made to improve our efficiency and effectiveness. If we do so, we will be able to reduce more flood damage in less time.

Managing for Change

Two fundamental concepts necesssary for a successful, long-term effort to reduce flood damage risks are (1) working together, i.e., forming teams to find solutions; and (2) looking for new and better ways of reducing the risk, i.e., being willing to embrace innovation and change.

Tom Peters, in *Thriving on Chaos: Handbook for a Management Revolution,* emphasizes the turbulent times we are in by writing:

> "If it ain't broke, don't fix it" needs revision. I propose: "If it ain't broke, you just haven't looked hard enough." Fix it anyway.[13]

In other words, we cannot rely on something working for us in the future just because it is not "broken" now. We must be open to new ideas, learn how to work smarter, and improve cooperation and communication. Discussing the need for cooperation and working smarter, Peters writes, "The power of the team is so great that it is often wise to violate apparent common sense and force a team structure on almost anything."[14] Private and public leaders at all levels need to make changes now for the challenges they will face in the future. Turning to Peters once more: "We must simply learn to love change as much as we hated it in the past."[15]

Competition provides more efficient production and delivery of services and products. In government, however, competition of the wrong type (i.e., not communicating, not cooperating, protecting "turf") can lead to duplication, wasted time and effort, and less effective delivery of services. Building teams among federal, state and local government agencies to find new and innovative solutions to water resource problems, as well as building on the best of the past, can retain the advantages of competition while reducing duplication and confusion.

Reducing flood damage risks requires not only a willingness to change and to develop intergovernmental teams but also an understanding of two important concepts, multiobjective planning and sustainable development. Let us consider each in turn.

Multiobjective Planning. For too long water resource planning has narrowly focused on such issues as water quality or quantity, open space, public access, and greenways, but there has rarely been a comprehensive integrated approach to planning. Multiuse is often confused with multiobjective as in multiuse reservoirs whose purposes or uses may include flood control, water supply, recreation, hydropower and navigation. Comprehensive planning is often defined in terms of the comprehensive river basin planning done under the auspices of the Water Resources Council and River Basin Commissions. This was a very "top-down" planning approach. Neither of these approaches from the past define multiobjective watershed and river basin planning.

Multiobjective planning varies with the interest or party defining it. At a minimum, it includes objectives for water quality, point and non-point sources, water quantity, habitat, open space, public access, and greenways. Multiobjective planning emphasizes "bottom-up" planning and the inclusion of all interested parties and interests, private and public groups, and different levels of government. Multiobjective planning involves more than just finding the most "economically efficient" answer to a particular water resource problem. It allows the integration of different and sometimes conflicting objectives and values of differing interests and establishes a framework for finding a broadly supported solution. Any comprehensive approach to management of surface waters must be multiobjective in focus.

Sustainable Development. Many look upon the 1990s as the decade of the environment, when the concept of sustainable development becomes a common

252

test for the rightness of our actions and activities. The strategy of sustainable development is built on a recognition that our natural and other resources are finite, that we must be good stewards of our resources, and that we should use and not abuse our resources—both human and natural. This requires us to forge a new partnership among developers, architects and engineers, between the regulated and the regulators, and between water resource managers at the federal, state and local levels. The concept of sustainable development recognizes that development is important and necessary for a society's well-being and that it should go hand-in-hand with using and not abusing our finite natural resources.

Prevention of New Damages

It is not a new concept that it is easier to prevent damage than it is to cure the results of damage. In many areas investment in prevention lags behind investment in cures. Investment in prevention produces the greatest return on the dollar and also reduces social and other disruption that continues to result from flooding.

As part of prevention we need to internalize costs. This means that we must relate the impact of the prevention activity to the particular activity increasing the risk, such as assessing impact fees that are related to increases in runoff or placing structures at risk. An example of this is a stormwater or drainage fee that is proportional to the increase in rate and volume of runoff caused by developing a piece of undeveloped property. The monies collected from the fee are used to construct and maintain the stormwater conveyance, storage, and treatment facilities related to the increase in runoff.

Wetlands Protection and Reconstruction. The historic and continuing destruction of wetlands has increased the volume of surface runoff, reduced the quality of stormwater runoff by reducing the availability of the natural water treatment provided by wetlands, and reduced the amount of water available in subsurface aquifers. The wetlands management program of the United States needs to be changed. It should not depend on federal dredge and fill legislation (Section 404 of the 1972 Clean Water Act) to protect wetlands but should be a cooperative, intergovernmental effort based on legislation specifically tailored to the protection of important wetlands. In addition, more cooperative approaches need to be developed, so that state and local agencies in cooperation with the private sector are encouraged to assume leadership and responsibility for a wetlands protection, reconstruction, and rehabilitation program.

With the significant loss of wetlands that has already occurred, wetlands protection is not sufficient. Watershed planning programs need to include wetlands reconstruction as a significant component of watershed protection work. Wetlands provide a multitude of benefits, not only to water quantity but to water quality and habitat. They are an integral part of the natural system and, in many cases, we should investigate the reconstruction of wetlands to replicate the benefits lost by the destruction of so much of this important natural resource.

Investment and Maintenance

Fragile Foundations: A Report on America's Public Works concludes, "Increasing flood damages coupled with development concentration in flood plains indicates a continuing need for investment in structural flood control, along with non-structural and compensation strategies."[16] We need to increase investment in flood damage reduction strategies, including both prevention and cure-related activities and structural and nonstructural solutions. Investment in flood damage reduction activities including public works produce short and long-term return on the investment. Delayed or insufficient investment defers dealing with the problem and results in greater total costs to society.

We need to reassess our approach to maintaining the system. Except for the national water navigation system, the federal government is reducing investment in water resource management. This does not reduce flood damage problems. As the national highway transportation system matured, greater and greater emphasis was given to rehabilitation and replacement. Consideration needs to be given to similar involvement at the federal level to maintain our major flood control facilities. The maintenance of these facilities is a national benefit. In many cases, rehabilitation and replacement are beyond the financial and economic capability of special purpose districts or smaller units of local government. Without federal assistance, important protection structures could be imperiled and threaten public safety.

Conclusion

The need for a comprehensive flood damage reduction policy is well-defined and recognized. Flood damages continue at a constant or increasing rate. People and property are at risk and social and economic well-being is affected. Investment in efforts to reduce the effects of flooding through prevention and protection produce immediate and long-term benefits to the economy and to society. The elements of an effective flood damage reduction program as discussed in this paper are:

- Cooperative, coordinated, and integrated programs involving all government levels, concerned interests, and affected parties (building teams and effective communications).
- A commitment to change and innovation (embracing change).
- Multiobjective, forward-looking river basin and watershed planning to reduce risks (deriving the greatest benefits from our investments).
- Decisions consistent with the concept of sustainable development (decisions we make today should not limit the decisions of future generations).

- Greater emphasis on preventing structures from being built that are or will be at risk from flood damage (an once of prevention is worth a pound of cure).
- Increased investment in the construction and maintenance of our infrastructure (pay now or pay more later).

The comprehensive flood damage reduction policy needs to be supported at the highest levels of federal, state, and local governments. Turf issues need to be set aside and teams formed to address the continuing problems of flood damage. There needs to be a high level of coordination and cooperation between federal, state and local agencies. This cooperation needs to extend to the prevention of increased damage and to the planning, design, construction, operation, maintenance, rehabilitation and replacement of the flood control system.

True cooperative actions of the types described will reduce the risk of flood damage if implemented now and continued in the future. It is our responsibility as water resource professionals and practitioners to take the steps necessary to make certain that the decade of the nineties is the decade remembered for turning the corner on flood damage reduction.

Notes

1. A floodplain is land subject to periodic flooding that may include areas of wetlands but is not limited to wetlands.
2. National Science Foundation, *A Report on Flood Hazard Mitigation*, (Washington, D.C., 1980), 30.
3. The period for the five-year running average starts in 1916 and shows the first average figure in the fifth year, 1920. In subsequent years, as one year is added the earliest year is dropped.
4. Kyle Schilling, Claudia Copeland, Joseph Dixon, James Smythe, Mary Vincent, and Jan Peterson, *The Nation's Public Works: Report on Water Resources* (Washington, D.C., May 1987), 50.
5. National Council on Public Works Improvement, *Fragile Foundations: A Report on America's Public Works* (Washington, D.C., February 1988), 120-22.
6. Northeastern Illinois Planning Commission, *Evaluation of Stormwater Detention Effectiveness in Northeastern Illinois* (January 1991), 16.
7. *New York Times*, 25 April 1992, 36.
8. Adam Smith, *An Inquiry into the Nature and Causes of the Wealth of Nations* (New York, 1976), 5: 681.
9. David Alan Aschauer, *Public Investment and Private Sector Growth; The Economic Benefits of Reducing America's "Third Deficit,"* (Washington, D.C., 1990), 1.
10. Bruce D. McDowell and Michael Bell, "The Value of Infrastructure to America; A Background Paper on Issues for Consideration in Developing a Federal Infrastructure Strategy," unpublished draft paper prepared for the U.S. Army Corps of Engineers, February 1991, 12.

11. U.S. National Water Commission, *Water Policies for the Future: Final Report to the President and to the Congress of the United States National Water Commission* (Washington, DC, 1973).

12. Schilling, et. al., *The Nation's Public Works: Report on Water Resources*, xiii.

13. Tom Peters, *Thriving on Chaos: Handbook for a Management Revolution* (New York, 1988), 3.

14. Ibid., 364.

15. Ibid., 55-56.

16. National Council on Public Works Improvement, *Fragile Foundations*, 182.

Where Do We
Go from Here?

Water Resources Development at a Crossroads

Bruce D. Long

Resource Limitations

The public's desires are changing and agencies are being forced to deal with increasingly perplexing physical, chemical, and biological issues. Resource limitations make this job even tougher, and there are some very serious constraints facing the water development agencies (Army Corps of Engineers, Bureau of Reclamation, and the Soil Conservation Service). The figures accompanying this article, taken from President Bush's 1993 Budget, illustrate the seriousness of this problem.

Most of the action in water resources development is funded from domestic discretionary appropriations. This means that a program or project is authorized and then funds are appropriated each year by the appropriations committees. Other sorts of domestic discretionary programs include funding for our national parks, space, and energy activities.

The evening news regularly reports on politicians warning us about the importance of reducing the deficit. This deficit is not being driven by domestic discretionary programs (Figure 1). For fiscal year 1993, discretionary expenditures are expected to be approximately $225 billion, about 14 percent of total outlays. In real terms, domestic programs have been relatively stable for a number of years, just barely holding their own. The same can be said of defense spending although there have clearly been ups and downs. Where the tremendous growth and resultant budget pressure have occurred is in mandatory spending—interest on the debt, health, social security, federal retirement, and other programs driven by formulas and legal obligations. Even in real terms, the growth is staggering.

The various components of the mandatory segment of the budget are interesting to analyze. Interest on the debt, for instance (see Table 1), is expected to be $214 billion for the fiscal year 1993, almost as much as total domestic

Table 7.1. *Outlays, Revenues, and Deficits*

Categories	1991 Actual	1992 Budget	1993 Budget	1994 Budget	1995 Budget	1996 Budget	1997 Budget
OUTLAYS, REVENUES, AND DEFICITS (Excluding Comprehensive Health Reform) (In billions of dollars)							
Outlays							
Discretionary:							
Domestic	195.4	216.2	224.7	229.3	232.2	236.9	236.8
Defense:							
Department of Defense	309.0	300.4	278.7	270.2	269.6	271.8	274.4
Other Defense	10.7	12.5	12.9	13.4	13.9	14.7	15.3
Total Defense	319.7	312.9	291.6	283.7	283.5	286.5	289.8
International	19.7	20.1	20.6	21.4	21.3	21.5	21.2
Total Discretionary	534.8	549.2	537.0	534.3	537.0	544.8	547.8
Mandatory:							
Deposit insurance	66.3	80.1	75.7	-25.0	-27.2	-21.7	-32.2
Federal retirement	75.8	78.3	81.1	85.6	88.7	91.2	96.4
Means-tested entitlements	62.6	74.8	77.4	82.5	87.5	89.4	95.5
Medicaid	52.5	72.5	84.5	98.2	113.7	131.1	150.7
Medicare	102.0	116.0	126.5	140.1	156.0	176.2	197.7
Social Security	266.8	284.3	299.7	315.1	330.8	347.4	364.8
Unemployment insurance	25.3	32.0	25.6	25.0	24.7	24.3	24.6
Other	-57.7	-10.9	-4.6	-12.0	-17.8	-28.2	-24.9
Subtotal Mandatory	593.7	727.2	765.9	709.5	756.3	809.6	872.6
Net Interest *	194.5	198.8	213.8	231.0	242.2	253.0	263.2
Total Outlays	1,323.0	1,475.1	1,516.7	1,474.8	1,535.5	1,607.5	1,683.6
Revenues	1,054.3	1,075.7	1,164.8	1,263.4	1,343.5	1,427.5	1,501.8
Deficit	-268.7	-399.4	-351.9	-211.4	-192.1	-180.0	-181.8
Deficit/Surplus (excluding interest)	-74.2	-200.6	-138.1	+19.6	+50.1	+73.0	+81.4
Deficit/Surplus (excluding deposit insurance & interest)	-7.9	-120.5	-62.4	-5.5	+22.9	+51.3	+49.3
Memorandum							
Deficit on an accrual basis	-268.7	-365.2	-332.7	-242.8	-217.8	-193.7	-203.3
Social Security (included above):							
Operating Surplus	53.5	50.2	63.4	75.9	86.9	101.1	115.0
Interest	20.2	23.9	27.0	31.1	35.7	41.1	47.4
Total	73.7	74.1	90.4	107.0	122.6	142.2	162.4

* Slight variation from estimates printed in appendices due to a late correction in the rate of redemption of State and local governments' holdings of Treasury Securities.

discretionary spending. Think about spending almost $1 billion more per day, 365 days per year, than we take in resulting in the $352 billion deficit projected for 1993.

If we are serious about balancing the budget, we must first get serious about controlling the cost of mandatory programs (Figure 7.1). These programs grow as more people become eligible for increasing levels of benefits. To control this type of cost increase, one must either limit eligibility or reduce benefits. President Bush proposed capping the growth in mandatory programs at the rate of inflation. Alternatively, the government can raise taxes. However, since there is little stomach for any of these options, discretionary programs are feeling an increasing pinch.

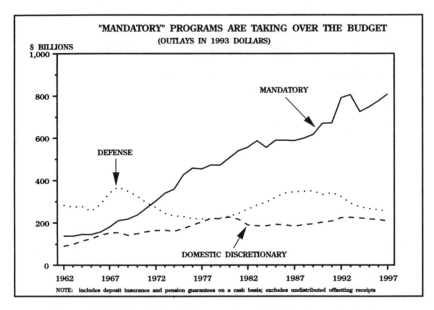

Figure 7.1. *"Mandatory" Programs are Taking Over the Budget*

Impact on Water Resources Programs

How should we, as water resources professionals, respond to these budget constraints? How many believe that reducing the deficit is important? How many support passage of a balanced budget amendment? How many believe that water resources programs would be strengthened by passage of such an amendment? How many believe that water resources programs will be better off if we just let current trends continue?

This is a very awkward way to develop fiscal policy. I think the answer, in the current circumstances, is fairly obvious. We must try to focus limited resources on projects that provide an honest return on the taxpayers' investment. This means: no phony benefit-cost ratios; no windfall benefits for small numbers of beneficiaries whether they be wealthy agricultural interests, shippers, or beach-front homeowners; and no exemptions from cost sharing, and no repayment of debt at subsidized interest rates.

It is time we all speak up for merit. The assistant secretary of the army for civil works and the U.S. Army Corps of Engineers have taken a hard line against projects which do not meet well-established economic, financial, and environmental criteria. Do they take heat? Sure. Have they been able to maintain a viable, forward looking program in spite of their resistance to pork?

Yes, they have. But what is going on even now? At the current stage of the appropriations process, the House of Representatives has found it impossible to include funds in the Corps fiscal year 1993 program for a modest number of new construction starts and for rehabilitation of inland waterway locks and dams that carry commodities basic to the functioning of the nation. Perhaps they were unable to find the money because of the tens of millions for flood control projects that are exempted from cost sharing and economic tests. Perhaps it is the tens of millions it has added for the Red River Waterway, a project which is exempted from traditional economic tests. Do you think the Tennessee-Tombigbee Waterway was the last of the dinosaurs? Forget it.

Perhaps there would be enough money to fund high priority water resources projects if Congress would not make more and more Reclamation investments nonreimbursable—a euphemism for free—and if agricultural water investments were repaid at contemporary interest rates as opposed to no interest at all. Many people may not be aware that the federal government still makes zero interest loans? It has a sort of Alice-in-Wonderland quality, does it not?

That is not all. Congress is in the midst [summer, 1992] of passing omnibus authorization bills for the Corps and Reclamation that contain billions of dollars in additional projects and programs, many of which are not subjected to even minimal tests for economic viability and require only minimal cost sharing or repayment. If we are going to sustain a viable water resources program in the face of limited resources and the declining support of broad segments of the public, we need to focus our resources on high priority projects that meet contemporary economic and environmental standards and that the beneficiaries cost share or repay at a reasonable level.

The Future

The future promises more of the same in terms of funding constraints. As a result, you can expect each successive administration budget to include additional efforts to increase cost sharing, user fees, or to obtain more favorable repayment terms. Programmatically, irrigation development is no longer a federal priority. Water supply is mostly a local responsibility, as is hydropower and they are only supported as part of multipurpose reservoir development— projects harder and harder to justify. Local flood control projects are a priority, but they should be relied on less and jurisdictions held more accountable for wise land use decisions. Storm damage protection is increasingly under the microscope because of greater understanding of coastal processes and skepticism about traditional answers. Navigation is a priority, but dredging in harbors is increasingly threatened by restrictions on the disposal of dredged material.

If you think I have painted a picture which deemphasises construction of new projects, you are right. We need to, and I think we are, turn our focus more and more to the operation of those projects already built. We must recognize the devastating impact of some projects on the environment. We must recognize new priorities that were often not included in the original authorizations. We must increase the flexibility of our laws and regulations to allow putting available water to its highest use.

We must also carefully examine new roles for the water development agencies. I support the Commissioner of Reclamation's efforts to redirect the energies of the Bureau of Reclamation. But can we afford to replace uneconomic irrigation projects with uneconomic desalination plants? Can we afford to clean up, at largely federal expense, the salts or even worse the toxic chemicals that run off fields which grow low value or surplus crops? I do not think so. There is no reason why farmers should not be expected to employ techniques to reduce the amount of runoff which is contributing to deformed ducks, poisoned fish, and possibly threatening human health.

We need to treat the environmental impacts of our projects as a cost of doing business just like the cost of fertilizer or tractors. We are subsidizing the water; we cannot afford also to pay to clean it up after it leaves the farm. Similarly, the Bureau and the Corps cannot have the value of their reservoirs impaired by non-point sources of pollution and then pay to clean it up. Whether it is agriculture, construction activity, or urban runoff there has to be a greater sense of responsibility at the source.

I am all for working with states, EPA, and polluters to identify problems and alternatives for their correction. But I cannot support the agencies' paying the lion's share for their implementation. You cannot be for a market system free of regulation and then turn around and ask for subsidies to clean up your mess. There is something wrong about that philosophically, and we cannot afford it.

Another point I would make about the future is that with budgets as tight as they are, there is less and less room for billion dollar projects. That sort of commitment squeezes out other activities and ties the administration's hands budgetarily for seven to ten years while the projects are being built. To the extent scarce resources are to be directed toward large projects, they should be those that present significant challenges beyond the capability of a single jurisdiction.

Whether we are talking large projects or small, it seems now that what project sponsors really want is financing. There are construction firms all over the country willing and able to design and construct projects. Look at the current direction of the reauthorization of the Central Utah Project (CUP) which will entail a transfer of hundreds of millions from Reclamation to the irrigation district that will construct a major feature of the project.

This trend will continue, particularly if the agencies do not get overhead under control. Spreading the costs of fewer and fewer projects over a stable workforce increases overhead rates. This in turn makes projects more expensive and the cycle continues. Sounds like business, does it not? General

Motors is finally facing this issue head on and is shedding management layers, closing plants across the country, and reducing the number of car models. Federal agencies must seriously consider similar action. The Corps' current success with work for others will dry up without cost control. CUP will be the tip of the iceberg for Reclamation for the same reason.

Without meaningful cost sharing or repayment pressure on agencies to control overhead, the taxpayer is poorer as a result. Neither alternative is very attractive.

Conclusion

The credibility and viability of the water resources development programs depend to a large extent on the positions we take on proposals to build new projects as well as the operation of ongoing projects. People are fed up with pork and business as usual.

The Reclamation authorization bill is being held hostage by an ongoing debate over a few projects and policies. How will the Central Valley Project deal with its significant harm to fish and wildlife? Will farmers continue to draw subsidies for crops grown with subsidized water? Will farmers have to implement meaningful conservation measures? Should not agricultural interests be required to live within the limitations envisioned by the Reclamation Reform Act? It is healthy that these questions have been made the subject of serious debate. We should insist on straight answers.

If you want to reduce the deficit and have a viable water resources program, we and the water resources development agencies must focus on projects providing high priority benefits having solid economics and real cost sharing. We must have the guts to resist erosion of those principles. If you are an advocate of a meritorious project, your chance of actually getting it built will be greatly enhanced if you work to reduce the competition from the turkeys.

The Federal Perspective

Bory Steinberg

In order to address where we go from here from the federal perspective, it is first necessary to review the present state of various water resources programs. Recent federal legislation, policies, priorities and appropriations, help shape this background. A number of speakers at the Forum focused on the past and present while other presentations eyed the future. Some skillfully discussed both where we have been and where we are going or at least in what direction the speaker thought a particular program should move. Thus, this summary is a blend of my own knowledge and assessment along with the stimulating input from a number of speakers at the Forum.

Flood Control

Since passage of the Water Resources Development Act of 1986 (WRDA '86) virtually all new flood control projects require non-federal cash in addition to the traditional lands, easements, rights-of-way and relocations. As a general rule, the non-federal share of new projects is at least 25 percent with a maximum of 50 percent and at least five percent cash. There is an allowance for reduced cost sharing in poorer communities based on the ability to pay provision contained in Section 103(m) of WRDA '86. The rule implementing this section made it difficult to apply the concept when a project had a favorable benefit-cost ratio unless the cost sharing was significantly higher than 25 percent. As a result, the law was modified by Section 305 of WRDA '90, but separate legislation prohibited the Corps from implementing the provision in WRDA '90. It appears that Congress will deal with this issue on a case-by-case basis in WRDA '92, given that neither the rule implementing WRDA '86, Section 103(m), nor the rule implementing WRDA '90, Section 305, is acceptable to *all* Congressional interests.

Physical opportunities, cost sharing, economic methodology and policies, and environmental considerations significantly limit the number of new reservoir projects which are likely to be built with federal and non-federal funds. Prior to WRDA '86, the federal government paid for lands and relocations, which generally constitute a significant portion of the cost of reservoir projects. This cost must now be borne by the non-federal sponsor. Further, recent Office of Management and Budget (OMB) policy prohibits the Corps of Engineers from formulating a reservoir project when the project is essentially for water supply. Bruce Long of OMB reiterated this position in his presentation.

There are other changes in the scope and design of new flood control projects. Sponsors are more sensitive to aesthetic considerations and stress their inclusion in the design, even when the Corps determines that extra cost sharing is required. In essence, this philosophy can be considered consistent with environmentally sustained development, given the long life of a structural flood control project.

Most local flood control projects constructed today provide a 100-year level of protection or less. Property protected by such a project will likely be flooded once or more over a 30-year mortgage. WRDA '86 requires that before a local flood protection project is constructed, the non-federal sponsor must participate in and comply with applicable federal floodplain management and flood insurance programs. Thus the public protected by a structural project will not have a false sense of security, or at least the individual home or property owner will have some coverage during a major event.

Perhaps the most dramatic change in cost sharing pertains to the 50 percent non-federal share required of sponsors for feasibility studies. This substantial non-federal contribution has had several major impacts. First, it significantly reduces the number of feasibility studies that are undertaken. Non-federal sponsors are reluctant to fund their share if the studies are not likely to produce a favorable report recommending the authorization of a new project. Secondly, we now find that the non-federal sponsor is much more of a partner in defining the scope of the project, including the work the sponsor will perform as part of the study effort. A very sensitive issue is the attachment of technical engineering appendixes to feasibility studies. This policy increases the cost of the reports, and thus the amount of money to be contributed by non-federal interests, but probably saves time and money during design and construction. An important program for the past 30 years has been Flood Plain Management Services (FPMS). The Corps of Engineers, the Tennessee Valley Authority, and other federal water agencies manage such programs which provide flood hazard information and guidance. The program also provides technical and planning assistance and develops and disseminates guides and pamphlets to foster public understanding of the options for dealing with flood hazards. The presentation by James Wright of TVA reflects the broader emphasis being stressed by administrators of the program. The single purpose emphasis on flood loss reduction through sound technical advice has broadened into a multipurpose program to meet several community needs. These needs include resource protection, i.e., wetlands, living resources and cultural resources. It is also characterized by better organized interest groups and increased emphasis on risk assessment.

Wetlands

Increased emphasis on protection of wetlands is reflected in both executive and legislative branch actions, ranging from budget and appropriations and new program authorizations to increased manpower resources at several federal water agencies. Better communications with the public is also stressed. The issue of private property rights versus wetland delineation and protection is receiving a great deal of attention in regulatory offices. However, discussion of a national strategy is still in its embryonic stage. Jon Kusler's presentation expanded our focus on such concepts as a national strategy, mitigation banking, and flexibility within a no net loss context.

Much attention has been focused recently on the restoration of the Kissimmee River, Florida. The proposal by the South Florida Water Management District to restore the Kissimmee River to its natural state received considerable attention during the Forum. The Kissimmee River Ecosystem Restoration Project was recently reported favorably to Congress by the assistant secretary of the army for civil works, recommending 50-50 cost sharing for ecosystem restoration. At this time, the Senate version of WRDA '92 includes a provision which would authorize this major environmental project. Len Shabman of Virginia Tech referred to this as market based environmental quality and believes there is political support for such proposals.

A broad range of programs and policy considerations affecting wetlands was presented by John Meagher, director of the wetlands division at the Environmental Protection Agency. He discussed wetlands protection in the context of "no net loss" and presented a broad range of policy reforms that are being developed or at least being considered. His view of wetlands as more than a water quality and habitat issue, but one involving flood control, recreation, and cultural resources as well, is important to future policies. Similarly, his point on the need for more information on trends, losses, pollution impacts and assessment tools is essential for future decision making.

Inland Waterways

There is no direct cost sharing for inland waterways by a local sponsor as there is for federal flood control or deep draft harbor projects. However, the fuel tax imposed on commercial users of the waterways generates substantial revenue. Section 1404 of WRDA '86, titled Inland Waterways Tax, provided for a gradual increase from 10 cents per gallon of fuel prior to passage of WRDA '86, to 20 cents per gallon by the beginning of 1995. This will generate about $100 million a year toward the 50 percent contribution to the cost of each new inland waterway construction project.

Based on funds currently available in the Inland Waterways Trust Fund, and reasonable projections of progress on new high priority inland waterway construction, the fund should have a positive balance until the year 2000. However, a careful analysis must be undertaken to determine whether replacement or rehabilitation of a particular structure is more appropriate. The Inland Waterway Users Board provides these analyses in its recommendations to the assistant secretary of the army for civil works and in testimony to congressional committees. Currently, rehabilitation work at existing locks and dams is funded entirely from operation and maintenance, general funds. However, the administration has recently attempted to treat major rehabilitation in the same manner as new construction. Such an approach could affect the health of the Inland Waterways Trust Fund and is an issue being considered by Congress.

Arlene Dietz's presentation pointed to the aging infrastructure and the implied shortfall of investment to maintain the system in the future. Clearly, new sources of revenue as well as operational efficiencies need to be considered now to avoid a crisis by the start of the twenty-first century.

Harbor Projects

WRDA '86 had a major impact on coastal harbor projects of all depths. For new projects, cost sharing increased from virtually zero non-federal cost for deepening work (where ocean disposal was the normal means of disposal) to as much as 60 percent non-federal cost (50 percent during construction and 10 percent to be paid back over time). This substantial increase in non-federal financing of new projects has resulted in the frequent use of separable elements wherein only part of the authorized project is constructed. The remainder is put on the "back burner," where it may not receive funding until several years have passed.

The heavy non-federal cost sharing has resulted in certain efficiencies in sizing of channel dimensions. For example, the authorized Norfolk Harbor deepening project was estimated to cost nearly a half billion dollars when authorized in WRDA '86. The scope of work consisted of deepening the inbound and outbound channels from 45 feet to 55 feet in depth. The scope also included protecting highway tunnels when dredging at the full 55 feet. depth. With the new cost sharing, The Virginia State Port Authority immediately decided that it would not propose to deepen the inbound lane (with the coal colliers coming in empty). Secondly, the Port Authority opted for deepening to 50 feet only as the first phase of construction. Subsequent separable elements are being considered for future implementation. This was a sound decision in my view, given that the five foot deepening generated substantial and immediate benefits and this dredging was completed at less than 10 percent of the overall estimated project cost reflected in WRDA '86. Similar incremental deepening at a small fraction of overall project cost was accomplished on the Mississippi River, from the mouth to mile 181.

We have learned several key lessons both from major harbor projects constructed in accordance with WRDA '86 cost sharing provisions and from other projects which have not proceeded on schedule. These lessons include the following, and to a degree have considerable broader applicability to other types of water resources projects, for which the non-federal sponsor's share has increased:

• Major deep draft harbors are apt to be deepened in separable elements, consistent with the non-federal sponsor's financial capability and assessment of the immediacy of project benefits. As a result, the new work dredging workload is considerably less than projections when WRDA '86 was enacted. Furthermore, with less deepening, there is less annual maintenance dredging.

• With the significant non-federal cost sharing, widths of channel heretofore accepted without question are being reevaluated consistent with safety considerations. This has resulted in less dredging for a given depth.

• Ports may elect to perform the dredging on their own and seek reimbursement of the federal share as provided for in Section 204 of WRDA '86. Two such projects have been implemented to date. St. Paul Island, Alaska, has completed the navigation improvements and has received reimbursement from the Corps. Miami Harbor improvement is currently underway. Section 303 of WRDA '90 extended this option to smaller harbor projects constructed under the Corps' Continuing Authorities Program.

• To assure that the project proceeds to construction in a timely manner, it is absolutely essential that environmental issues are addressed during the study stage and that a strong coalition in support of the project be developed during this early phase. The non-federal sponsor must take a leadership role in building the coalition. Failure to achieve this support can add years to the overall project schedule. Examples of critical harbor projects which have incurred significant environmental delay are the Oakland Harbor project (authorized in WRDA '86) and the Galveston Bay navigation improvement project, which should have been authorized by WRDA '90, having had a timely Chief of Engineers' report. The plan now calls for authorization of the Galveston project in WRDA '94, allowing time to resolve environmental issues. A portion of the Oakland project is now being implemented after several years of post authorization negotiations to find an acceptable location to dispose of dredged material.

The vast majority of annual dredging accomplished by the Corps is in connection with its maintenance responsibilities. Typically the Corps must manage funds appropriated for this purpose so as to assure that adequate depths are available consistent with authorized depths and the depths required for ships entering and exiting the harbors. In accordance with WRDA '86 and WRDA '90, rather than the federal treasury financing maintenance work, funds are now derived entirely from the 0.125 percent ad valorum tax placed on the value of goods exported, imported and transshipped from one port to another. It is not clear whether future appropriations ceilings will allow the full expenditure of funds collected. In any case, the fact that users are paying for the maintenance work will undoubtedly result in increased demands for full project dimensions throughout the year. This new source of revenue also reflects considerable ingenuity in that expenditures on a port by port basis are in no way compatible with collections. Nevertheless, the compromise assures equal treatment and a reliable source of revenue and, most importantly, is politically sound in that ports with heavy annual dredging requirements are not taxed more heavily than those with minimal average annual sediment loads.

Hazardous and Toxic Wastes

There is a growing sensitivity to the impact of hazardous and toxic wastes on groundwater sources and on fish and wildlife habitat. While there was only limited discussion of this issue at the conference, Paul Bailey of ICF, Inc., presented us with an overview of the magnitude of the problem and the risks to groundwater sources. Locating and identifying hazardous and toxic wastes and assessing the risk they pose to water supply sources is a growing problem. Even when water supplies are not threatened, there may still be a potential adverse impact to human health, a degradation of natural resources, and a decrease in property values. Further, the cost of cleanup, containment, and remediation may add substantial costs to various types of water resources projects not specifically designed to improve water quality, e.g., flood control, harbor dredging, inland waterways, etc.

It is clear to me that a better understanding is needed of the legal, regulatory, and policy issues pertaining to hazardous and toxic wastes, whether governed by the Resource Conservation and Recovery Act of 1976 (RCRA), the Comprehensive Environmental Response, Compensation and Liability Act (CERCLA), or other legislation and regulations. We have seen water resources projects delayed, modified, and occasionally terminated as a result of the discovery of hazardous and toxic wastes. Procedures are being developed to investigate subsurface conditions prior to project formulation, particularly if prior uses of the land, often a number of years ago, would have resulted in the likely presence of such substances. This is gradually becoming a normal part of engineering investigations much in the way that geotechnical subsurface explorations determine the nature of the soil, groundwater, and other natural conditions. There is probably a need to more clearly define the extent of these investigations based on prior uses. Today, procedures and degree of investigation are somewhat subjective.

Here is an area where new technologies are sorely needed. Major General Arthur Williams, Director of Civil Works for the Corps of Engineers, discussed sustainable development, and he emphasized the need for new solutions, where technology is the key. In the case of hazardous and toxic wastes, we need innovative solutions for the problems we created by our past actions. We must also focus on such concepts as waste minimization in future endeavors.

Opportunities for Management Improvements

Operation and Maintenance of Reservoirs and Other Completed Projects

There is considerable opportunity for improvement in the operation of existing flood control and multipurpose reservoirs, particularly under drought conditions. In a drought, not enough water is available for hydropower, water supply, recreation, water quality releases and releases for navigation. However, there is ample storage capacity for flood control. Since many reservoirs (particularly those built and/or operated by the Corps of Engineers) were authorized primarily for flood control, the operating rules favor flood control, with operation, even during periods of drought, difficult to change. In the coming years, the management of reservoirs with a broader range of objectives in mind requires increased attention.

Considerable discussion during several sessions focused on management of reservoirs, particularly during drought. The conflicts between water quality and quantity and traditional users and distribution is complicated. It certainly requires considerable focus in the future, at all levels of government. Bureau of Reclamation Commissioner Dennis Underwood characterized the Bureau's program as evolving from infrastructure development to one of resource management and protection. He stressed the need for innovative methods of meeting demands and avoiding periodic shortages, for eliminating conflicts among uses, and for preventing the loss of natural and economic resources.

Whether dealing with new water resource projects or the management of existing projects, it is essential to recognize the politics of water resources and the role politics plays in the decision-making process. Economic and environmental tradeoffs cannot be viewed without considering watershed boundaries and competing uses. The political nature of water resources decisions makes it imperative that engineers involved in water management have a broader background than merely a technical one. As Neil Grigg pointed out, future engineers must gain a knowledge of policy, planning, communications, finance, and public involvement. My experience with the Corps of Engineers certainly reinforces this approach.

Evaluation of Environmental Benefits and Costs

A cursory review of recent authorizing legislation and appropriations acts points to the significantly increased emphasis on environmental protection, mitigation, and enhancement. Yet the tools for evaluating the benefits and costs of such projects have yet to be adequately developed. Questions such as how much mitigation is justified for a particular project are frequently a matter of dispute. The value of one wetland restoration project versus another of comparable cost has yet to be defined. The willingness of non-federal sponsors to share costs provides some indication about the worthiness of a project. However, with the federal government bearing 50-75 percent of the cost, greater rigor in evaluation of benefits is needed.

Project Management

A dramatic and meaningful change in the way an agency conducts its business has taken place within the Corps of Engineers over the past four years. Project management was introduced in 1988 and, by 1992, was firmly established as the method of managing feasibility studies and projects. This was in contrast to functional management prior to 1988, in which project responsibility was transferred from the planning division to the engineering division to the construction division as a study or project moved from one phase to another. Cost estimates were frequently understated and baseline schedules were rarely met. Constrained budgets and substantial non-federal cost sharing make project management the only proper way of conducting business if concepts such as partnering and customer satisfaction are to be taken seriously. This approach has been well received within the executive branch and by many non-federal sponsors who have seen commitments met once agreements have been signed. The fact that implementation of project management and the new cost sharing has proceeded reasonably well over the past several years has been a major factor in the Corps' healthy budgets during this period of constrained discretionary spending.

Another benefit of project managment, partnering, and cost sharing has been the completion of feasibility studies with considerably more engineering effort. While this procedure is relatively new, the result has already been noteworthy. Preconstruction engineering and design (PED), which constitutes the design effort prior to initial construction, can begin as soon as a favorable feasibility report and accompanying engineering appendix are forwarded by the division engineer (the engineer officer, commonly a general, to whom several district engineer officers report) to the headquarters in Washington for review. This concept—called "seamless funding" because no gap exists between the feasibility report and PED funding—can considerably expedite engineering and design work without sacrificing quality. It has worked well for several years. At the district office, even before the feasibility report is formally sent

271

to the division engineer, various Corps management levels as well as representatives of the Assistant Secretary of the Army for Civil Works review the district's work in technical review conferences and the Feasibility Review Conference (FRC). Seamless funding, the FRC, the technical engineering appendix, and procedures that reduce the required review time in Washington all serve to ready projects for construction in less time than in the past. We are actually seeing new projects being recommended for funding in appropriation bills in the same year that they are recommended for authorization in the biennial water resources development act. This achievement serves to refute critics who continue to point to the extended period it has taken historically from study to completion of construction.

Further, improvements are being realized in cost-estimating procedures. The cost of each new project recommended for authorization is more carefully analyzed through the micro-computer aided cost-estimating system (M-CACES) that the Corps has developed. Only a few projects have exceeded the 20 percent growth limitation allowed by Section 902 of WRDA '86, and they are less likely to exceed the limit in the future. These achievements, combined with timely signing of local cooperation agreements and construction contract awards, are the best evidence that project management is working and producing tangible beneficial results. The concept of project management is most suitable in our complex environment, where a great deal of horizontal and vertical integration of efforts is required and a team approach drawing from several organizations or divisions is most appropriate. Traditional organizational structures in federal and non-federal water resources agencies make the forging of such project management partnerships difficult. However, moving in that direction, in my view, is a necessity and worthy of broader consideration in the federal and non-federal sectors.

Appropriate Role for the Federal Sector

An appropriate role of the federal government is to determine priorities, develop policies, and in turn support these priorities and policies. Ed Dickey, Principal Deputy Assistant Secretary of the Army, Civil Works, indicated that there is a lack of consensus on relative values and, in fact, in understanding the complex relationship in the integration of water quality and water quantity. This is the major challenge at the federal level—arriving at consensus. Several participants, both as presenters and as commenters, pointed to the lack of a high level group at the federal level for water policy development. At a time when controversies abound and discretionary spending is limited, there simply is no replacement today for the Water Resources Council. Today, each agency develops its own policies through a complex relationship with Congress and the non-federal sector and through interpretation and reinterpretation of administration positions. Each agency bears certain "baggage" in terms of laws, implementing policies, and a bureaucracy that does not change rapidly.

This "baggage" is both the strength and weakness in the federal sector. It assures that programs and policies are carried out with some degree of consistency and according to certain standards. Yet, it complicates and delays achieving interagency consensus among water resources agencies on issues of mutual concern. Even when new policies are adopted, we now find Congress occasionally prohibiting their implementation. Thus, we have in limbo such issues as wetlands delineation and ability to pay (for flood control).

In conclusion, I believe there is a void created by the demise of the Water Resources Council. While, there was not unanimous agreement on the policies that body helped shape during its two-decade life, it did provide a forum for addressing issues and seeking consistent interpretation of laws and application of policies. Today the issues are more complex and federal investments focus more on the environment than on water resource infrastructure development, In comparison to the 1960s and 1970s, federal discretionary spending for new water resources projects is considerably more constrained. Yet the non-federal sector is not receptive to more federal policies and restrictions without adequate federal financing of programs. The solution lies in a strong federal and state organization, where sensitive issues involving the two levels of government can be discussed.

The State Perspective

Holly E. Stoerker

The struggle both to redefine national water policy and give it full expression in the decision-making process has become more earnest. Increasingly more complex threats to our natural resources, coupled with severe financial limitations and a heritage of incongruent water and related environmental policies, have led to near gridlock. The growing frustration over our collective ability to meet the challenges of the future and more effectively manage the nation's water resources has given rise to a renewed exploration of our options. The American Water Resources Association (AWRA) National Forum on Water Management Policy is one of a growing number of assemblies which offer an opportunity to engage in both reflection and debate on the form and substance of national water policy.

As one of the closing presentations at the AWRA National Forum on Water Management Policy, the purpose of this paper is two-fold. The first assignment was to share the "state" perspective on the theme of this meeting—national water policy—and to reflect, from that perspective, on where we are or should be heading. The second challenge was to critique the Forum and offer some observations on both its strengths and weaknesses. Rather than attempting to respond to these two questions independently, the intention is to integrate the remarks in a fashion that will accomplish both of the objectives.

By way of background, it should be understood that the "state" perspective would perhaps more appropriately be termed a "nonfederal" perspective. Local, interstate, and regional water management agencies, as well as states, play a unique and increasingly important role in water policy planning and management. Furthermore, just as it is difficult, if not impossible, to define a "federal" perspective, it is equally challenging to articulate a singular "state" perspective. While there are unique circumstances which contribute to the differences that are apparent in states' views of their role in water resource management, there

274

is also a growing convergence toward generally accepted principles among the nonfederal water community.

These general principles serve as the benchmarks upon which the contributions of this Forum were judged. In particular, three criteria were used to evaluate the AWRA Forum:

- Were the fundamental principles of water policy that are taking shape within the nonfederal water community validated and reaffirmed or were there new or different perspectives embraced by the participants in the AWRA Forum?
- Did the AWRA Forum serve to advance the discussion of these principles and thereby offer enhanced definition of our collective vision for the future?
- Did the AWRA Forum expand the on-going dialogue on national water policy to a broader community of interest groups, stakeholders, and disciplines?

All of these questions are based on the premise that the AWRA Forum is one of a series of meetings, hosted by a variety of organizations, that are addressing many of the same fundamental water policy issues. In particular, over the past year, the Western Governors' Association and the Western States Water Council sponsored a series of workshops in Park City, Utah, to explore the challenges faced by western water managers. Punctuating this series was the National Water Policy Roundtable sponsored by the Interstate Council on Water Policy (ICWP) in February 1992. The purpose of the ICWP Roundtable was to provide a national "test" of the principles emerging from the western states' Park City workshops and to further explore the need for reform of the national water policy framework. The AWRA Forum is the most recent meeting in what is emerging as an on-going series of water policy debates.

There are five fundamental principles that appear to capture the "state" perspective on water policy. These principles are essentially the "Executive Summary" of both the recent Park City workshops and ICWP Roundtable. While a number of these principles reflect widely-recognized time-honored fundamentals of water management, others reflect the more contemporary challenges of a management system in gridlock. That is indeed their strength and precisely the conclusion that the AWRA Forum appears to have reaffirmed. The keys to sound national water policy include partnerships, a watershed approach, an integrated natural systems framework, a balance between flexibility and predictability, and state leadership.

Obstacles to Meaningful Intergovernmental and Interinstitutional Partnerships Must Be Overcome

Intergovernmental relationships have long been the cornerstone of water management in this country and indeed are the basis for the federal system of governance. Collaboration among various levels of government and among single-purpose agency units of those levels has always been a matter of concern. While the states and federal government have long been financial partners in the delivery of services and development of water projects and regulation, the term "partnership" has only recently become part of the water community's vocabulary. Most notably, the 1986 Water Resources Development Act, which set forth a cost-sharing framework for Corps of Engineers' projects, brought the term "partnership" into common usage. Unfortunately the term still frequently connotes merely a financial relationship, and nonfederal project sponsors continue struggling to inject the term with more substantive meaning, including shared decision making. Despite the fact that the word "partnership" may be falling into disfavor due to its vagueness and the difficulties associated with implementing it, it would be unfortunate if it were to be abandoned. The term still comes closest to capturing the relationship to which we aspire.

At the AWRA Forum a variety of speakers made reference to the value of partnership. Both Dennis Underwood of the Bureau of Reclamation and Bill Richards of the Soil Conservation Service used the term in describing the solution to increasingly limited financial resources. In his comment, Bill Whipple noted that, since the demise of the Water Resources Council, no single federal agency has the lead for setting up partnerships and the institutional means for achieving partnership are not obvious. Although other speakers did not necessarily use the term "partnership," their comments suggest that it is a concept which is indeed widely embraced. Dean Mann, in his discussion of the politics of water resource management, described a system of "multiple centers of power." From the engineers' perspective, Neil Grigg discussed the need for "cooperation, coordination, and communication." And finally, Bill Goldfarb said "read my lips—no new institutions." All these remarks suggest that there is indeed a recognition of the need for partnerships even if we do not always label it as such.

Despite the fact that there appeared to be a strong affirmation of the partnership theme at this Forum, there was, regrettably, limited discussion of the existing obstacles to, and limitations on, our capacity to them. If we expect to create meaningful partnerships, we must at some point more fully understand the reasons why they do not naturally emerge from our existing institutional framework.

The Most Appropriate Unit of Analysis for Water Resources is the Watershed or "Problemshed"

Water resource professionals, elected officials, and the public have always been confronted with the dilemma that our government institutions and political boundaries are incongruent with the natural system of watersheds. Perhaps that explains the fact that the term "problemshed" is increasingly in vogue. While new jargon is not the answer, it may be helpful to begin thinking in terms of "problemshed," meaning the area that encompasses both the problem and the affected interests. Regardless of which term (watershed or problemshed) is used, it was abundantly clear that the concept was heartily affirmed by the participants at the AWRA Forum. There were no less than a dozen of the distinguished speakers at this meeting who remarked on the need for a watershed perspective and acclaimed the virtues of this approach. Indeed, Rutherford Platt reminded us that the watershed concept was one of the primary contributions that geographers made to the history of water resource policy development. Yet the remarks of Ken Rubin were perhaps most compelling. Rubin suggested that the watershed approach "is a must, not a cliche." He identified a number of reasons why we are closer than ever before to the reality of a watershed approach, including the fact that many programs which historically served as disincentives have been eliminated, that other alternatives are simply too costly, and that public awareness of the value of a watershed perspective is at an all time high.

An Integrated Natural Systems Approach is Necessary

Similar to the watershed perspective, the concept of an integrated natural systems approach is not a particularly new concept. However, it has become an increasingly important one insofar as it reflects the dynamic interdependence of hydrologic, ecological, and biological systems and emphasizes the relationship of water to the landscape. This increasingly popular perspective was another of the ICWP Roundtable themes that was widely affirmed at the AWRA Forum and was in fact the topic of one of the technical sessions at this meeting. While the concept was not always described with the same terminology, examples from this conference abound. General Williams called it "ecosystem thinking." Bill Goldfarb referred to "comprehensive, coordinated, multipurpose, basin-wide water and related resource planning and management." Bill Richards called it "total resource management." Jim Wright discussed "multiobjective management," while John Meagher termed it "natural resource planning." In describing natural or ecosystem restoration, Leonard Shabman observed "it is not a plumbing problem anymore." In short, the principle of an integrated natural systems approach was widely endorsed.

However, our major failing at this meeting was perhaps the limited range of disciplines represented in the discussion, particularly with respect to the concept of an integrated natural systems perspective. As has been the case in numerous other recent water policy forums and conferences, the natural sciences have been conspicuously absent. If indeed we embrace a more holistic natural systems framework for water management, we must begin to engage biologists and other natural scientists more fully in the policy dialogue.

277

Balance Between Flexibility and Predictability in Water Management is Necessary

We must be better equipped to adapt to change—not only changes in the conditions of our natural systems but also changes in our political culture and values. Management systems that can accommodate complexity and allow us to act in the face of uncertainty are becoming increasingly necessary. However, this flexibility must be tempered with predictability. The timeliness and certainty of decisions is equally important, not only to meet the needs, for example, of those responsible for making economic investment decisions, but also to bolster public confidence in both the process and the result.

The notion of flexibility was frequently discussed by participants in the AWRA Forum. In the session on sustainable development, Myron Fiering commented on the limitations of many of our analytical tools because, in essence, we are "shooting at a moving target." Major General Arthur Williams, in describing the challenge of balancing local needs and federal priorities, used the example of the Kissimmee River where public values have changed over time. Dennis Underwood described the benefits which can be achieved with more innovative and flexible operational rules at existing Bureau of Reclamation projects. Jon Kusler very aptly described our dilemma in wetlands regulation and policy when we ignore flexibility and rely instead on prescriptive uniformity. While the discussions at this Forum appear to have validated the merits of flexibility, there was little if any reference to the countervailing concept of predictability, which has surfaced in many of the previous water policy dialogues. This may suggest the need for elaboration or further discussion of the significance of this balance.

States Play the Fundamental Role in Water Planning and Management

In our federal system of government, responsibility for water resource management is vested in the states, including such responsibilities as water quality standards and water rights. The notion that states play a pivotal role is, however, much broader than the simple recognition of the precepts of federalism. What ICWP and other state organizations are suggesting is that it is at the state level where both leadership and innovation are emerging. The federal government, which has long been the arena for water policy development and technical expertise, has become increasingly incapable of providing the necessary leadership and has through a "top-down" management style, contributed to the gridlock which we now experience. State and local leadership is becoming more the rule than the exception.

While the first four principles, which ICWP and others have espoused, were largely reaffirmed by the discussions at the AWRA Forum, support for the fifth principle—the fundamental role of states—was less clear. A number

278

of speakers promoted the idea that states play a key role. Bruce Long of OMB, LaJuana Wilcher of EPA, and Dennis Underwood of the Bureau of Reclamation all proclaimed the primacy of and acknowledged the expertise of states. Ed Dickey, the Principal Deputy Assistant Secretary of the Army for Civil Works, candidly acknowledged his pessimism about the ability of the federal government to provide leadership for institutional reform. Interestingly, representatives of the federal community were the most vigorous proponents of state leadership. One of the few nonfederal representatives to comment on the state role was Jon Kusler of the Association of State Wetland Managers, who called the innovative work being done by states in protecting and managing wetlands "more rational than the federal approach" and offered a number of examples of creative and effective state programs.

In contrast to these observations about state leadership, many of the recommendations that took shape in the issue group discussions at the conclusion of the Forum appear to be cast in terms of federal initiatives. While acknowledging the failings of the Water Resources Council and federal river basin commissions, a preference for federal leadership seems to persist. How this approach is reconciled with the equally persistent disposition to a "bottom-up" approach is not clear.

There are a variety of reasons why mixed reviews exist on the concept of state leadership, even by those who espouse it. To advocate state leadership suggests that states have both the capacity and will to exercise that leadership. However, there are a number of limitations on state capacity. The complexity of our water problems requires substantial investment in research, technology development, and data systems, all of which are frequently beyond the ability of states to support or are impractical and inefficient to pursue unilaterally. In addition, states are often as fractured in their institutional composition as the federal government. Moreover, there are interstate water issues beyond the geographical scope and authority of single states. Finally, there are national public interest values, such as endangered species or commercial waterway transportation, that are difficult for states to integrate or fully recognize in their authorities.

On the other hand, states are often on the forefront of innovation, frequently having higher tolerance for experimentation. We see this in the fields of health care and education and increasingly in the water resources arena. In addition, states are better positioned to understand the unique and variable natural resource problems in their area and possess more direct political accountability. Most importantly, states have a unique relationship to local units of government. And it is at the local level where many of the most difficult water issues arise and must be resolved. Insofar as states are empowered to create and transfer authority to local units of government, whether they be municipalities, counties, or special water or natural resource districts, states are in a unique position to facilitate and nurture the partnerships which are so widely acclaimed.

Although many of the principles just described are not particularly new, what distinguishes them is the attendant sense of urgency among state, regional, and local water professionals, and, for that matter, among the public. If indeed we accept these principles as the foundation for national water policy, then the challenge becomes to find ways to attain these objectives, discovering why it is that we do not necessarily act in ways in which we all agree we should. The prescription for change remains elusive. There were, however, a number of very interesting and exciting ideas that emerged from the issue group sessions at this AWRA Forum. While these recommendations do not constitute a comprehensive strategy for reform, they certainly embody a number of key ingredients. Many of the ideas which surfaced in the AWRA Forum issue groups parallel the conclusions of ICWP's National Water Policy Roundtable. In short, the Roundtable identified the following needs.

1. Building Comprehension at the Problemshed or Watershed Level. It is not sufficient that water resource professionals use and understand the term "watershed approach" and strive to manage water as part of an integrated natural system. It is becoming increasingly important that the public-at-large and our political leaders more fully comprehend these concepts and develop an appreciation for the uncertainty inherent in managing large complex natural systems. While it is difficult to convey the complexity of these issues in a communication environment that relies on mass media sound-bites, we must become agents for building broad-based comprehension.

2. Networking. If we subscribe to the notion that the days of substantial dependence on the federal government are long past and that what is emerging is experimentation and innovation at the state and local levels, then we need to learn from each other. Networks for exchanging information on our historic successes and failures need to be enhanced. Insofar as many of the imaginative approaches we seek are rooted in the environmental movement of the 1960s and 1970s, we must preserve the lessons that have been learned and build upon our heritage.

3. Capacity Building. There is a need to explore new models that will allow us to integrate all the principles we espouse—partnership, flexibility, integrated natural systems management, watershed perspective, and market-like structures. While the concept of capacity has a variety of dimensions, the most challenging issue appears to be providing our institutions with the capacity to reflect these principles in their actions. Institutional and legal obstacles should be evaluated in addition to financial and technical capacity.

4. Leadership Development. It is becoming increasingly important to develop constituency-based leadership at the grassroots level. Citizen leaders who are informed and have the necessary resources to participate in the decision-making process will be critical to the success of any new water policy framework. Likewise, the water community must cultivate political leaders at all levels who appreciate the value of holistic approaches to water and natural resource management and can credibly engage in public policy debates on these issues. Outreach and communication with political leaders has typically focused on gaining support for specific projects or programmatic adjustments. The challenge will be to nurture political leaders who can serve as spokespeople for more integrated management systems and fundamental policy reforms.

Conclusion

Perhaps the most authoritative spokespeople for the state perspective are the governors. At the annual meeting of the National Governors' Association in February 1992, the governors adopted a revised water resource management policy statement. Its significance lies not only in *what* it says, but *who* is saying it. Because the ideas it embodies were the very theme of the AWRA Forum, it is perhaps fitting to close both this overview of the state perspective and the conference as a whole with an excerpt from the governors' policy statement:[1]

> Historically, this nation has approached water resources as isolated and categorical, with programs designed specifically for certain waters depending upon where they are found. Now we know that our water resources are part of an interrelated hydrologic and environmental system that demands systematic management. The governors believe the future demands a new model for managing water resources, based on well-defined geographic units such as basins or watersheds, that recognizes all the interconnections with the watershed that define the hydrologic cycle in that area, including surface and groundwaters as well as wetlands. The management of any watershed should reflect all of the things that make it unique, including specific precipitation patterns, topography, soil and geological characteristics, and land use.

> A systems management approach would involve the development and operation of a comprehensive water resource management program—though ultimately it need not be limited to water resources—within the specific geographic area encompassing the basin or watershed. Components of such a comprehensive program would include water supply, water quality, water conservation, flood protection, land use, and protection of fish and wildlife resources.

> There are few, if any, significant scientific barriers to the transition from our current collection of categorical programs to this kind of comprehensive, systems-based approach to water resource management. However, the Governors recognize that there are significant institutional obstacles, and that the new model needs to be developed in an evolutionary fashion. It will require unprecedented cooperation among many state and local entities, among state and federal agencies, and between states in the case of watersheds crossing state lines.

Where Do We Go from Here?

The Governors reaffirm their commitment to the restoration and maintenance of the chemical, biological, and physical integrity of the nation's waters and water ecosystems and the protection of its availability and acknowledge that the nation's water and related resources are increasingly central to our economic and environmental well-being. The nation's strategy for achieving these objectives should remain founded upon a vigorous federal-state partnership that recognizes that limited resources for water resource management demand enhanced intergovernmental cooperation.

. . . As our government policies transition to a systems-based, comprehensive approach to managing water resources, we must introduce increased flexibility and latitude into current programs so that cross-categorical management of resources can flourish.

Note

1. Water Resources Management Policy, National Governors' Association, Adopted August 1991, revised February 1992.

Appendix A

Issue Group Reports

Presented below are summaries of the eight issue group reports resulting from the National Forum on Water Management Policy. Each group met for a total of three to four hours. All registrants were encouraged to participate. Issue group participants chose one or two policy issues to address dealing with their group's topic. The recommendations represent the views of the participants and not necessarily of the American Water Resources Association or co-sponsors of the Forum.

I. Regional Water Management

A. *Policy Issue*: The development of comprehensive regional water planning

B. *Discussion Summary:* Participants identified 22 specific components of what they considered to be an optimal regional water resources planning program. These components can be divided into three broad categories: 1) the planning process to be followed, 2) the priority issues to be considered, and 3) the mechanisms needed for planning and implementation.

   1. Planning Process: Regional water resources planning can be successful only if it is conducted with full local initiative and public involvement. The selection of alternatives, and the products, must be arrived at openly and be fully reviewable by all parties. To prevent later challenges, there must be a level playing field for all participants (i.e. no disenfranchised interests). The process should be interdisciplinary, and it should foster state and local involvement. There should be incentives to encourage innovative managerial actions for state and local involvement. Although the focus would be on water resources,

the relationship with related resources (e.g. land) should not be overlooked. Where possible, the planning process should make full use of prior experience and precedents at appropriate geographical scales. In all cases, those engaged in the planning should be as sensitive to social, political, economic, as well as resource concerns.

2. Issues: Issues deserving special attention include cross-media and regulatory overlaps. Impediments to regional water management should be identified and addressed. The plan should be sensitive to occasions when managerial flexibility may be limited by external constraints. It was felt that a regional water resource plan built around functions and/or decisions actually needing to be carried out would provide legitimacy to the products. Matters of organization, admiministration, funding and cost sharing would be crucial. A fair share of a particular water management action should be allocated to the beneficiaries. It is also important to have the regional plan provide a common meeting ground for local, state, and national concerns.

3. Mechanisms for Planning and Implementation: First and foremost, involved parties should be fully committed to the planning and implementation. Thus, the plan itself needs to contain built-in mechanisms for follow-up and implementation. These can range from informal arrangements to test out the ground for action to formal compacts or other intergovernmental agreements where sovereign powers are modified in the interest of implementation. There may be a need to streamline regulatory procedures in order to attain plan objectives. Finally, participants agreed that planning and implementation must be viewed as a dynamic process with allowance for changing conditions and periodic updating to meet new and unforeseen needs.

C. *Policy Recommendations:*

1. The principles set forth above should serve as a preliminary guide for regional water management activities.
2. The AWRA Committee on water, law, science, and policy should receive, refine, and further develop these principles and encourage participation in a variety of settings, scales, and sponsorships.
3. If any council or commission is established relating to national water policy, a component of its work should be aimed at fostering bottom-up, comprehensive, regional water management planning.
4. The AWRA should consider convening a working conference on

the experience, precedents, and techniques for regional water management, including the definition of viable regions in more than simply hydrologic terms.

II. Sustainable Development

A. *Policy Issue*: Valuing environmental systems

B. *Discussion Summary:* The group spent considerable time discussing the definition of "sustainable development." The general view was that the term was ambiguous and in need of explicit definition if it were to be used as a guideline for planning and management processes at federal, state, and local levels. Furthermore, it was noted that the definition should include both human and natural system dimensions. Accordingly, the following definition was proposed:

> *Sustainable Development* is a process of pursuing world-wide social welfare in a manner that enhances the natural resource, health, and environmental quality of life requirements of future generations.

Several participants wanted to add the following to the definition, but time did not allow discussion:

> The principles of pursuing worldwide social progress in a manner that preserves the natural resource should be applied by managing water resources at a watershed or ecosystem level. The evaluation of aggregate and cumulative consequences of water usage and future water system development shall reflect public values at local, state, national, and international levels and shall also reflect environmental and ecological values as outlined in the proposed national environmental accounting system.

While the participants identified many issues relevant to sustainable development, they chose to focus on valuing environmental systems in the limited time allowed. However, they noted that many other issues were critical in both a national and international sense.

It was unanimously agreed that population and institutional constraints were compelling issues deserving of considerable attention.

C. *Policy Recommendations:*

1. The Congress or Administration establish (modeled after the 1971 National Water Commission) a national commission on environmental values for the purpose of developing a common structure for measuring and reporting environmental values. This commission should be supported for a period not to exceed five years and should be funded at a level of $8 million for its entire period of operation.

2. The Congress or Administration establish a council to develop and recommend a coherent national water policy, which includes a water valuing structure. Other missions of the council would be to identify areas needing further research and to develop and maintain an effective decision support system. Furthermore, the council should be charged with examining local/regional water-shed-specific factors that are relevant to practical natural system valuation designs and with forming recommendations for incorporating the appropriate level of flexibility into these designs.3. The President charge the Council on Environmental Quality with developing a national accounting system for environmental resources. The results of this accounting should be reported annually to the nation in the President's State of the Union address. It is expected that this accounting system would serve as the basis for a national pollution taxing system to compensate for costs imposed by pollutants on natural systems.

4. The Congress appropriate funding to the National Research Council to support a nation-wide study of U.S. institutions (political, economic, social, environmental, and technological) which constrain, interfere with, or encourage the conduct of effective sustainable development programs. A recommendation of this study should be to establish a public education program to promote understanding and to overcome constraints.

5. The Congress authorize and fund five regional laboratories for the purpose of developing and testing sustainable development planning processes. These laboratories should be funded in a manner similar to that of the long-term ecological research sites supported by NSF. It is proposed that these laboratories be funded for an initial period of five years and that individual laboratory budgets be set at $1 million per year.

6. The Congress appropriate funds to the water resources research institutes established under the Water Resources Research Act of 1964 for the specific purpose of conducting basic and applied research, and technology transfer focused on providing scientific, economic, and other bases for valuing environmental systems and facilitating multiobjective water resources planning and management. Budget requirement: $12.5 million per year for five years.

7. The U.S. government recommend that the United Nations convene the next round of international forums on economic development to focus on valuing environmental systems worldwide.

III. Present and Future Water Infrastructure Needs

A. *Policy Issue* 1: Needs are often unnecessarily determined by legislative, regulatory and administrative practice.

B. *Discussion Summary* 1: More local/nonfederal flexibility to deal with end results and achievability within the scope of a total "problemshed" considering costs. Unfunded mandates and the separation of water quantity and quality issues in areas like stormwater and combined sewer overflows were part of the issue as well as the dichotomy between planning and guidelines and regulatory approaches.

C. *Policy Recommendations* 1:

1. Educate legislative bodies and others better as to the needs, impacts, achievability, costs and other alternative approaches to achieving end results.
2. Introduce more flexibility to recognize costs and performance including achievability, local circumstances, risk and overall end results into practices.
3. Streamline and coordinate processes.

D. *Policy Issue 2:* How do we establish, prioritize, and pay for needs.

E. *Discussion Summary* 2: While we cannot afford to do everything we might want to do, no matter whose "needs list" it is, work on benefits and valuation processes could help increase the willingness to pay. These processes include performance indicators such as economic return, international competitiveness, as well as capital budgeting.

F. *Policy Recommendations* 2:

1. Need to deal with local community values and ability to pay, as well as incremental costs and benefits of achieving legislative mandates.
2. Need to deal with cross functional, cross media and alternative impacts.

IV. Risk and Uncertainty in Water Resources

A. *Policy Issue:* Need for statistical rigor in data collection and modelling for decisionmaking. These data define the hydrologic cycle, surface and ground water quality and usage, geomorphology, ecology, and the social and economic systems.

B. *Discussion Summary:* Management of multipurpose water resource systems involves estimation of risks and uncertainties. To estimate these, system managers use a variety of techniques, including mathematical models whose solutions serve the multiple objectives of the system. An overarching issue is the communication of these uncertainties, and of their impact on objectives, to the decision makers for their explicit consideration. Participants believe that the multiple sources of uncertainty and risk in water resources development need to be reduced before decision makers can make appropriate and well-informed decisions. Significant additional data and better understanding of systems will be required. In this context, the participants identified the following needs:

1. The need for statistical rigor in data collection and modelling for decision making.
2. The need for improved tools for measurement, evaluation, documentation and communication of risks and uncertainties for decision makers.
3. The need for long-term planning/management that recognizes risk and uncertainty, rather than repeated crisis management in response to extreme events.

C. *Policy Recommendations* (Although the participants did not identify the levels of government or agencies that should assume leadership for each recommendation, the group recognized that identifying a lead agency and initiating appropriate implementation actions are the first steps needed):

1. Identify priority data needs.
2. Develop standards or protocols for data collection.
3. Assure funding for collection of priority data.
4. Coordinate interagency data collection in accordance with other recommendations.
5. Establish interagency clearinghouse(s) for data/models.
6. Develop and use statistical methods to express to decision makers the uncertainty in model outputs.

V. Changing Institutional Relationships

A. *Policy Issue:* Institutional design should be driven by particular water resource problems. Problems are customarily defined through the political process; but problem definition and resolution may be enhanced by early professional involvement. Improved institutional design will improve the delivery of water related services.

B. *Discussion Summary:* Once the water resource problem has been defined, the following criteria should be used to guide institutional design:

1. Structure and Function: The institution should be structurally and functionally suitable to solving the problem. This includes

resolution of intra and interagency conflicts. Some problems may require solutions involving a number of institutions. The institution should possess management capacity and institutional culture consistent with problem solution.

2. Spatial Scales: Each problem exists over a particular geographical scale. Complex water resources problems can be multiscale. For example, a proposed multipurpose impoundment may extend over a hydropower scale (the relevant power grid), a recreation scale (local boaters and fishermen), and a wildlife habitat scale (the appropriate ecosystem), among others. Each institutional solution should possess a suitable scale or set of scales. In water resources management the hydrologic basin (watershed) is frequently the most appropriate unit to use in establishing management scale.

3. Temporal Scale and Viability: The institution should possess a lifespan that is equal to the phase of the problem at hand, without either assuming a life of its own independent of the problem requiring solution or being captured by clientele groups.

4. Finance/Economics: The institution should possess sufficient available resources to solve the problem. Market solutions should be applied whereever appropriate.

5. Laws: The institution should possess adequate legal authority to cope with the problem.

6. Politics: The institution should be validated by a political consensus constructed through a "bottom-up" planning process including bargaining among all possible stakeholders. Higher levels of government play important roles in the bottom-up approach (e.g., technical assistance, guidelines).

7. Equity: The institution should be capable of assuring equity with regard to politically weak stakeholders, ecosystems, and future generations.

8. Implementability: Delivery systems should be feasible, efficient, and effective.

C. *Policy Recommendations:*

1. Responding to the problem of haphazard and politically-driven water resource institutional structures, water resources professionals should have significant input into the governmental process of problem definition and institutional design, so that water resource problems can be addressed and managed in a rational, comprehensive, and multidisciplinary way. The water resources professional community is to some extent fractured by sector (e.g., AWWA) and by discipline (e.g., ASCE). Those water resources professional organizations that are multidisciplinary by nature

should organize a Water Resource Professionals Advisory Group to advise governments on problem identification and institutional design in the water resources field. This new institutuion should be designed based on the foregoing criteria.

2. AWRA should facilitate the understanding of the history, social content, and evolution of water resource management institutions.

3. The federal government should establish an environment that will facilitate the development of local water management institutions and capabilities.

4. There should be a high-level federal policy coordinating institution for federal water resources policy.

VI. Urban Water Management

A. *Policy Issue*: The appropriate federal role to help communities develop the capacity to efficiently, effectively and equitably manage their urban water resources.

B. *Discussion Summary:* The federal role should be to:
1. Encourage cooperation and facilitate partnerships at all levels of government, as well as between and among public and private associations, agencies, and groups.

2. Facilitate the development of networks and other appropriate forums for exchange of ideas, thoughts, and technologies.

3. Encourage and fund research and development.

4. Be the focal point to monitor and disseminate information related to urban water management, domestically and internationally.

5. Encourage land-use planning by nonfederal entities on regional and watershed basis, based upon demographics and projected future water needs.

6. Provide incentives to encourage innovative approaches to solve local urban water problems.

C. *Policy Recommendations:*
1. The most contentious issue regarding the federal role in urban water management is the setting of standards. The setting and implementation of standards should:
   • Incorporate best available scientific and technological research and risk analysis.
   • Include an assessment of net local impacts.
   • Not be set in a vacuum, but should incorporate whole system impacts and all interactions.
   • Recognize that a uniform standard may not be best to meet all needs in all cases.

290

- Be based upon input from all affected constituencies.
- Be sufficiently flexible to allow mid-course corrections, as needed and justified, to meet changing conditions and priorities.
- Be based upon solution-oriented approaches.
- Be informed by an ongoing research effort.
- Give local communities a role in determining what risks are acceptable.
- Be flexible and allow tradeoffs to meet local priorities and resource needs.
- Include standards based upon accurate cost/benefit estimates of their implementation.

2. The federal role in research should be to facilitate, coordinate, support and, in some cases, perform research on urban water resources issues. To meet the goal:
   - Greater support and funding is needed for water resources research, especially applied research related to urban resource problems.
   - User needs should be considered in setting research priorities;
   - Research should assist and improve the standard setting process;
   - A mechanism needs to be in place to facilitate exchange of information and research between end users and academia and research facilities;
   - Research priorities should be set based on larger objectives.

3. The federal role is to work with and be responsive to interstate, regional or watershed-based associations to:
   - Help resolve interstate water disputes;
   - Facilitate coordination in interstate resource issues;
   - Help identify regional resource issues and develop strategies to meet objectives;
   - Encourage multistate cooperation and planning.

VII. Managing Natural Systems

A. *Policy Issue*: Facilitating interdisciplinary, intergovernmental approaches to management.

B. *Discussion Summary:* Participants identified several philosophical issues that underlie the policy recommendations given below. They are not all inclusive and could be refined with further discussion. These issues are:

1. Practice triage: a prioritization of sites/issues based on needs, practicality, economic feasibility, etc.

2. Environmental democracy: people should have a vote in how much they want to "pay" (money, loss of rights, etc) for environmental protection. There should be more public involvement in the process than there is now.

3. Recognize that natural systems are public trust resources (fish, wildlife, and water) that are to be managed for the benefit of the public.

4. Promote ethical ecology and environmental responsibility.

5. Recognize that landowners have an important role to play and must be involved in these issues.

C. *Policy Recommendations:*

1. Promote a common language and a common core of knowledge through the use of databases, maps, etc. For each particular project, basic information would be made available to all parties (through a pre-education system or basic primer). This "common language" (which may be heavily reliant on graphics) is necessary to provide a measure of environmental health and determine the impacts of projects on the environmental health of watersheds (riverbasins or ecosystems).

2. Support legislation outlining a CCMBPM (comprehensive, coordinated, multipurpose, basinwide water and related resource planning and management) or MOM (multiobjective management) approach. Legislation would establish a structure for this approach (similar to a water resources council) and would require all disciplines to be represented but would not give any one agency authority to make all regulatory decisions. The process would involve the use of interdisciplinary experts as facilitators. The group should have clear goals and objectives.

3. An interdisciplinary approach would require more environmental scientists with broader, multidisciplinary training, instead of specialists with technical training in only one field. Specialists are needed as part of this planning and management process, but it is important to involve more generalists with broad training in such a process. Cross-training, through special assignments and conferences and seminars, should be required of those involved in the planning and management process.

4. This process would involve a consensus approach through mediation and negotiation, with an alternative dispute resolution process built into the framework. All participants should be committed to an objective consideration of all disciplines involved.

VIII. Public Participation

A. *Policy issue:* Why initiate public participation and how to involve the public?

B. *Discussion Summary:* Public participation has become an accepted activity associated with the development of government-funded water resources projects. Public participation can and should be used positively. It can provide valuable information for project planning and can assist senior officials in making decisions and carrying out their duties. The process can be time-consuming and costly to carry out. Skilled, competent management is required for success. There is a responsibility to find broadly acceptable solutions to common problems.

While public participation is becoming increasingly accepted and, indeed, is often mandated by various local, state, and federal laws, there are still obstacles to it:

1. It involves facing value differences, which can be very unsettling.
2. Sponsors could lose control.
3. It is very difficult to do effectively; there is the enormity of "trying to do it right."
4. Lack of public interest complicates the task.
    • There is competition of other issues—crowded agendas.
    • The public is accustomed to officials doing it all.
    • The public perceives it does not make a difference.
5. Mid-level managers are not trained to use consensual processes or consider consequences of public not being involved. They generally analyze technical issues and make value judgments.

C. *Policy Recommendations:*

1. Public agencies and organizations should provide sufficient resources, including appropriate personnel and adequate offical and scientific support to properly plan and execute public participation activities.

2. Public agencies, when inviting the public, should:
    • Define the issue and identify problem
    • Provide an open agenda—no secrets
        - Fully display data and information, clarify limitations, and define boundaries
        - Establish credibility and create a "good faith" environment
    • Build trust
    • Provide sufficient time for effective citizen participation
    • Openly recognize the potential and existing sources of discord
    • Establish common goals with which parties can identify

- Reach the public
  - Seek out existing, organized groups
  - Seek out existing community leaders
  - Identify and involve other impacted parties and individuals
  - Organize open meetings for citizen participation
- Give status recognition to any group
- Overcome cultural barriers
- Beware of communication barriers created by cultural differences
- Sell the process
- Know when to call in a third party neutral
- Include identified stakeholders and the general public in the problem and process definition o Use and share self-help material such as
  - "Riverwork" (NPS)
  - *Managing Public Disputes* (Carpenter and Kennedy)
  - *Coming to Public Judgment* (Yankelovich)

3. All parties must:
   - Identify and involve major stakeholders
   - Be flexible and sensitive but must understand the constraints of federal regulations and statutes
4. The question of whether the costs of public participation are too high in terms of the benefits gained should be objectively explored and guidelines developed.

Appendix B

Authors and Commentators

STANLEY A. CHANGNON: Principal Scientist and Chief Emeritus, Illinois State Water Survey

ARLENE L. DIETZ: Director, Navigation Data Center, U.S. Army Corps of Engineers

RUSSELL EARNEST: Deputy Assistant Director for Fish and Wildlife Enhancement, U.S. Fish and Wildlife Service

MYRON B. FIERING: Gordon McKay Professor of Engineering and Applied Mathematics, Harvard University, until his untimely death in October 1992.

FRANCES H. FLANIGAN: Executive Director, Alliance for the Chesapeake Bay

ELLEN L. FRAITES: Formerly with the Coastal and Environmental Policy Program, University of Maryland

THOMAS M. FRANKLIN: Chief, Technical Services and PENNVEST Unit, Division of Drinking Water Management, Pennsylvania Department of Environmental Resources

KENNETH D. FREDERICK: Senior Fellow, Resources for the Future and Director of their Renewable Resources Division from 1977 to 1988

NEIL R. FULTON: Study Director, Levels Reference Study, International Joint Commission; formerly Chief, Bureau of Resources Management, Division of Water Resources, Illinois Department of Transportation

WILLIAM GOLDFARB: Professor of Environmental Law, Cook College, Rutgers University; author of *Water Law* (1988)

NEIL S. GRIGG: Head, Department of Civil Engineering, Colorado State University; formerly Assistant Secretary for Natural Resources, North Carolina, 1979-1982; Director, University of North Carolina Water Resources Research Institute (1977-1982); Director, Colorado Water Resources Research Institute (1988-91); Director, International School for Water Resources (1985-1992); author of *Water Resources Planning* (1985).

ROBERT KELLEY: Professor of History, University of California, Santa Barbara; among his many publications are *Battling the Inland Sea: American Political Culture, Public Policy, & the Sacramento Valley, 1850-1986* (1989) and *Gold vs. Grain: The Hydraulic Mining Controversy in California's Sacramento Valley* (1959)

ALLEN V. KNEESE: Senior Fellow, Resources for the Future; author or principal co-author of sixteen books dealing with environmental and resources economics

BRUCE D. LONG: Chief, Water Resources Branch, Office of Management and Budget; formerly with the Office of Policy, Planning and Budget, Tennessee Valley Authority

DAVID C. MAJOR: Staff Associate, Social Science Research Council; formerly Senior Planner, New York City water supply system; author of *Multiobjective Water Resource Planning* (1977)

DEAN E. MANN: Professor Emeritus of Political Science, University of California, Santa Barbara; author or editor of seveal books and articles on environmental policy in the United States including *Environmental Policy Formation* (1981) and *Environmental Policy Implementation* (1982)

FREDERICK A. MARROCCO: Chief, Division of Water Supplies, Pennsylvania Department of Environmental Resources

RUTHERFORD H. PLATT: Professor of Geography and Planning Law and Director, Land and Water Policy Center, University of Massachusetts at Amherst; author of numerous articles an monographs on water resources and *Land Use Control: Geography, Law, and Public Policy* (1991)

DON L. PORTER: Chief Engineer, Floodplain Management, Flood Protection Section, Tennessee Valley Authority

MARTIN REUSS: Senior Historian, Office of History, Headquarters, U.S. Army Corps of Engineers, specializing in the history of U.S. water resources policy and technology; General Chair, AWRA National Forum on Water Management Policy

KENNETH I. RUBIN: President, Apogee Research, Inc.; formerly (1981-86) the principal analyst for the U.S. Congressional Budget Office in the Natural Resources Division

THEODORE M. SCHAD: Water resources consultant; formerly the staff director to the U.S. Senate Select Committee on National Water Resources (1959-1961) and Executive Director of the National Water Commission (1968-1973)

WILLIAM J. SEDLAK: Statistical Analyst, Division of Water Supplies, Pennsylvania Department of Environmental Resources

LEONARD SHABMAN: Professor, Resource and Environmental Economics, Department of Agricultural Economics, Virginia Polytechnic Institute and State University; formerly, Visiting Scholar, U.S. Water Resources Council (1977-78) and Scientific Advisor, Office of the Assistant Secretary of Army for Civil Works (1984-1985)

BORY STEINBERG: Partner, Steinberg & Associates; formerly Chief, Project Management Division, Headquarters, U.S. Army Corps of Engineers

HOLLY E. STOERKER: Executive Director, Interstate Council on Water Policy; Executive Director, Upper Mississippi River Basin Association

L. SCOTT TUCKER: Executive Director, Urban Drainage and Flood Control District, Denver, Colorado

CHRISTOPHER D. UNGATE: Projects Manager, Water Resources, Tennessee Valley Authority

GILBERT F. WHITE: Gustavson Distingished Professor Emeritus of Geography, University of Colorado; Interem Director, Natural Hazards Research and Information Center, University of Colorado; served at various times during the period 1934-1942 on the Mississippi Valley Committee, National Resources Board; National Resources Planning Board, and the Bureau of the Budget; President, Haverford College, 1946-55; Professor of Geography, University of Chicago, 1956-69

LAJUANA S. WILCHER: Assistant Administrator, Office of Water, Environmental Protection Agency, (1989-1993)

ARTHUR E. WILLIAMS: Lieutenant General and Commanding General/Chief of Engineers of the U.S. Army Corps of Engineers (August 1992 to present); Major General and Director of Civil Works, Headquarters, U.S. Army Corps of Engineers (July 1991-August 1992).

JAMES M. WRIGHT: Senior Technical Specialist, Floodplain Management, Flood Protection Section, Tennessee Valley Authority; Project Manager of the Federal Interagency Floodplain Management Task Force that published *Floodplain Management in the United States: An Assessment Report*, 2 volumes (1992)

Index

A

Ackerman, Edward A., 39, 41
Africa (country), 122, 129n.10
agriculture and water resources, 23
Alabama, 41, 223, 226
  Auburn University, 41
  Mobile, 226
Alaska, St. Paul Island, 269
Alexander, Richard B., 43
Almond, Gabriel, 20n.7
Alternative Dispute Resolution (ADR), 74, 98, 128
American Public Works Association, ix
American Society of Civil Engineers (ASCE), 70, 289
American Water Resources Association (AWRA), ix, 1, 5, 67, 135, 177, 296
  and national water policy, 274, 275, 276, 277, 279
  Forum issue group recommendations, 283, 284, 289-90
Anatal, E., 198
Anderson, Senator Clinton, 17
Annapolis, Maryland, 111
Appalachia, 210
aquatic systems restoration, 174-76
  monitoring, 176
aquifers, 184
Aral Sea, 41, 132
Argentina, 178
Arizona, 24, 47, 153, 167
  Phoenix, 167
  Scottsdale, 153
  Tucson, 47

Army Corps of Engineers, 2, 12, 123, 136, 276, 294-96
  Federal perspective on national water policy, 264-65, 268, 270-72
  Flood damage reduction policy, 245
  Sustainable development, 125-28, 134, 136
Aschauer, Dr. David, 249
Assistant Secretary of the Army for Civil Works, 221, 225, 264, 265, 270, 277, 294
Association of American Geographers, 41
Atlanta, Georgia, 198
Auburn University, 41
Ausubel, Jesse H., 179
American Water Works Association (AWWA), 290

B

Bailey, Paul, 269
Baker, Richard Allan, 17,
Baltimore, Maryland, 223
Banks, Harvey O., 41
Barrier islands, 142, 149
Barrows, Harlan, 38
Bates, Sarah, 67, 68
Baumann, Duane D., 42, 45
Baumol, William J., 179
Bay/Estuary Program, 176
Benefit-cost analysis, 9, 185-87, 188
  computer systems technology, 27, 29
  consumer surplus concept, 25

298

national environmental accounting
system, 287
Nature Conservancy, the, 88, 109, 116
population growth problems, 120-21,
137, 231
Save Our Streams, 108, 110, 111, 115
Sierra Club, 110, 111, 113
Valuation of Environmental
Investments Research Program, 25
Environmental Monitoring and Assess-
ment Program, 176
Environmental Policy Institute, 109-11
Environmental Protection Agency (EPA),
2, 43, 58, 62, 93n.16, 106-7, 125, 130,
133, 136, 137, 149, 152, 154, 176, 262,
279, 296
flood control strategies, 159, 167,
168-69
Office of Water, 239
wastewater goals, 233, 234, 236, 239
Environmental quality (EQ), 28
estuaries, 174, 176, 184
Chesapeake Bay, 44, 105-118
Ethics and values, 96, 293
"Earth Ethic," 120
Ethiopia, 121
Exxon, 131

F

Fairfax, Virginia, 107
Feasability Review Conference (FRC),
272
Federal perspective on the future of water
resource development, 264-273
Federal agencies
26 involved in flood damage reduction,
244-46, 249-52
Federal funding, 4
Federal Insurance Administration, 143
Federal Reclamation Act (1902), 23, 25-26
Federal Reserve Bank, 249
Federalism, 3, 14, 15, 17, 18,
creative, 4
Fiering, Myron B., 295
Flanigan, Frances H., 295

Flood
100-year, 187, 265
5 federal agencies in damage reduction,
245-46, 249-51, 258, 259, 260, 261,
262, 263
control, cost and cost sharing, 264-65
coordinated interagency damage
reduction, 250-55
damage prevention, 255-57
damage reduction policy, 250-55
interagancy partnership, 250-55
damage reduction, 244-55
damage reduction: multiobjective
planning, 254-57
Flood control, 10-12, 19n.1, 68, 90, 125,
174, 187, 203, 244, 245, 246, 254-55,
261
costs and benefits, 171
economics and, 25-26, 29
federal perspective of the future,
264-65, 269-70, 273
floodplain management and natural
systems, 142-56
geographers and water policy, 37, 39,
41, 42
National Environmental Policy Act 0f
1969 (NEPA), 143, 146
National Flood Insurance Act (1968),
143
publicly owned treatment works
(POTWS), 169
Sacramento Valley systems, 10-11
stormwater systems, 168-72, 244,
247-48, 253
stream corridors, 142, 155, 158-172
urban corridors and streamways,158-172
Flood Plain Management Services
(FPMS), 265
floodplain
biological monitering criteria, 176
Biomonitoring of Environmental Status
and Trends (BEST), 176
cultural resources, defined, 148
defined, 255
Federal Interagency Floodplain Management Task Force, 146, 152, 154

302

Snake, 33, 127, 134
South Platte (SPR), 137, 159-62, 164, 165
Susquehanna, 40
Tar-Pimlico, 102
Tennessee, 50, 204
Truckee-Carson, 59
Upper South Platte, 137
Vistula, 132
Volga, 40
Yuba, 10
Zambezi, 41
See also: River basins, Water
Roberts, Rebecca S., 44, 46
Robinson, Sid, 228
Roosevelt, President Franklin D., 6
Roosevelt, President Theodore, 38
Roper Organization, 134
Rubin, Kenneth I., 277, 296
Ruckleshaus, William, 130, 133
Rutgers University, 44

S

Saarinen, Thomas F., 42, 45
Sacramento Valley, California, 10-12, 19, 19n.1, 170-71
Sacramento-San Joaquin Delta, 84
Salt River Project, the, ix
Salveson, David, 102n.15
San Francisco Bay, California, 84-85
Save Our Streams, 108, 110, 111, 115
Schad, Theodore M., 38, 41, 296
Schaefer, Governor William Donald (MD), 107
Schoolmaster, Andrew F., 47
Schultze, Charles, 249
Scientific Committee on Problems of the Environment, 137
Scottsdale, Arizona, 153
Sediment, 44
Sedlack, William J., 296
Seinwill, Gerald D., ix
Shabman, Leonard, 266, 277, 297
Shaeffer, John R., 42
Sierra Club, the, 110, 111, 113
Sigma Xi Society, 137
Siltation, 37

Silverstein, Michael, 134
Smith, Adam, 248, 249
Smith, Richard A., 43
Smithsonian Institution, 112
South Dakota, 24
Southern Illinois University, 45
Spain, 59
Sofford, W. O., 217n.3
St. Angelo, Douglas, 7n.5
State of the Union address, 287
Stegner, Wallace, 37
Steinberg, Bory, 3, 297
Stewardship, 4, 115, 125, 152, 253
Stillwater National Wildlife Refuge and Wetlands, 86, 88
Stoerker, Holly, 5, 297
Stone, Donald C., 70
subsidies, federal, 31, 44, 261
Suison Marsh, California, 84
Sustainable Development, 2, 120-28, 130-40, 252, 253, 254, 270
  environmental challenges, 130-135
  ergodicity, 138
  Forum issue group recommendations, 285-86
  framework (9 concept), 123-24
  technology's role in, 120-28, 139
  World Commission on Environment and Development, 121
Swampbuster provision, the, 99
Systems analysis, 27, 71, 72, 74, 281-82
  Decision Support System (DSS), 71
  water resource management, 281

T

Taylor, Frederick, 70
Technological innovation, 232, 270
Templer, Otis, 47
Tennessee, 78, 91, 154, 203, 204, 226
  Chattanooga, 204
  Conservation League, 154
  Memphis, 226
Tennessee-Tombegbee Waterway, 260
Tennessee Valley Authority (TVA), ix, 5, 39, 50n.14, 77, 91, 97, 127, 153, 204-8, 207, 208, 265, 295, 296

U

V

W

federally supplied, 31, 32
filtration, 213-14
geographers and resource policy, 36-49
groundwater, 24, 36, 37, 39, 46, 60,
    62-63, 67, 69, 73, 91, 148
human use of, 36, 37
hydrodiplomacy, 69, 71
hydroelectric power, 36, 39
infrastructure needs, 208-57, 287
instream flow, 24, 31, 32, 48, 60, 63,
    68, 72, 82, 90, 183
interdisciplinary approaches to policy,
    36, 37, 38, 66
investment in development of, 25, 29, 237
irrigation, 82, 86, 87, 91
law, 31, 47-48, 61, 62, 82-118
marketing, 30-31, 34, 94, 99-101
non-agricultural use, 24, 37
offstream flow, 24, 183
politics, 56-64, 95
pollution control, 62, 95, 96, 99-102,
    105-110, 112, 116, 165-72
quality, 82-91, 130, 178, 183, 184, 204,
    235, 248, 252, 253, 270, 272, 287
quality costs, 233, 240-42
quality as a national goal, 231-42
quantity, 23, 41, 45, 62, 68, 83-85, 88,
    89, 93n.16, 130, 154, 178, 183, 248,
    252, 272
recreational management, 43-44
research, 4, 23, 36, 49, 287
resource geography, 36-49
resource planning: economics of risk,
    182-91
resource planning: multiple objective,
    28, 68
resource systems, 138
rights, 24, 30-31, 32, 34, 47-48, 58, 59,
    60-62, 72
river basins. *See*: River basins
runoff, 182
salinity, 184
salt water intrusion, 85
stormwater, 287
streamflow, 182
subsidies, 60, 68, 99
surface, 174, 250

systems analysis, 71, 72, 74
the value of, 59-61
transbasin projects, 23
transfers, 187
transportation system, 218-228
treatment, 88-89
unit removal curve (water quality),
    235, 236
urban management, 291-92
watershed restoration, 94-103
Western United States, 23, 24, 30, 31,
    32, 37, 39, 47-48, 58, 61, 62, 68, 99,
    275
withdrawal, 187
See also: Policy, rivers, water resources
water districts, 23, 59, 84-90, 92n.14, 94,
    158
    Carson-Truckee Water Conservancy
        District, 86-88
    Central Valley (California), 59, 84,
        85
    Metropolitan Water District
        (S. California), 16, 19, 56
    North Colorado, 59
    South Florida Water Management
        District, 92n.14, 94
    Spain, 59
    Urban Drainage and Flood Control
        District (Colorado), 5, 158-166
    See also: Policy
water management, 10-16, 36, 38, 41, 49,
    66-77, 82-83, 88-89, 196
    CCMBPM (comprehensive, coordi-
        nated, multipurpose, basinwide water
        and related resource planning and
        management), 90
    effective, 82
    engineering perspective, 66-75
    evolution of, 10, 11, 14
    intergovernmental, 274-75
    issues, 285
    judicial integration in, 82-90
    judicial/legislative solutions, 82, 91
    litigation, 10-12
    multidisciplinary aspects, 10-19, 70, 72,
        76
    natural systems, 292

waterways, 216-28

watershed
management, 2, 94-95, 99-102, 111, 155, 167, 175-76, 274, 275, 278, 286
management, market-based, 99-102
natural systems approach, 277
planning and management, 238-39, 253-55
pollution, 101-2, 167, 175, 231, 235, 238
"problemshed," 276, 277, 280
restoration and water policy, 94-103, 103n.3, 106

watersheds
Catskill, 93n.16
Croton, 93n.16
Delaware, 93n.16

Waterstone, Marvin, 48

Watt, James, 86, 87

Weinberg, Edward, 41

Wescoat, James L. Jr., 41, 47, 48

Western Governors' Association, 275

Western Michigan University, 40

Western States Water Council, 276

wetlands, 2, 104n.16, 131, 175, 240, 248, 253, 266, 271, 278
1977 Executive Order on Wetlands, 149-50
EPA Office of Wetlands Protection, 152, 154
fee permits, 100-1, 104n.16
floodplain management, 142, 149-50, 154, 155
geographic Information systems (GIS), 154
joint venture areas, 175
protection, 253-54

Research Program, 125

Stillwater, 86, 87, 88

sustainable development's role, 121, 125, 126

watershed design, 100

watershed restoration, 86-88, 94, 96, 99-101

Wetlands Division, Environmental Protection Agency, 266

Whipple, William Jr., 68, 276

White, Gilbert F., 38, 39, 40, 41, 42, 297

White, Stephen E., 46

Wilcher, LaJuana S., 2, 139, 279, 297

Wildavsky, Aaron, 185

Williams, Arthur E., 2, 130, 134, 138-39, 270, 277, 278, 297

Wilson, "Engine Charlie," 77, 78

Wilson, President Woodrow, 5,

Wilson, Robert, 193n.25

Wisconsin, 126

Wittfogel, Karl, 56

Wollman, Nathaniel, 41

Wolman, Abel, 6, 8n.12, 38, 41

Wolman, M. Gordon, 42, 43

Wong, Shue Tuck, 42

World Commission on Environment and Development, 121

Wright, James M., 5, 266, 278, 297

Wyoming, 226

Y

Yankelovich, 294

Yellowstone Park, Wyoming, 198

Yuba City, California, 10-12